WELCOME TO THE NEIGHBORHOOD

Welcome
TO THE NEIGHBORHOOD

An Anthology of American Coexistence

EDITED BY SARAH GREEN
Foreword by David Baker

Swallow Press / Ohio University Press ⠸ Athens, Ohio

Swallow Press
An imprint of Ohio University Press, Athens, Ohio 45701
ohioswallow.com

Printed in the United States of America
Swallow Press / Ohio University Press books are printed on acid-free paper ⊗ ™

29 28 27 26 25 24 23 22 21 20 19   5 4 3 2 1

Hardcover ISBN: 978-0-8040-1216-4
Paperback ISBN: 978-0-8040-1217-1
Electronic ISBN: 978-0-8040-4105-8

Library of Congress Cataloging-in-Publication Data
available upon request.

LCCN 2019040362

For Alan P. Grimes

[W]e are each other's
harvest:
we are each other's
business:
we are each other's
magnitude and bond.

—Gwendolyn Brooks

Contents

Contents

Foreword

WE LIVE IN FAMILIES AND IN VILLAGES. We live in clans and teeming cities, in tribes, in regions, and in nations. We live in these social formations gladly sometimes; at other times reluctantly. But either way they are among the primary communal and geological structures we inherit—the bloodlines and borders. There's another arrangement where we live, too, and it's a considerably less talked-about form of identity and placement. That is, the neighborhood. We live in neighborhoods of all kinds.

I live in two of them, in fact. Since 1984 I have resided in or near the village of Granville, Ohio, population 3,600, give or take. But I also spend lots of time in Greenwich Village—the East Village—in Manhattan, in New York City, where my partner Page has lived since 1980. You might think there would be polar differences between our two neighborhoods. Granville is small and quiet, green, with lots of unbounded space all around; I know many of the people here, and they know me. When I'm in New York, I frequently grow dumbfounded by the pounding, the sirens and speed, the intense press of bodies and looming buildings. Yet Page and I live in similar orbits. Each of our neighborhoods in our villages is really just a few-block sphere, with a grocer and a bank, a shoe repair shop and dry cleaner, a hardware store, a deli in easy walking distance. We pass many of the same people every day, nodding to some, not meeting the eyes of others.

That's what a neighborhood is, the living and working proximity of others. My trusty OED confirms that a neighbor is someone who lives nearby. The word combines the Old English *neah* with *gebur:* a nigh peasant. A neighbor is a nigh farmer, a near peasant, a close-by dweller. Maybe your neighborhood is a block or two long; maybe it's a hillside or a couple of valleys or a cluster of houses or buildings. Neighborhoods are as ubiquitous and as actual as families. In fact, we may know more about our neighbors than our own family members; we may spend more time among neighbors than kin. But equally sometimes we know virtually nothing about the people who live next door or down the corridor or over the creek.

Such complexity is part of the joy and wisdom of *Welcome to the Neighborhood*. I rejoice in Sarah Green's soulful and hospitable work in giving us this new book. It's high time we looked with such eyes—artistic as well as critical—at the neighborhood. In the very first poem, Jamaal May writes of one neighborhood—it could be any neighborhood—that it's "as tattered and feathered as anything else." And he's right as rain. Like each of us, like every resident neighbor, May's neighborhood embodies a doubleness common to most: it is worn, and yet it is capable of soaring.

Elsewhere in *Welcome to the Neighborhood,* among these marvelous poems and prose works (even a comic strip!) that Sarah Green has curated so astutely, we see the diversity of the neighborhood as much as the shared qualities. A neighborhood is a playpen, a skating rink, a garden, a "corridor of maples" from a "simpler time," as some of these pieces celebrate. But there's rupture and danger, too, that require what Dora Malech calls "a neighborhood watch." Gary Jackson concurs: "it's exhausting / work / to keep a watch out in my city." And Wayne Miller, watching, sees a common neighborhood affliction: "the flight path / painted over your neighborhood / is killing your property values."

Neighborhoods are defined by proximity but also, as these writers testify, by economic and social class, where we find like-minded people living next to like-salaried people. Some are walled in, even as others are walled out. Money, race, religion, education, all the evident and covert affiliations of cultural identity and likeness—and difference—are part of Sarah Green's sharp-eyed neighborhood watch. That is, for every commune, every garden and greenspace, there's an underworld urbanity as figured in Carolina Ebeid's subway with its "world- / sorrow drafting through the hyaline / shell of myself in thought." Ebeid's catalog records a neighborhood beyond nature, post-pastoral, with "reconstruction-delays, / the stench of piss & nothing / weather shaped, nothing ocean spun."

That is, there's beauty and trouble alike in *Welcome to the Neighborhood,* just as there are experimental and traditional works, poems that clarify and stories that complicate—the dear, the dingy, the documentary. Maybe Sarah Green's book is itself a great kind of neighborhood, where we all gather with our myriad voices and lives to sing together for a while. We sing of marriages and families, of losses and sorrows. We sing our solitary nightmares, and yet, in each other's company, we sing our "meteor dreams."

David Baker

Preface

I FIRST HAD THE IDEA FOR THIS ANTHOLOGY in January 2017, when the "Muslim ban" and the proposed border wall between the United States and Mexico were novel and disturbing news items, and the frequency of police brutality headlines across the country showed no sign of lessening. That winter, as xenophobic acts and divisive rhetoric reached their then-peak, I was afraid that as a country we might forget, or future generations might never see, what it looks like to truly—and with humility—"welcome the stranger." It seemed to me that the gesture of being not just a neighbor but *neighborly,* that is, the gesture of hospitality based solely on and earned solely by proximity (and not necessarily based on cultural or ideological symmetry), was the gesture we were missing.

While I had an inkling that my vague nostalgia for a golden age of the more harmonious American neighborhood was likely based in cultural myth, I knew that in my lifetime I had experienced a tangible shift in tone when it came to local and national leaders' vision of a country strengthened (or not) by its cultural heterogeneity and ideological variation, and committed (or not) to its citizens' freedoms. I felt an almost desperate pull to compile a book of contemporary American poetry, fiction, and essays imagining and witnessing the neighborhood. I suppose the idea was to pin down some set of images and stories in which such grappling happens constructively, kindly—some attempt to both record and envision how "we the people" *could* be.

But we live in the real world, with gentrification and "lost dog" posters, late-night assaults and new-baby meal trains, spray-painted swastikas and block parties. At certain times, to be a neighbor means to reach out with warmth and aid, out of solidarity; at other times, the intense proximity of neighboring with its predictable trespasses (or perceived trespasses) provokes fraught vigilance and even violence. The title of the book, *Welcome to the Neighborhood,* is meant to have a double tone, both sincere and sarcastic, implying both offers of casseroles and shrugs of nonsympathy to newcomers. While I briefly considered editing a collection that represented only ideal neighborly encounters, I soon realized that such a controlled approach would be the literary equivalent of a gated community—a bubble of denial—when the very mode I wished to celebrate was a mode of openness, curiosity, and engagement with complexity and discord. Such a collection would also be overly limited, both in its literary depth and in its ethnographic, reflective, and civic usefulness. American ambivalence about other people takes root close to home, after all, before it ripples out farther. What could we learn about the country as a whole, I wondered, from examining the smaller site of the American neighborhood as seen through literature? What is this character, this simultaneously imagined and embodied, sealed-off and invaded, community? These "contain[ed] multitudes"? This "we"?

I shifted my editorial attention to choosing pieces that reflect various points in the human cycle(s) of harmonious and conflict-filled coexisting. I was especially drawn to pieces that, as Emily Dickinson encouraged us to do, "tell it slant," or approach the theme in an unexpected or nuanced way. It became clear over time that this book itself was a "neighborhood" of sorts, and that the editorial process was a form of world-building. I began paying special attention in the later stages of submission reading to collecting pieces that rounded out some of the less-represented experiences of the neighborhood, especially experiences of estrangement. My hope is for the pieces here to open up possibility—to encourage curiosity about whom we live among and how we go about it. Some of these poems, stories, and essays will warm and feed us, yes, but many will rattle us out of what we think we know.

There are seekers: "We woke in the parked car aslant in the field Cory's grandmother had found for us to sleep in" (Christine Schutt); "I've been searching to find that net again, that [. . .] citizen body" (Liz Stephens). There are activists: "I don't police // my protection" (Leora Fridman), skeptics: *"Why should I help this creep?"* (Dinty W. Moore), and enthusiasts: "Even my bitch-ass neighbor a gift" (Jill Mc-Donough); "Praise the 606-pound squash at the county fair" (Daniel B. Johnson). There are women who crave solitude: "She wanted a little room for thinking" (Rita Dove). There are cautious women alone at night: "I tell myself I will wave" (Ladan Osman). There are animal neighbors: "I see Candy / squirm out of his collar again" (Fred Marchant), criminal neighbors: "no one thought that my neighbor would become a serial killer" (Katrina Vandenberg), and hustlers-turned-altruists: "I tell him I have no cash on me, but when I get out of the shower I see that he's shoveled it anyway" (James Miranda).

I have attempted to cast a wide net aesthetically with this multigenre collection, to the extent that a narrative-leaning theme can cast widely, and I have intentionally selected pieces by authors whose backgrounds and identities reflect the diversity of this country. The anthology call went out on general social media pages for creative writers and I received submissions that way; at the same time, I solicited writers whose work I knew and admired. Pieces were chosen for thematic relevance, precision of craft, and complexity of tone and argument. The result is a mixture of emerging and highly established authors, each of whom I am proud and honored to showcase here.

I am writing this one year after the release and box office success of *Won't You Be My Neighbor?*, the Fred Rogers documentary; less than three months after the synagogue shooting in Fred Rogers's actual neighborhood, Squirrel Hill; one month after a girl died in border patrol custody in New Mexico. The question of how to live peacefully and ethically with one another remains urgent. I am grateful to Ohio University Press/Swallow Press for making room for the literature here that both answers and raises it. This book is full of flawed and vulnerable characters, just like us—just like our country. What these poems, stories, and essays assert, however, is a refusal to retreat to separate, self-reinforcing corners: these are imperfect narrators and authors with the courage and discipline to stay engaged, be wrong, and keep learning.

Sarah Green
March 3, 2019

There Are Birds Here

For Detroit

There are birds here,
so many birds here
is what I was trying to say
when they said those birds were metaphors
for what is trapped
between buildings
and buildings. No.
The birds are here
to root around for bread
the girl's hands tear
and toss like confetti. No,
I don't mean the bread is torn like cotton,
I said confetti, and no
not the confetti
a tank can make of a building.
I mean the confetti
a boy can't stop smiling about
and no his smile isn't much
like a skeleton at all. And no
his neighborhood is not like a war zone.
I am trying to say
his neighborhood
is as tattered and feathered
as anything else,
as shadow pierced by sun
and light parted
by shadow-dance as anything else,
but they won't stop saying
how lovely the ruins,
how ruined the lovely
children must be in that birdless city.

Hungry

This time the jay, fat as a boot, bluer
than sky gone blue now that the rain has
finished with us for a while, this loud jay
at the neck of the black walnut keeps cawing
I want, I want—but can't finish his clause.
Hard runoff has spread the driveway with seeds,
green talcum, the sex of things, packed
like plaster against shutters and toolboxes,
sides of the barn, while the force of water
pouring down from the stopped-up gullet
of gutter has drilled holes deep in the mud.
Yet the world of the neighborhood is still just
the world. So much, so much. Like the bulldog
next door, choking itself on a chain
to guard the yard of the one who starves it.

GAIL MAZUR : poetry

I'm a Stranger Here Myself

Sometimes when you stop for directions,
when you ask someone who doesn't look
threatening or threatened the way to a gas
station or restaurant, the person stares at you,
dumbly, or seems apologetic or guilty,
and says these words as if they'd been
scripted: I'm a stranger here myself—, shaking
her head, or his head, and you're especially struck
by the bond between you, your strangeness,
and the town, or city, changes to unnumbered
anonymous facades, but generic, unmistakably
New England—white clapboard houses, black shutters;
or Texas storefronts—low porches, two-by-four columns,
longhorn arches; or even Southern California,
the faces its bungalows make, the expressive mouths
of, say, Los Angeles doors—and suddenly you want
to live there, wherever there is, to belong
in one place, to read the surviving daily,
you want to get a grip on the local mores,
to pay taxes, to vote, you want to have cronies,
be tired together in the Stormy Harbor
Coffee Shop, to be bored with the daily specials:
you want not to be like him, or her, not the outsider
who's never sure where things are; so you say,
"Thanks, anyway," and find the worn face of a
native who'll point you to a real estate office,
which hadn't been where you were going—
But then, you stop cold, scared, wanting
only your own room, the books under the bed,
the pencils, the snapshots, what's left
of your family, the dead flies on the windowsills,
the exhausted scorched-coffee smell of your city,
familiar as your own particular dust—and you turn

on a dime, shaking off Church Street and School Street,
the allegorical buildings, the knickknack bookshelves
in the glowing blue family rooms blind to the moonlit
Main Street night, the lonely, confused, censorious
American-ness of places you drive through, where
you can get ice cream or a flat fixed, places where
strangers get hurt, so you jump back into your car
and head out to the highway, until the town,
that stage-set that almost swallowed you,
disappears at last in the fogged rearview mirror,
and you drive to the next and the next and the next,
fleeing that vicarious life for your life.

My Summer Next Door to the Serial Killer

I was not afraid of him. He was twenty-two or so, bird-boned, childlike. He kept the fence between us when he asked, "Aren't you afraid to live in that big house all alone?" I said I had a lot of friends. It wasn't big. It was yellow, with a porch swing. A street of rental bungalows with frenzied honeysuckle yards: hippies with a VW van that never worked and a jazz band that did; an ex-lawyer who ground lenses for eyeglasses; the serial killer. The ex-lawyer listened to Jehovah's Witnesses describe the Kingdom of Heaven for forty-five minutes one day, too polite to finish changing his oil. The serial killer said, "Not me, I'm an asshole," cha-cha-cha-ing with an imaginary partner on the gravel driveway. The ex-lawyer said he had the time. His wife had died, then he had gambled away everything. Fine.

The first summer after my husband had died, and I slept with the windows shut, without a/c. The dollhouse of my life had a love seat, a double bed, and too many dishes even for two. I missed the sound of recess from the nearby school. I learned to repair my washer, to catch a mouse. The last time I had recess, I owned a set of Trixie Belden mysteries, a Rockin' Barbie tour van, an Easy-Bake Oven. I knew back then the rock star and mystery-solving parts were fantasies.

No one thought that my neighbor would become a serial killer. He said he taught music in the next town, was finishing a master's; he told Lens Grinder he mixed paints at the hardware store. He flew a Navy SEAL flag. He was a police buff in the way they say to watch for, with detachable gumball lights for his car, a German shepherd. He strutted with his cop flashlight and handcuffs on his belt and said that the tea I sipped on my porch looked very good. He made guest-star appearances all over town—browsing the university library and wearing fraternity letters; teaching Death and Dying at a nursing home; wolfing free eggs and links at Jerry's while wearing a minister's collar; filling his tank in hospital scrubs. A cop, searching young women's cars. A baseball player. A dress-up boy doll.

He left in the middle of the night. I walked through broken glass and trash in his abandoned house, looking out at his yard. That fall he was arrested for trying to search an off-duty cop. An anchorwoman listed his disguises in a bright. He was a year away from his first murder. It was nearly time to close the windows, and the children were walking home from school in new shoes, asking each other, What will you be for Halloween? What are you going to be when you grow up?

Tonight

Tonight is a drunk man,
his dirty shirt.

There is no couple chatting by the recycling bins,
offering to help me unload my plastics.

There is not even the black and white cat
that balances elegantly on the lip of the dumpster.

There is only the smell of sour breath. Sweat on the collar of my shirt.
A water bottle rolling under a car.
Me in my too-small pajama pants stacking juice jugs on neighbors' juice jugs.

I look to see if there is someone drinking on their balcony.

I tell myself I will wave.

Watch

tonight my mother calls
                               You better keep a watch out
                in your city

I remind her *I don't go to church   so you knew*

     I was safe

You need to stop
        she reminds me of fear
older than me

            that if given the chance
    to argue   for my own right   to live
I could still be denied
                       we drove cross-country

       in a U-Haul & a car

      & when the cop pulled each of us
                 over   he asked the same questions

Where are you going
What do you do for a living   & when my mother told him
                   her son was a professor
you must be proud

       it took a week to calm her down   as if being
                calm
  helped anything

       tomorrow I will try to teach
poets they should bear witness

to the world
they walk through

but we all hesitate
to confront so much white space
tomorrow

my wife will sob in her sleep
& wake up & grab me & when

I ask if she had a bad dream   she will say   *yes*

there are two women   in my life
who will always
fear
what happens to my body &

this awareness makes me   more aware
of my own body

than I have ever been
& there's no
way to communicate this
to you
who are not in this body

you just
have to trust

when I say   it's exhausting

work
to keep a watch out in my city

to keep watch
in every city
we have ever lived

Neighborhood Watch

My back porch looks out on an alley
into which a neighbor's consumptive sump pump
coughs violently and sporadically at all hours.

Sometimes I pretend the alley's leaves and litter
stand in for Pharoah's army, rendering the effluence
a dramatic player in a biblical tableau.

Sometimes I fancy the flow some misguided New Age appropriation,
a feng shui fountain—and at the north end of my home, no less—curative
imbuing elemental prosperity, blessing my "career and life path area."

Sometimes taking the trash out in the dark quiet of a Monday night,
I screech and leap at the sudden gush, my reflexes puppeteering me,
B-movie heroine to the drainpipe's poltergeist.

I seethe a little as I nod a greeting to my neighbor
on the rare occasions when he shuffles past, stepping
over his brown-green scum stream as he exits my scene stage left.

We engaged in the perfunctory name exchange when I moved in
years ago, but in disuse, those hinges between us rusted shut.
Mr. Whomever—I can't remember. Perhaps I should consider

my stage left as his stage right, and in his theatre, the conflict is
my music, my laughter, my little dog's loud demands, my penchant
for pantslessness and open windows on warm nights.

Can I call this a watershed and thus trace thoughts and follow
feelings sourceward? Try to imagine his basement,
how wet it must be to warrant such round-the-clock diligence.

Try to imagine our whole block is one leaky boat
and he's the only one bailing, not standoffish
as he seems, but just immersed

in the thankless necessary work, only emerging on occasion
to take the air and remind himself that we're worth saving,
though he's the only one who seems to see the sea.

Shelter

Oh Death! Oh Death! Won't you spare me over to another year?
Please spare me over to another year.
—Traditional

On the day I met Wilbur, the snow was coming down so hard and fast I had to walk to work. My battered old car and its bald tires couldn't be trusted on icy pavement and already the snow lay in drifts as high as the front bumper. I was pulling a double at Bartlett House—8 a.m. to midnight—and figured that even if I could get the car there, I'd have to leave it when my shift was over. The weather report called for another foot or so of snow. So, bundled in my mother's hand-me-down parka, my roommate's too-big snow boots, and the keffieyeh I wore then as both a scarf and a political statement, I walked the few miles between home and the homeless shelter through the beginnings of what would come to be known as The Storm of the Century, The Great Blizzard of 1993.

Bartlett House was new then, with only a handful of dormitory rooms, a large communal area for watching television and serving meals, an industrial kitchen, and three offices. The shelter had a men's room and a women's room, each with two toilets and two showers, and another half bath behind the locked door of the general staff office. We had room on the bed assignment sheet for forty people. By the time I got to work that morning, forty-seven people had checked in for the day.

"Police are bringing everybody in," said Rich, who had worked the overnight. "Not just the guys off the riverbank, either. I mean everybody." He gestured to the hallway packed with people just milling around, pointing to one guy in particular. Melvin. We'd kicked him out of the shelter a few months before when, after the other residents had complained of a terrible smell coming from his bunk, we'd discovered several decomposing squirrel carcasses and a hunting knife tucked inside his rucksack. He'd refused to give up either, saying the food we served was full of poison and he preferred to eat what he could kill on his own. Even the police were a little wary of Melvin, who was rumored now to be living off feral cats and roadkill in a sewer pipe near the Wal-Mart.

"Did they take his knife away?" I asked.

"Said they did," Rich answered, in a way that suggested there was a good chance they hadn't.

"The cops said we couldn't turn anybody away until the weather breaks." Rich handed me the bed assignment sheet and the cordless phone, our only link to outside help in an emergency. "I ran out of blankets. I've been giving out the towels and extra mattress pads, but we're almost out of those, too. There's maybe a little room left on the floors in rooms four and five, but other than that, we're past full."

Rich left. I gathered a small corps of long-term residents and, together, we worked out a strategy for dealing with the demands of the sudden influx of so many people. Traveling Jack and Cat-Eye sat guard near the door in exchange for the privilege of coming back into the shelter after a few beers later that night. They escorted the people who came in throughout the day back to the kitchen so I could find them a place to sleep and write their names in the margins of the bed assignment sheet. Rita and Star peeled fifty pounds of potatoes, Errol boiled them off in batches, and a woman called Granny Lynn mashed them with commodity butter and tins of evaporated milk. Carthelius helped me pull pounds and pounds of ground venison out of the freezers and defrost it in the microwave. Granny Lynn mixed it with powdered eggs, dehydrated onions, ketchup, and cornflakes, making four giant meatloaves in five-gallon metal steam-table trays. Everyone in the kitchen was sworn to secrecy. The venison was the only thing we had enough of to feed this crowd, but it turns out beggars can be choosers. It'd been languishing in the freezers for months, because when we told the residents what it was, most of them refused to eat it.

Just before dinner Cat-Eye walked in with a sick, gray-haired man wearing a light jacket and torn sneakers with no laces. He was carrying a sheaf of paperwork in a wet brown paper bag. There was a bloodied bandage at his throat, and his eyes were rheumy. "Cop said they found him sitting at the bus stop in front of the hospital. Says his name is Wilbur, but other than that he don't talk much." He put a hand under the old man's elbow to steady him. "Don't look so good, either." Wilbur swayed a little and then fell back into Cat-Eye's arms.

WILBUR SPENT the night on the floor of the office, wrapped in the least worn mattress pad I could find and my mother's old parka. He seemed too frail to put in the hallway with the other latecomers, who were restless with drink or delusion and hadn't wanted to come in at all. I didn't sleep, but sat perched in the desk chair after lights-out, listening to him breathe. It seemed possible that, at some point in the night, his breathing would stop. The bag of papers turned out to be prescriptions and discharge orders, and the bloody bandage covered the place where he'd had a feeding tube until just that morning. There was a tumor the size of a bread loaf hanging over the belt of his pants. Stomach cancer, he told me. "Probably won't live till spring," he'd said during the intake process, as if it were just another piece of information for the form. "But the medical card only pays for so many days in the hospital, and I guess my days must have run out this morning." He smiled, and then turned his hands up in a gesture of helplessness.

Wilbur either never had been, or always was, homeless, depending on how you feel about private property. He lived in the same tar-paper shack he'd been raised in, but he didn't own it. His family had been squatting on unused coal company land for three generations. He'd worked odd jobs and done some jack-leg coal mining, but mostly he lived off what he could grow, hunt, and—since his sixty-fifth birthday a few months before—buy with his meager Social Security check. He was country poor, and this was before Oxycontin and crystal meth destroyed what dignity came with that. He drank some but wasn't a drunk. He didn't read well but had never needed to learn. He wasn't much of a churchgoing man, because the church was a long walk from his home and he'd never owned a working car, but he said his prayers and figured he was mostly right with God. His was a simple life, but one well enough lived to suit him. Or it had been, until the cancer forced him into town.

I'd heard a lot of tragic stories in my year at Bartlett House, and I knew that almost everyone who ended up there could have avoided it if jobs doing manual labor were easier to find. If we hadn't stopped building low-income housing. If we still believed it was the obligation of the middle class to offer a hand up to the impoverished. If we'd followed up on the promise to build full-service Community Mental Health Centers after we released the people who'd been held prisoner in our system of asylums and state hospitals. But I also knew the parts of their stories that made the reasons for their homelessness more than just the inevitable result of a failing social welfare system: the women who used the shelter to get away from one abusive man only to leave a few weeks later with another, the old men who had to drink just to get by, the young men and women who were mentally ill and augmented their craziness with street drugs but didn't take the pills that would have made them better. The people who lived here had difficult lives and complicated stories. My job was just to feed them, assign them chores and beds, and keep what passed for peace among them as best I could.

Wilbur's story wasn't complicated. He was a single man from the country who'd gotten by until cancer made him too weak to hunt or farm. He hadn't ended up at Bartlett House because he'd drunk himself there, squandered his money, or been caught cheating on a disability claim. No, Wilbur had ended up at Barlett House because he'd never married or had children, and kin was how a man like Wilbur got through his dying years. And because I, too, am from around here, I know that when there is no kin, neighbors are supposed to step up and help, so it wasn't hard to decide to offer Wilbur a place to live.

I'D BEEN, since my late teens, the sort of hippie who tries to save the world by doing bong hits and going to Rainbow Gatherings. Before coming to Morgantown, I'd lived for a while on something that was almost a commune—though, because we all kept day jobs or took classes, and so also had in-town homes, not really much of one—in rural Wayne County, West Virginia. We had electricity but no running water; we showered by dribbling lukewarm water out of a bucket on a hook; woke up freezing in the early morning hours to add logs to the woodstove; tried and failed to feed ourselves on what we could grow on the one small patch of bottomland near the well. It'd been fun, but the world stayed the same in spite of us.

I was trying, then, in my late twenties, to be the sort of hippie who changes the world by being actively engaged with my community. I put "Think Globally/ Act Locally" and "Who Is Your Farmer" bumper stickers on my car. I stopped shopping at grocery stores in favor of the local co-op, bought clothes only in thrift stores, and traded my Grateful Dead bootlegs for demo tapes from local bands. And still, the world was as it had been.

It was only after I got the job at the shelter that any of what I was doing had clear and immediate results. I knew, when I cut off the boots Cat-Eye had duct-taped together and soaked his feet in warm water with Epson salts on the night of the blizzard, that at least one person wouldn't lose a toe to frostbite. That when I sat down with Mary to fill out her application for HUD housing, a mother and two young children were one step closer to having a home of their own. Even the dinners I cooked, lousy as they often were, meant that forty or so folk wouldn't be hungry that night. And suddenly the world stopped going on as if nothing I did mattered, even if the things I did only mattered in the smallest of ways to a very few people. That was, finally, enough for me.

And so, when a man dying of cancer showed up one snowy night in a thin jacket and with no place to go, it didn't take much thought to decide he should move into the empty apartment. The doctors said he had weeks to live, and how much of a burden are a few weeks when one is presented with the opportunity to do something so wholly and obviously good? I was young—younger than I should have been at twenty-seven—and it seemed a simple thing to do.

IT TOOK surprisingly little convincing to get the social worker, then the executive director, and finally the woman who administered our primary grant at the state capital, to let me break every rule about client/staff interaction and take Wilbur home with me. We moved him into the empty basement apartment in my house less than two weeks after he'd been brought to the shelter by the police. Even people with long careers in social services, and the disillusionment that goes with them, understood that Wilbur's story shouldn't end at Bartlett House, and that if we allowed the rules to stop us from making sure it didn't, then we were not the good people we held ourselves out to be. My parents would have been harder to convince, and so I didn't tell them. I can't remember when they found out, but by then, Wilbur had settled in and there was nothing to discuss.

The basement apartment was a dump, even compared to the rest of my ramshackle little house. When I'd first bought the place, which had no central heating and cost less than a new car, I had rented the apartment out to a local writer, who thought it was romantically disgusting, for a hundred dollars a month. After he moved out, I'd left it empty with the vague plan, but neither the skill nor the money, to fix it up. The floors of the apartment were concrete poured directly on dirt, the walls crumbling drywall or exposed cinderblock. The bathroom had only a toilet and a miner's shower: a showerhead attached directly to a pipe in the ceiling over a drain in the floor. But Wilbur's shack had neither running water nor electricity, and the apartment had its own street-level entrance with a wide porch shaded by an apple tree and a row of forsythia sepa-rating it from the road, both of which seemed to bloom almost the instant the snows from the storm had melted. "I like to sit out on the porch of an evening and have me a sip of beer," Wilbur'd said upon seeing the place. I understood that to mean that he would take it.

Wilbur was fastidious about his apartment. He spent his Social Security check on new curtains and a slipcover for the old sleeper sofa in the living room, big bot-tles of bleach and boxes of steel wool. The social worker from the shelter found him dishes, sheets, a half-busted vacuum cleaner, and a television. The grants director from the state sent him two ferns as a housewarming gift. Virgil Peterson, one of my English professors, produced a mattress and box spring he said were used and just lying around his house, but still smelled like the plastic wrappings in which they had been packaged. Rich, the overnight shelter worker, borrowed a truck and drove Wilbur deep into Preston County to retrieve what he wanted from the tar-paper shack and, less than a month after he'd been released from the hospital, Wilbur was as much on his feet as he had ever been.

He was also fastidious about his appearance. He wore his thick white hair in a pomaded pompadour and favored Western shirts and jeans, both of which he kept ironed, large brass belt buckles that he shined, and white leather tennis shoes that he polished. "Man doesn't want people to treat him like a bum, he can't look like one," he said. And he didn't look like a bum. He looked like an aging country music star. The kind who had a storied past and who'd grown temperate and dignified with age.

THE CANCER didn't kill him by spring of that year, or the next. For as long as I lived in the little house on Hite Street, he did, too. He was rarely any trouble. Once in a while, he'd go downtown and forget that, since the cancer, he couldn't tolerate more than two beers. He'd have four or five, and then start the walk home only to discover he was too tired to make it. The police would find him asleep on a bench in the courthouse square. When they woke him, he'd say, "Call my daughter Sarah." And the police, who knew I wasn't his child, would call and say jokingly, "We need you to come and get your father." When I'd arrive to pick him up from the station, he'd hug me and wink, as if he thought we'd really pulled one over on the man. The police winked, too, as if we'd just pulled one over on old Wilbur. And I would smile, because for one of the few times in my life, I knew nobody was getting the raw end of this deal.

On Wednesdays, when I was working at Bartlett House, he let himself in to use the wringer washer in my kitchen and hung his clothes to dry on a line he'd strung from the apple tree to the side of the house. When the washing machine broke down, which it did every few months, he fixed it. He was handy, and often came upstairs to tinker with the plumbing, the old Warm Morning heaters, the fuse box. He said he'd never owned a car, but he kept my oil changed. And although he couldn't push the lawnmower, he kept the blades sharp and made sure it was full of gas so that I could.

Every Saturday, I brought him his groceries: twenty-one cans of chocolate Ensure, two Hershey's chocolate bars, and seven forty-ounce bottles of malt liquor. We'd sit on the porch for a while, or in winter stand in the kitchen, and gossip about the goings-on at the shelter. The folk who cycled in and out were as close as he had to friends since moving into town. Two or three times a week, he'd go to the soup kitchen for a lunch he couldn't eat, just for the company. He would warn me when Traveling Jack was on a drinking binge and ought to be put out at night, when Pamela was off her meds and needed looking after, when there was someone new in town he thought was up to no good and warranted a little extra scrutiny. He knew, without being told, that he shouldn't bring these friends back to the house. If they gave him grief about this, he never let on, though I imagine they did. Apartments were communal among the frequently homeless. It was bad form to have a place and not let other folk crash there. This was part of why it was so hard for them to hold on to apartments once they had them.

Welcome to the Neighborhood

During his courses of chemo, I would take Wilbur to the hospital twice a week to have the little pump he wore in a fanny pack refilled. Because he got the poison so slowly, he said it never made him ill, but he refused radiation treatment after the first course. Given the odds, he didn't think the sickness it caused was worth it. "If I was a dog, it wouldn't be time to put me down, but there wouldn't be no use in taking me to the vet, neither," he used to joke. He was proud of outlasting his prognosis. He refused pain medication because the doctor told him he couldn't drink while taking it and that offended his sense of autonomy. Most nights, he said, he fell asleep while the bottle was still mostly full and dumped out the rest in the morning, but it was the principle of the thing. "Ain't nobody," he'd say, "should tell an old man he can't have himself a beer at night excepting his wife, and I never wanted me no wife."

Wilbur was accustomed to solitude. He didn't ask much, and preferred to tinker with the car or the washing machine when I wasn't home, so early on I gave him a key to my door and an extra set of keys to the car. It never occurred to me to wonder about the wisdom of this. Because he couldn't write well, he left artifacts instead of notes: empty oil cans, the busted belt he'd replaced on the washer, sometimes in spring a bouquet of wildflowers wrapped in a paper towel on my kitchen table. That he asked so little, and was so completely trustworthy, made it easy to have him there. Very soon, we began simply to think of ourselves as neighbors, though the helpful and concerned sort that even then seemed something of an anachronism. A blessing, really.

AFTER I finished college, in the summer that I was twenty-nine—long after Wilbur should have been dead, according to his doctor—I sold the house and moved to Alabama. I felt guilty leaving Wilbur behind, with nobody to drive him to chemotherapy or do his shopping.

"Do you want to come with me?" I'd asked, once the decision was made. "You can. And it's always warm there, which would be easier on you." We were standing in his kitchen, both in aprons. I was making pies for a bake sale and he was teaching me to make the crust with lard, the way his mother had.

"Nah," he said, cutting the lard into the flour with two knives. "I like it here just fine, and I can get along. The ladies from Christian Help will carry me to the doctor, and I'm sure I can get someone to do the shopping." He passed me the mixing bowl. "Here you go. I can mix it, but I ain't never been any good at rolling it out. Always tear it up."

He didn't seem sick, just worn out. He'd never really seemed sick after that first night in the shelter.

"I feel like I'm running out on you, though. Maybe I shouldn't go?"

"Now you're just talking crazy," he said, taking off his apron. "Well, my part's done. You gotta finish them pies yourself. I'm gonna go lie down for a nap. Just let yourself out when you're done." He ducked out of the kitchen without even saying good-bye and, just like that, the matter was settled.

I knocked five thousand dollars off the price of the house and sold it to some friends with the understanding that Wilbur could stay there, rent free, for as long as he lived. They promised to be kind to him, though not to take him to doctors' appointments or do his shopping. But it was okay, because he'd arranged for "the charity ladies" to do those things. I called to check on him as soon as I'd moved into my new place. The friends who bought the house carried their cordless phone down to him. "You just get on with your life," he'd said. "I've got everything under control over here. Now quit bothering me, and these nice people, and get you some rest. Alabama is a long drive."

Wilbur died two weeks later, sitting in an old armchair that he'd found in a neighbor's trash and moved onto the porch just that afternoon. It was a quiet, easy death. He had a pauper's burial. The social worker at Bartlett House filled out the forms, even though it had been years since he was her responsibility. There was no service. No headstone. Just a small prayer before lunch at the soup kitchen on the day he was interred and a three-line obituary in the local paper. It would have been enough for Wilbur, though, I think. He wasn't much for ceremony or making a fuss.

THE BASEMENT of my current house is empty except for boxes of books and a washing machine. What little world-changing I do happens in the college class-room, although I like to think that—as at the homeless shelter—what few changes I can help bring about make some small difference. As I write this, the winter storms are receding and the forsythia has gone to bud. I have my own chair on my own porch now, beside my husband's, where we too like to sit of an evening and have a beer. Sometimes, I raise my bottle to the memory of Wilbur. Mostly, though, I just get on with my life, as Wilbur said I should.

The House on Congress Street

Lee never came out. I will always remember this.

The year was 2002 and we were living in the house on Congress Street—the first place Ben my husband and I lived together—in the quaint seaside town of Newburyport, Massachusetts. We were not alone, however; our apartment was on the first floor of a multifamily home and so, in addition to hardwood floors, high ceilings, and lovely bay windows in the living room that looked out on a park across the street, we had neighbors.

In the apartment directly above us was Rob, a single man in his forties with four cats and a passion for *South Park*, cigarettes, and smoking pot. On the top floor were two studios, one belonging to a woman named Savannah, and the other to a petite, older-looking man named Lee.

With the exception of Rob—who asked us to watch his cats when he went on vacation or brought us corned beef and cabbage on St. Patty's day—we didn't see our housemates much. I met Savannah only once in the year and a half we lived there; rumor had it she stayed at her girlfriend's house most of the time. And I only saw Lee during fire alarms, when we would all wait on the sidewalk until the firemen arrived and gave us the okay to go back inside. I remember shaking hands with Lee once: the feel of his sweaty, delicate palm.

⁝

This was the house with the spider problem. First, it was only a stray here and there, unfortunate wanderers from the basement into the living room where they were quickly extinguished by a shoe or an old magazine. Soon, however, as summer gave way to autumn, they migrated to the outside of the house. The spiders came in all shapes and shades—blacks, browns, grays. I was told the ones shaped like fiddles were the ones to avoid, and I'd taken up the habit of running to the front door and fumbling with my keys while keeping one eye out for anything that moved and resembled an instrument.

When I bought four bags of candy on Halloween and no children rang our bell, I blamed the spiders.

"The kids are scared," I told Ben, who refused to exterminate them with the can of Raid I had purchased for that purpose. He shrugged and said, "Spiders need a place to live too . . . besides they're good. They eat the other bugs."

The next day, I saw Rob outside with a broom, knocking the spiders down, pulling at the sticky webs with his fingers. I waved from the window and mouthed the word, "thanks." But by the next afternoon, to my surprise, most of the spiders, and their webs, had returned.

Wanting to understand more about spiders, about why they lived here, at our house, I did research and jotted some notes in a journal:

> *Spiders can live anywhere. They are highly adaptable.*
> *A spider's web is its home . . . many species of spider rebuild their web, or home, each day.*
> *An interesting fact: the Native Americans believe that the spider represents connection between the past and future . . . A symbol of possibility.*

The week we had three fire alarms in a row, the firemen speculated it was because of the spiders.

"Yeah, probably a spider setting off the sensor . . ." but I suspected it was because they could come up with no other explanation.

I had noticed, when waiting for the truck to arrive three chilly evenings in a row, that Lee never came out of the house.

"Do you think he's home?" I'd said to Rob on the third night. We could see a light on in his apartment. His beat-up blue Ford Escort on the street in front of the house, where it always was.

"I don't know . . . but if he is, I don't know how he could stay holed up in his apartment with the sound of that alarm. I'd have a heart attack."

"Maybe we should call the landlord," I suggested to Ben. He agreed.

But neither of us called.

Maybe we each thought the other had done it.

Maybe we both had the same thought: we're overreacting.

But I can only speak for myself. And even then, I find this question difficult to answer. Why didn't I call? Just to be sure? Not only was Lee a neighbor, but he was living under the same roof. Did this mean I had an even greater responsibility to make sure he was okay?

Or maybe it's because at thirty-one, I was selfish. And naïve. Because I didn't believe yet that the worst could happen, a notion that would change quickly, only a few months later, when my mother would die of ovarian cancer and nothing would ever be the same again. I remember returning home to Congress Street after her funeral and staring into the cupboards while crying, seeking some sort of comfort, or nourishment that could never be fed.

⋮

Three days after the final fire alarm, we awoke to a banging on the front door. It was Lee's boss.

"Have you seen him?" the man wanted to know. "He hasn't shown up for work in four days."

We called our landlord, who came and, after glancing curiously at the spiders on the outside of the house, found Lee in his kitchen, dead of a heart attack.

The next morning I saw Rob and Rick talking outside the house. It was snowing, an unexpected flurry, the first of the season. I dug my hat and boots out of the hall closet to go out and meet them.

Although I didn't know Lee, I felt bad and wanted to go to his funeral. But for a moment, I couldn't even remember his name. I quickly ran as many three-letter names through my head as possible: Tom, Tim, Jim, Joe. Then I just said, "Will there be a funeral?"

"Nope, none that I know of," our landlord said. "We haven't been able to locate anyone. It seems he had no family . . . no home, like he didn't come from anywhere. It's weird . . . sad, really."

"I think Lee was in the witness protection program," Rob half-joked.

Lee. That was his name. I repeated it in my head several times, hoping to commit it to memory.

I looked up at his dark window for a moment and then over at Lee's car. It would remain in its spot in front of the house for about another month until one day, like the spiders, like everything, it simply disappeared.

The Invincible

Delano rode like wind, like death was rumor not to be trusted. He'd shift his grip wide on his handlebars and lift his feet to the bike's saddle, and when he was certain he had your attention, he'd raise one leg in the air, his body like a forward-fallen *K*.

We'd build ramps with planks the builders left behind when they abandoned their construction projects in the acres behind our house. We leaned plywood against boulders that must have dated back to when Florida was still underwater; wave patterns riddled these rocks. Bits of shell and coral stuck to their surfaces. If you peeked in the hole-pocked face of one, you knew you were looking into the homes of sea creatures. When Delano's wheels lifted from the wood-and-rock ramp, he loosed his grip and spread his arms like wings, like he knew one of these times he was destined to fly.

When we could find no plywood, we raced our bikes in the stony terrain that was our backyard, alongside trenches, which extended like roofless catacombs for what felt like miles.

"This is where they'll lay the plumbing," Delano told me, "if they ever come back. This is like how the allies fought the Germans."

"This is like my ant farm," I said.

When it rained, we dared each other to swim in the trenches, then checked each other for leeches and signs of ringworm.

Once, we followed these channels to a dead end near the woods that spread between the construction site and my elementary school. Sheetrock stretched loosely over the channel's top where it ended, making a roof, making a dim cave. A rusted yellow chair, the kind we had in kindergarten class, was pushed up in one corner. Grit-speckles covered a black garbage bag at the chair's feet.

Cukie was with us this time, I think. Cukie was our fatherless cousin, so we took him adventuring with us when Aunty Daphne needed time.

Anyway, we had experience inspecting these garbage bags. What we needed was one good stick. We'd found dozens in the acres behind our home, the bags I mean. When Delano flicked one open, you knew to hold your nose. Really, you were holding it already. Slaughtered animals, many unidentifiable, some cats, or cat-like, rotted into the plastic. But a good find consisted of a crucifix, or a rosary, or a Bible with the bones. Sometimes, the bags contained just the Bible.

"Devil worshippers," I liked to say.

"No. It's Santeria," Delano corrected me.

"Santa Maria?" Cukie asked on at least one occasion.

This time, though, when the stick flicked bag, there were no bones or Bibles, no gag-inducing funk, just magazines; half a dozen, displaying full-on sex in glossy stills. We collected those magazines and dusted them off. Pored over them for days. Afterward, and I can't say for sure, but I'd guess none of us were the same.

Occupants

First there is Brandon, whom everyone calls Squeaky B because of his big body and small voice. Also his sixteen-year-old cousin, Duncan, who opts out of high school and instead sits on the front porch of their house with a laptop while someone corn-rows his hair. When their power gets shut off, Duncan charges his laptop at our house. One night he wakes me up asking for a charge at one-thirty and I tell him enough is enough and close the door.

Brandon's getting his degree in sports management and I edit his papers on Kobe Bryant and Mike Tomlin. He volunteers as an assistant football coach at the high school. He wants to do anything for the NFL. His teachers ask questions when his grades improve and I tell him to tell them he has a tutor, or, if he wants to fuck with them, to play the race card.

Some afternoons after teaching I sit with them and their other cousin, John, and we drink an anti-energy drink called Drank (which tells us to "Slow our roll") and Steel Reserve (which tells us it is "High Gravity"). I tell them that I think the Ramones once wrote a jingle for Steel Reserve but they've never heard of the Ramones.

In the spring, they agree with their landlord to paint the entire peeling and collapsing Victorian they call home for a one-time rebate of two hundred dollars off their rent. They choose charcoal-gray with forest-green trim. They borrow my ladders and drop cloths. Half of the house is painted when someone shows up with an orange notice that says the house is being condemned.

⋮

Strings are pulled.

A new family comes in a convoy of pickup trucks and Chevy Cavaliers.

The goateed father in the trucker's cap and the toothless mother won't make eye contact with me over our shared chain-link fence. But the kids—a little boy and a littler girl—love our dog with shrill voices and sticky hands.

Ten-year-old Jeremiah is the envoy. He asks for the cans and bottles in our recycling bin once a week and then steers them down to the corner store slung over his shoulder in great black sacks, the front tire on his BMX wobbling over every crack in the sidewalk. When our recycling bin is empty he asks us for money.

Eight o'clock Tuesday morning and Jeremiah, red-headed and gap-toothed, stands on our back porch with an econo-sized can of SpaghettiOs and a dinner plate. He wants to know if we have a can opener. Then he wants to know if we could heat this up for him.

Two weeks after Christmas, Jeremiah arrives again with a gift for my wife: a clear plastic bird on a string. If you unscrew the bird's head it becomes a wand through which you can blow small bubbles. He asks if he can shovel our driveway. I tell him I have no cash on me, but when I get out of the shower I see that he's shoveled it anyway.

They are evicted after seven months and the following tenants find the oven door missing, used crack pipes in every room, and small orange mushrooms growing out of the bathtub.

$$\vdots$$

The last family arrives in a flurry of box-trucks, beaters, and one giant jacked-up Ford pickup that they use to go mud-bogging behind the bowling alley off Stadium Drive.

Gary and Rick are half brothers. Their elderly mother is Mee-maw. She sits out on the front porch with a box fan and watches the kids: a string of babies and toddlers who visit on the weekends, dropped off by ex-wives and ex-husbands, and spread their bright plastic toys across the hard-packed dirt of the backyard.

There are also James and Monica and their fresh fat baby everyone calls Butterbean. James is quiet, polite, and covered in the shaky scrawl of his own tattoo work. When he goes missing for a few weeks Monica explains, through the thick cut of her lisp, that he's in jail on charges of kidnapping and possession, bullshit charges, she says, that are *really* all about a bad rap from when he was fifteen and accidentally shot his best friend to death back in North Carolina.

Rick is six years clean but looks like he just got off a weeklong amphetamine bender because of a spinal injury he suffered when he was gang-beat in his sleep in prison. His teeth are one solid fused mass of brown and blue. On the day that we're moving out, he waits until after carrying a dresser and a queen-sized bed down the stairs of our place and into the moving truck before telling me that he really isn't supposed to lift anything over fifty pounds on account of he could end up paralyzed. When I yell at him he says, "What am I supposed to do, stop living my life?"

Gary chases away the pregnant girl from down the street—the one who knocks on our door asking for money and/or a ride to the McDonald's on East Michigan—when she tries to break into our bathroom window one night while we're out of town. He calls the cops and files a report.

Gary also shows up on my porch one morning, two hours before I have to teach, with a pint of Dubra vodka and a six-pack of Mountain Dew. When I open the door and say, "Mountain Dubra?" he says he knew I would get it.

The night before we move, Gary and Rick and I pitch horseshoes in the long dirt stretch of their back lot. The house is being condemned again. Around midnight their power cuts out, killing the mechanic's drop-bulb they'd strung up to light our game. I run back to my house and grab a bag of votive candles and we place one ablaze in front of each stake. We don't mind having to relight them every time someone scores a point.

Daystar

She wanted a little room for thinking:
but she saw diapers steaming on the line,
a doll slumped behind the door.

So she lugged a chair behind the garage
to sit out the children's naps.

Sometimes there were things to watch—
the pinched armor of a vanished cricket,
a floating maple leaf. Other days
she stared until she was assured
when she closed her eyes
she'd see only her own vivid blood.

She had an hour, at best, before Liza appeared
pouting from the top of the stairs.
And just *what* was mother doing
out back with the field mice? Why,

building a palace. Later
that night when Thomas rolled over and
lurched into her, she would open her eyes
and think of the place that was hers
for an hour—where
she was nothing,
pure nothing, in the middle of the day.

House near the Airport

1

The next plane enters its final approach,
enlarging by degrees its shadow—

which warps as it combs the canopies
of leaves, the knocking veins of traffic;
it climbs and descends

the angled roofs one after the other,
falling to the yards, the streets
between them, a shadow dividing

and re-forming, a swatch of it sliding
through window after window—
through my kitchen window, where,

for a quarter-instant, the room
darkens. Then the roar rolls over—
an empty wave. I hardly notice.

2

Plane like a massive firework:
upon landing, its contents sealed
those hours in the fuselage

explode into a hundred separate
rooms of the city. This happens
a thousand times a day.

3

Those strangers inhabit
not just the plane
but the shadow—which floods

how many windowed rooms?
I was in this shade as it carried you,
you were in my house

as it held me. Don't say that
means nothing, America—! To which
you reply: The flight path

painted over your neighborhood
is killing your property values—
and it's easy to calculate

with rudimentary physics
the height at which a plane ceases
to cast its shadow against the earth.

Aubade in the Old Apartment

I wake inside the old apartment. No—I wake
in the apartment two doors and one floor
down, in the 1920s building slightly past
its prime, but still charming, with its rust-
colored trim and wide, wooden staircase, the foyer
tiled and smelling intermittently and vaguely
of piss, the electronics store underneath,
next to what was once cheap and decent
Korean food, now gone. I wake today to
the artificial dawn we learned to love
through acclimation, early mornings
of our early twenties when
I rode the BART and my bike
to teach and you sold people succulents
and lemon trees. I wake to
that familiar aurora of pink
neon signage reading *glamor*
in two different spellings, the street-
lights on their sturdy green posts
winking like girls, soft sigh then hum
of the bus coming to a stop at the curb.
Through the blinds, sky still black
as asphalt and the dependable sing-song
of the crosswalk. A woman shuffles
down 40th with all her possessions
in a wheelchair, her shadow
dragging behind her like a tide, a siren
shrill in the distance, so far I can imagine
all danger a dream, and
it does not wake you. You are still
asleep in this just-breaking morning
I have been so lucky
to wake to like any other, your face

turned towards mine on the pillow we share.
I know it will not always be like this: you and I
so poor and wise or desperate
enough to think anything we own is beautiful
just because it's ours. But for now,
we are here, back in the old apartment
building where we came at 21 and now
again at 26, the same
subways rattling into the station
just down the block, the donut shop and the wig shop
and the pizza place no one goes into
and the neighbors who remembered us and will
stir in a few hours to tramp through
nearly identical rooms above us, everything so similar to
how it was I could almost forget
this life isn't endless—not a series
of these simple and good enough days.

House Hunting

1

FIRST AD. 2 fam. 10+4, 1 house off Cambridge St.,
24′ kit., 24′ master bdrm. Low $100's.

"Fixed it all myself. Tore out some walls—
opened it all up; new tiles . . . Beautiful!
She wanted a dishwasher, I put in
a dishwasher, disposal—everything!
Beautiful!
                    Thirty years we lived there . . .

                                                  How's

seven o'clock?"

                    A waxed black Coupe de Ville
pulls up at seven sharp; he heaves himself out
on the huge upholstered door . . .
                                        Small, yet stooped—
a little human question mark.
                                        His short
white summer shirt at least a size too big;
his pressed, but oily, olive gabardines
bunched under his belt . . . He pastes his few, sad,
last grey hairs straight back across his freckled,
sweaty scalp.
                    (Was this the wound-up, do-it-
yourself voice on the other end of the line?)

She's even smaller. Not much younger (sixty?)
but in superior repair. Blonde; lipstick
and powder; a real figure moving under
the sheer white blouse and pink pants suit;
a Star of David—
                    (Morelli? Could *he* be
Jewish too?)

"We moved up the North Shore
just a year ago" (her hoarse rough voice
preceding us up the narrow hallway stairs)
"when he retired. Nice place.

I hated leaving.
Thirty years, did he tell you? . . . time!

I still
can't keep him home. He misses work—but, you know,
they don't miss him . . .

If we stayed, it would've
killed him.

This is the first time I've been back!"

She unlocks, and shows us in; he shows off
his handiwork: the glazed "Italian" tiles;
a dusty niche "built in for the Frigidaire."

A doll house:
the "24' kitchen"'s just
a showroom strip of white appliances,
partitioned by two drainpipe "columns" ("Tore
out some walls") from a playpen living room . . .

Some magazines (glossy, technical) lie strewn
on the dark-green, winestained wall-to-wall;

upstairs, a home computer crowds one long
(24'?) and very narrow bedroom . . .

Four—tiny?—Chinese MIT grad students
rent; a widowed sister-in-law (they don't
say whose) "has the downstairs."

A shade is torn;
a cardboard mobile dangles motionless.

"Look what they've done!"
She's shaking. "—It's
scarcely been a year! I told him we

should've cleaned it up before we took
that ad.
            I'm so ashamed. In thirty years
it's never looked like this! . . ."

                        Downstairs, it's worse—
a rabbit hole: low dusty ceilings; narrow
windows; soiled wallpaper; worn linoleum.

A labyrinth of shopping bags and cardboard
cartons stuffed with clothes. No place to move.

How long since anyone had looked down here? . . .

He doesn't say a word; she blots a tear;
I nearly hit my forehead ducking out.

We say we'll call to let them know. They know.

                        2

        IMMED. OCCUPANCY. Exceptional high-ceilinged,
        fireplaced, lge rms, detailed woodwork, mod. bathrooms,
        3 new kitchens, 3 story house plus basement & gar & parking.
        Make offer. Must sell.

"I'm not in real estate; I'm a lawyer—I've
got to be careful. My parents gave me this house
when I was still in law school. Now I'm tied up
in a New York deal worth over a million;
I can't waste time here. I want to sell
this weekend.
            Why do you think I'm asking
so much less than the market value? . . ."

                                    Look
at the fluted marble mantels, those intricate
ceiling medallions (hand-carved mahogany),
the high-arched Victorian windows: our own
mansion—

        and a steal—
                        with "rental units"
and a parking lot . . . Could we scrape up
a down payment?

                    "Four rooms here, two bathrooms;
a five-room flat—three baths—upstairs; three rooms
with bath in the attic." There's even a rusty tub
down cellar.
                    Seven bathrooms? (What *was* this,
a monastery? Or a brothel—)
                                The sinks
and johns look new . . . and pasted in; a lot of
broken windows, and warped frames.

                            "Not safe?
There hasn't been a break-in since I've been here.
It's a good neighborhood—I don't know where
it gets the reputation. We've had great parties!

Don't worry about rent control. The rents
are high enough to pay your mortgage!" (He quotes
figures we like.)
                    "—Besides, they don't control
how much you can charge for parking. No one asks,
no one complains;
                    there's always a loophole . . .

                                    Look,
I've got another couple coming back tomorrow.
I don't want to pressure you (I *like* you), but
you want the house, you'll have to decide soon . . .

How much did you say you planned on putting down?"

He's not too keen about *our* figure; he wants
thirty percent—no waiting. He says
he'd even do the financing himself . . .

We'll have to make some calls tonight.

                                        Meanwhile,

we think we'd better do a little sleuthing . . .

At City Hall, the deed isn't registered
in a name we recognize (though a name we do
turns up on a lot of other properties—
whose house *is* this, anyway?)
                             and last
changed hands less than two years ago (how long
did he say he lived there?).

                         The Rent Board says
the rents are *quite* controlled. Too controlled
to help us meet a mortgage? (How much would *we*
have to charge for parking?)
                          No one's reported
the recent plumbing and "improvements": why
didn't he want to raise the legal rent?
(What *isn't* "legal"?)

                    Our shady dream house . . .

                                  Good
we checked. Weren't we *right* to be suspicious?

But who could afford a dream house market rate,
no loopholes . . .
                Why can't we make those loopholes
work for us?

            We're wasting time. Where can we
get our hands on ready cash?
                      He said he
liked us—maybe he'll reconsider; that other
couple might be just as strapped . . .

We'll call

in the morning—

        tell him we want the house (*don't* we?)
and that we've got to find some way to work this out.

        3

    SOMERVILLE. Solid 2 family in superior
    location. Cedar-shingled beauty with
    spacious aptmts & contemporary updating,
    big sun deck & 2 car garage.

 "They're not speaking to me upstairs. My
stepdaughter. We haven't spoken since
the Doll died last year. They even
forgot my birthday . . . Seventy-three today—
would you believe it? *Cheers!*

                Go on, look
around. I've got nothing to hide."

—It's oddly "tasteful" for this florid,
garrulous grandpa:
             low-slung, plastic-covered,
blonde '50s "sectionals"; a couple of
yellow brick planters ("Built 'em myself—
not bad for an old man, eh?"); fine-grained
walnut paneling; and sliding glass-door cabinets
suspended over the long oak kitchen counter . . .

The master bedroom, once evidently two ("I
knocked down that wall with my own two hands!"),
looks unslept-in . . .
            In the spare, rumpled den,
an unmade daybed, a closetful of shirts.

A few tiles missing in the shower.

 "To tell you the truth, I lost interest when
the Doll died. That's why I'm selling . . . I used to
fix up every little thing—now I don't care.

I could call my son, and move in with him
tonight—he keeps asking. Don't you believe me?
Look, I'm picking up the phone . . ."

●

"Twenty-five years—and he's selling the house
right out from under us!
                              All my friends
live on this street; my kids' friends . . .

                                        My husband
had a restaurant around the corner, three blocks
from here. It burned down two years ago—
we still haven't collected the insurance;
now he's driving a cab. We'd buy the house
ourselves if we had any money.

Who thinks they'll ever have to move . . .

                                        There's so much
stuff! We've still got all the kids' toys.

                              At least
we won't have to pay these heating bills. Winters
it's freezing in here! This year
we were going to close off the living room
on account of the cold.
                          I feel sorry for anyone
moving here!

              It's all his son's idea . . . If
he died, my sister and me would get half
the house; but if he sells it, he could leave
all the money to his son!

                    What can you do—
you have to make the best.

He drinks, did you
notice? A certified alky! Even before my
mother died . . . Believe me, he was never the
greatest husband in the world.

We get so
worried about him, alone down there . . . He's
fallen a dozen times, and he won't
let us in—thinks we're spying on him.

He just can't be trusted. Changes his mind
every five seconds—

you know, at the last minute
he could decide not to sell!

I'll be glad
to see him taken care of, though; I just hope
that son of his knows what kind of a bargain
he's getting . . .

Listen, is there any chance
you could let us stay? We've been good tenants—
fix things ourselves; always pay the rent on time . . .

Of course, it would depend on how much you were
planning to raise it. We could even squeeze in
downstairs, if you needed *our* place; put in
a daybed until my son leaves home;
make do!

We've done it before . . . At least we could stay
in our own neighborhood, our own house.
It would be
awful to have to move—awful to move away."

Writing the Kingdom on Skates

We had lived in northern New Jersey, an area that would soon be peppered with homes, but when my family moved there—from a flat in a slightly more urban part of Bergen County—it resembled wilderness. We were third to be settled on a development of new houses, split-levels with just the essentials, but it was my mother's dream to have a family room, with a fireplace, and bookshelves installed on either side. It would take a few years to pay for its completion. For a long time, it was simply a concrete floor with cinderblock walls about three feet high and painted white. It was large enough to have housed a swimming pool, and the concrete floor became my rink for roller skating with my good friend Lisa.

Our old metal skates were fashioned like cars, with two sets of wheels; they could be shortened and lengthened by means of a key. A soothing sound, that of two girls careening on cement. The paint on the walls was thick. We could grab the top of the wall, if we wished to or needed to, slide our fingers on the edge without tearing any flesh. My friend and I solved many world problems while skating in eights and circles, forward and back. We engaged in serious discourse. We often did, us girls—there was a bunch of us all around the same age. Mine was one of the three Jewish families in the neighborhood, and I had questions that could not be resolved by my parents. I did not understand Jesus, how he could be God and human at the same time. I asked my friend about Jesus, and she dutifully answered me, as we skated.

Words like "crucifix" and "salvation" don't come up in the early indoctrination of Jews.

"We believe in Jesus, that he was the savior."

I'm remembering a progression, as I recall this—not the precise conversation. Surely too many years have passed—but this is generally how it went, how I remember it.

"What's 'savior'?"

"Means he saves us."

"What's saving?"

"From Hell."

"Hell?"

"Damnation?"

"What's that?"

"Fire and the devil?"

"You're kidding? Where is that?"

"After you die."

"But where is it?"

"Down there," she said, my friend, pointing at the concrete floor. Early on Lisa established herself as someone who was both fun and trustworthy. I would watch her read on her porch. She was not someone whose parents kept goading her on about it.

IT WAS no small enterprise for the seven-year-old me to grasp the idea of this Hell. For me, it had neither history nor ritual, but it was helpful to know that Hell was where they buried the bodies of the dead. As someone who accompanied her father in his rounds to place pebbles on various headstones in Newark, New Jersey, and in Queens, I was acquainted with the graveyard, even though I had not known those whose graves I visited. What I do know was that I embarrassed my father by mistaking the paid mourners for Santa Claus. When my father took me in the men's room (I had no brothers), I questioned him about what exactly it was that "those men were doing to the walls." The only death I had really known about was the mother of one of our friends in the group who was a little older. I believed her mother was still around somewhere, just unseen. However, I also knew very well the story of Pompeii, which would solidify itself on the shelf and torment me when I became a solid reader. Still, I'd heard all about lava and the word "petrify" and its relationship to the word "volcano," and so it meant that I had to renew my attempts to question my mother about Hell and salvation and Jesus, which I did, endlessly, but to no avail.

The skating conversation continued. "So how does he save you?"

"When you get baptized."

"What's baptized?"

"They sprinkle water over you. People do it differently. Some people actually swim in the water, and some people get sprinkled, even before they have an opportunity to agree to it."

"Agree to what?"

"Becoming Christian."

"What did you do?"

"I got sprinkled. As a baby. I don't exactly remember it."

"Jesus. He's a Christian, then?"

I DIDN'T realize I was piecing a religion together. It's probably a little like the way I was and am once again piecing this memory together. Except—the opposite.

The child that I was was like the reader. I was given words and concepts—and as can be seen, the way I was given to understand the concepts came by way of images. They made a splash in the simplicity of my mind. Now, on the other hand, I have this memory, which is like an old film. I have some images stored in that murky mind, not so simple, but instead polluted, radioactive, transgressive, water that's hard to swim in without pulling up netting and slime and algae. It's not easy to restore that scene. I've been back to that town, and my hometown is so far gone, I'm better off trying to simply remember it. One time I saw that my little patio cum skating rink was now a solid foundation surrounded by more than sixty years of shrubs. The last time I drove by, all the shrubs and most of the trees in the yard had been unearthed, chopped down. And while I certainly do not recall the exact conversation, I do remember the back and forth; I remember my own drive to understand, and I remember that it came about. I recall that feeling of satisfaction as well as I recall the texture of the cement, the careening, the brightness of the day, Lisa's hair flying about, her braids. I recall the way she held her face, and I recall a mix of honesty, humor, and intelligence in her eyes that were brown. I recall joy.

I recall looking out my bedroom window mesmerized by the Christmas lights that were strewn around her porch door. I remember that there was no discernible pattern to the lights. I loved them.

Looking back, I see a simpler time. If only I could go back there. I knew about Jesus, even sang about him because I loved the tune of "Jesus Loves Me." I found it so catchy that I sang it on the toilet until my father hollered for me to stop. I'd mixed it up with the Mickey Mouse Club Song. So by the end it went something like this: *We are weak / and He is strong / That's how Mouseketeers are born.*

Santa Claus, Christmas ornaments, blinking lights around doorways, the Tree, Easter dresses and hats, Easter candy—I learned to accept that those treasures would never be mine, much the way I understood that I wouldn't have long blond hair or pale blue eyes or speak with the accents of Midwesterners or Southerners, or grow large tomatoes the way my next-door neighbor from Nebraska did.

But suddenly, now, at this moment in the setting of my quasi-roller-skating rink, the notion of suffering in the afterlife haunted me, vying as it did with my fervent belief in everlasting life. As we were skating that day, something congealed, and it became painfully clear to my seven-year-old mind that unless you were Christian and baptized, you were going to Hell someday. Even though it didn't penetrate my inner world enough to absolutely terrify me the way the story of the Lindbergh kidnapping did, or the story of Frankenstein did—or this fear that I had that the electrical saw in another friend's basement might get loose and attack me when I slept over at her house—certainly not the way it got all my

Welcome to the Neighborhood

friends pasty white and respectful—still I knew Hell wasn't something I wanted to experience firsthand.

How could these two ways of seeing the world coexist? In my child's mind, only one could be correct. Did I know then that we would come to some kind of philosophical peace treaty? It was the kind of conversation that was to be continued, and roller skating, such as it was, was the perfect venue.

Still it gnawed at me to see the extreme differences in our perceptions. I had a stubborn nature. If there were no reconciliation, I would create one. At a later point, I would reject much of what I held dear. I would see the contradictions of Judaism. I would see movies with heroic nuns and wish to be one. I would find the very idea of "the chosen people" anathema. But now I was firmly identified. I loved my Hebrew School teachers, the sweet-smelling, smiling women who hugged us and joked as they tried to pass on the goods, and they fed us and sang and danced with us. Anything that mixed eating with singing was as close to God as I required. The aftermath of the Friday night service, drinking heavily sugared weak tea in the basement of the synagogue with platters of cut cakes, was my idea of heaven. I loved the songs and had known all the words before I even knew how to read. I attended services with my father. Religious gatherings were tied up with familial gatherings, the wild games and hushed conversations with cousins, and meshing of delicious food with the beloved apartments of my grandmother, or the beautiful homes of aunts. My mother, an agnostic until the end, thought praying was voodoo, but I loved praying.

Of course, there is plenty of darkness in Judaism. Did I know it then? It would all turn for me, turn around and around, and it is still turning. It's not in a stable place, but it was in a stable place then. I loved my Judaism, would not forsake it, even for the Christmas tree. There was no way I was going to become Christian for fear of Hell.

Jesus is God's son. Why was this such a fascinating idea, though? Why did they make so much of it? *Of course* he was God's child. Who wasn't? This tidbit was a thing I chewed on for a long time, the way children do—really mulled it over, until one day it just popped out. I said to my friend again, when we were roller-skating on the foundation, "So what if Jesus is God's son! I'm God's daughter."

"You can't be God's daughter."

"Why not?"

"Jesus is special."

"I know, but you can be God's daughter, too," I said.

"Really?"

It was hard to read her face.

"We all believe the same thing, then," I said.

"I guess," she said.

"So this way I don't have to go to Hell anymore, right?"

"Right," she said.

"Well, it's the same thing, then." I wasn't thinking about baptism anymore. I was thinking—okay, now. Okay!

We kept skating and repeating the thing, because I needed to know she agreed with me. It was something that had to be made clear, and the way children make things clear is by repeating it. Adults do it, too. With a little less grace.

"What's the same thing?"

"Jews," I said. "And Christians. We are all God's children—so the way I look at it, Jesus was God's son, and I'm God's daughter. And so are you."

THE TENETS of Christianity are among those things I still find puzzling. Grace is something that I wouldn't begin to approach until I read Flannery O'Connor— and I wouldn't really get to the bottom of it until I taught the story, "A Good Man Is Hard to Find," and the truth is I'm not sure I'll ever truly get it until I have it, if you know what I mean.

It amuses me now that I was focused more on the idea rather than on the ritual of baptism. Otherwise, why not perform some compromising act, like a little sprinkling of water to prevent my descent, my demise. But I did nothing of the kind. It was the idea, the reconciliation, that settled. It was the concept, after all. The dialogue. The words.

And the skating.

Religion

We woke in the parked car aslant in the field Cory's grandmother had found
for us to sleep in, turned earth in front of us, almost houses behind, frames and
unpoured sidewalks, abandoned machines and wheelbarrows left anywhere in the
thin light that was afternoon light we know for spring in the county. We had lived
through these long, wrong seasons before; we knew this cold, how even the fruit
trees went on pouting, unwilling as girls to unfurl their crimped leaves, show their
blossoms. Too cold to have even unrolled the windows before we fell asleep—on
the instant—the car driving itself over the ridged site and tender, penned-off,
seeded yards to settle safely at an angle on higher ground.

Here it was, awake again, we hushed the unmade house that we had left
behind, the sorrowful impressions of bodies in beds, blankets, curtains, clothes
bunched and flung away, my sister's crying when what was there worth crying
about?

"Did you want to go on peeing in a pan in the basement," we asked my sister,
"no running water?" Food greasing the goosenecked paper bags the women gave
us for the afternoon when they remembered there would be an afternoon with us
children
left to draw in the common room; nothing but gobby pens and squared-off pencils
sharpened by a knife to make our names with—we used erasers. We could blow
off what we wrote: our names and our mothers' names and where we had come
from or been to, which was no place you would want to be once you had learned
how to spell it.

But the stuttering boy, he couldn't even say where it was he had been to. Lem-
on-water yellow color of someone sickly, he slunk about the compound, brushing
his hand across his brush-cut hair, worrying his father's dying in that *tuh-town* he
couldn't say—his mother in the bleeding room with our mothers, keeping clean.

"Do you remember at all?" we asked my sister, who did not answer and might
have been sleeping when we were in the front seat saying, "Yes, it was a good
thing we had left our mother—who knew what they were doing?"

Kneading his feet with their spatulate thumbs, salving the raised skin of
wounds.

"How he suffers!" they said, walking among us with his terrible vision when
the grasses shudder on an intake of breath and cattle list, and all things roosting

or rooting lift off, move away, flame on flame taking up the field and us—but not by name. This man named Jerry, he was not always sure of our names. Jerry called us after others, or else it was we were the children, although I was not child. I had been to the bleeding room. I knew what the mothers inside were doing, washing one another and applying hot waxes. Three, four, five days shut off, standing in the steam of the herbal boil, we came out clean and nearly hairless, our knuckles pinked from scrubbing rags with stones.

The compound was so primitive. There was a spigot in the greenhouse where the shot-out panes were taped with plastic, moaning in the wind. We made the stuttering boy or the older Ruth go there to the greenhouse—"Although it could have been you," we told my sister. "Would you have liked that, the florist spikes and prickly markers at your feet, talking to the spigot, saying, Hurry, please hurry?"

We did not like to be alone on the compound, but we were often alone on the compound with the babies in sodden diapers, licking dirt. My sister found a dead rat and thought it was a kitten and came carrying it back to us in tears. We beat the dead rat with a shovel. We beat Naomi, too. We each took a whack at that stalk of a girl, running in the heat in just her underpants. The oppressive summers in this county—you need some way to stay cool.

"Don't you want air-conditioning?" we asked the baby, my sister. "Don't you like the comforts in this car?"

"I miss Mother," was what my sister said. "I want to go back."

But we told Cory's grandma, "Don't pay attention to her. She doesn't know what she is saying. Drive on, please," which she did, with Cory wheezing again in the front seat, and Cory's grandma asking, "Where's that thing you suck on, Coreen? Was there no one in that place to think of you?"

No one, no one, we assured her, with the mothers stapling pamphlets and driving to the mall. They looked like messy girls to us, and I was surprised at my mother. She let her hair grow lank and her wide-slung self swing free. She jostled underneath her clothes when she walked. Hoisting herself into the cab of the truck, never turning, as some others turned, to wave good-bye.

"Is that your idea of loving?" I asked the sniveler, the baby, my sister.

The mission was *stu-pid* was what the stuttering boy always said, worrying his real father was already dead in his bed up north where the stuttering boy had seen him. The stuttering boy had said his good-byes before his mother had put herself and him in that same truck as ours, had boarded and ridden to the compound, ridden to the mall, ridden to the old towns strung with bunting on the holidays.

OUR MOTHERS, butting tambourines and crying out, "Amen!" and crying sometimes—oh, we were embarrassed!

"Weren't you embarrassed?" we asked my sister, which was a feeling she didn't understand, I think, wearing her mopey face, saying, "I liked dancing with Mother. We put cracks in the ceiling from our dancing. Mother showed me the damage," my sister said, and she was crying again, but we weren't embarrassed this time—only angry.

"Drive faster, please," we said to Cory's grandma. "We are too many in this car. It is hard to breathe."

Under the driver's thumb all the windows hummed down at once period.

"Air!" we said, and breathed.

Scabs in the spring air on the compound, cotton-seed and petals, early bees and trembling webs, dews, worms, some stones in the sun already warm in the sun against our feet—remember spring there? How Jerry caught us in our night-gowns, how he stared? I was ashamed—we all were. We never went outdoors again quite so undressed.

Summer, the last, the insects hung in the air unmoved, the fine threads of their legs just a riffle. We went looking for water beyond the fields, broke through pokered plants in the mudbank, wet-bark brown that was a river. There, crouched, we spit white spit to watch the fish puck at the surface to eat it. I was next to the older boy, the one we never asked to come along but who sometimes came along, took his pants off, made to swim. The older boy dangled his martyred feet in the river. I watched them drift in the sluggish current and saw, too, the dark sacs of his sex, legs apart, water to his knees. Unmuscled arms and narrow shoulders, tender neck and skull, near bald he was, that older boy, ghostly border over nuded ears. We knew which mother had done that to him—and she in tears. But the older boy was a dirty boy; we saw that much against him. Chewed-up lips and blood stars on his cheeks from scratching, the older boy was angry. We were right to leave him.

Cory's grandma said, "Not if I had had more room in this car. If I had had more room in this car, I would have gathered up all of you children."

Jerry used to say things like that, too. On a painfully bright day, when I re-membered I might otherwise be in school, I stood—we all stood—at the bleached field under a dark blue sky and listened to him loving us; surcease and promise. Jerry's throat tightened when he spoke, and he unbuttoned his shirt, and we saw the flushed and grizzled heart he beat when he was speaking to us as Jerry was speaking to us. Children, he said, and we were all children—even the mothers—we belonged to him, which was belonging to something more than to a man.

"What are you crying about, you baby, you sister? You didn't even understand what he was saying. You were winding yourself in Mother's skirt. You said you were cold; you said you couldn't see," I said, although we all had to admit it was hard to see him with his back to the sun and our own eyes dazzled from wherever in the sky the sun was shining. Jerry was just a cutout; even his face was black, and his hair, wet slash in his pacing, water dripping off his chin—we never knew a man could dribble as though he were a spigot you could drink from.

I wanted to be his favorite, but when it seemed I might be, I grew afraid of Jerry's snouty fingers sniffing in the dark, his gentling, "You, is this you? Have you been waiting?"

"Oh, I am glad you children wrote me," Cory's grandma said, and we said we were glad, too. The winter had been hard, cindered mouth and blank dawning, we slept near to fires and woke, crying, "Water!" running after it to the greenhouse with a jar, jumping over babies, their puckered hands smudged black. We wouldn't touch them, though the mothers stomped and cried out, "Will you take that baby with you!" But we were after water, running over frozen earth in the fossilized boot tracks of someone's earlier departing in the thaw, in a hurry—our mothers had it been not ours. Ours were in the common room, waiting for water. They were waiting for Jerry's instructions: what to do next.

Sell your plated silver; close your thin accounts.

"Don't you remember our first house?" I asked my sister. Father's indentations in the soft couch yet not cold, and already on the curb that Jerry.

"But I liked him," my sister said. "I was carried when I didn't want to walk. He promised he would show me things outside the county."

"Jerry had nothing in his pockets for us," we said. "His hands were empty and hairless."

"Soft," my sister said, "warm."

"Moist, maybe," the fingernails cracked, stained. I remembered, too, the fingertips steepled, pressed against his lips as he considered what to do with the stuttering boy when the stuttering boy cried at the table, his face a leaky sore at the mention of a father—anyone's father—when his was dying, was probably dead. "I thought you were grown up," is what Jerry had said, before he took him to the greenhouse and left him bleedy at the spigot.

Cory's grandma said, "Lordy, Coreen, where was your mother in all of this? How was it this Jerry had such a hold?"

"The mothers were easy," we said. They only wanted a word—a *sweetheart* or a *honey*.

The mothers said Jerry's gentleness had reminded them of fathers who had had to do hard things for which they yet seemed sorry.

But the man we're talking about was never sorry. Jerry backed up over the older boy's old dog and left the bitch for us to bury. He took the money that our grandparents sent—it was lucky someone knew how to sneak us a stamp!

"Lordy," Cory's grandma said, "lucky."

"It was lucky you came," we said, when at the windows he said he saw faces—but looking in on what? Mothers putting waxy sacks of white bread on the table, sticks of softened butter? The babies in the common room were licking the TV while the in betweens were slunk on bunk beds, playing who will you marry and what will you be. Not a lot to look on, although we hoped someone was looking in on the stuttering boy with his mouth taped shut so that his sound was all blurred howling—and that to rouse his mother from what the man had done to her when she had said, "But Jerry, the boy only wants to see his father before the man is dead."

We said to Cory's grandma, "We knew our letter to you could mean trouble, and we kept some children out of it. We didn't want anyone to get hurt."

"Do you understand," we asked my sister, "we made some sacrifices. Not everyone is here, you'll notice. Some are missing." Some are in the greenhouse still, ripping sheets to strips to stuff the holes with, stop the moaning. The piss pot in the basement, the slops beneath the sink, some child is there, too, cleaning and sweeping the way he had us do to cover the boot tracks and clean the greenhouse of the flowers stood on end, their ganglia of dark roots wire-stiff, their leaves dissolving.

"Have you forgotten," we asked my sister, "those others were left to their suffering? The stuttering boy and his bleeding tongue, Naomi with her bruises were only some of what we left behind. There were babies and crawlers, children after mothers, mothers far away if it is a mall day—remember them?" Fluttering inky dittos, the mothers wander malls, seeking others like themselves. What is it that brought us here, they may wonder, but the vacant face in the darkened window, the one we saw in passing and had to claim as ours?

"The mothers sounded drugged," Cory's grandma said.

Sometimes, yes, they moved that way. In the river, after standing an eternity cut off at the ankles, they walked—dared to walk—along the shallow stony bottom, moving as mystics move with feet turned out over nails or coals: when pierced by some sharpness or benumbed by the cold, the mothers kneeled into the water and swam out. White necks and weedy hair on these mothers who squealed in the open air, sharing worn soaps and saying, "Doesn't this feel good after such a winter?"

"Stop crying!" I said to my sister. "You and your tears—you sticky baby, you aren't the only one who misses Mother."

"Of course," said Cory's grandma, "but see here," and she pointed to the street trees outside the car windows. "Look, children, what we are coming to!" Tasseled shrubbery and ragged bibs of lawn, snow shovels on front porches, narrowing blocks, less green and higher buildings, chips of colored light blinking on for evening—and us driving into it. April this was, mid-April, May, when the cold rains keep the earth black, before anything could burn.

BRAD AARON MODLIN ⋮ nonfiction

The Summer of the Commune,
and Some of the Summers before That

I.

At the commune, he chose the yellow bedroom because he wanted to live a
year inside that color, because of the color-theories people assume are true. He
hesitated to unpack his boxes because he planned first to paint additional shapes
in a lighter shade, one called *Corn Silk*, so that the walls would provide a depth of
yellow. (The old, one-person apartment had failed him with its tiny windows and
hunting-lodge dark paneling.)

The members at the commune didn't like the word *commune;* they preferred
intentional community, which they didn't much like either. They did not ask him
to give up his books or sneakers or money, but they did live by rules, and this im-
pressed him as a sign of high ideals. Everyone at the not-commune was required
to assemble at six-thirty in the morning and six-thirty in the evening to recite
Psalms; everyone ate together at noon and seven; and everything was organic. "If
you want donuts, you'll have to get them yourself," he was told when he moved
in. (If he wanted donuts, he had to hide them.) At weekly meetings, decisions
were made through discussion rather than voting. And what mattered most, why
this farm was special, was that they grew produce for the poor. He put his cereal
boxes and spices in the common pantry.

And the next morning, when the sun rose in the way it does on first days,
with that earlier-than-expected white light that says, *Today is going to last won-
derfully long,* he woke before his alarm clock for the Psalm meeting. And in the
evening, when he walked up the driveway and one of the members called out the
house window, "Welcome home," he felt somehow flattered.

He chose the yellow bedroom because he wanted to be happy his whole year
there. He hesitated to unpack his boxes.

II.

One summer he worked at a day camp for children with autism and Down's. For
two months he sang songs about sharks and showed them how to toss baseballs.

One summer he listened to teach-yourself-to-speak-Spanish recordings in the
garden and taught himself to grow tomatoes, and eggplants, and cucumbers, and
green beans, and carrots (which never came up), and potatoes that he must have

Welcome to the Neighborhood

buried too late or upside-down, and he overpacked the little bed (which the land-lord had intended for only a few flowers), so that the plants killed each other.

He secretly hoped someday to marry someone who would help him finish all his projects, and in this way, he hoped to be a completely clingy but charming husband. One summer when notebooks were on sale, he bought twenty, meaning to fill all the empty lines as if soup bowls, thinking that on future days he could reread them. He wanted to be a person whose thoughts were worth saving. He wanted all his ballpoint pens to dry up.

III.

He chose the not-commune because of how, at dinner, the day's cook would often have forgotten to set the silverware, and someone else would slip into the kitchen for the forks before she noticed. He wanted to eat food without pesticides. He wanted to come home to a house full of people who knew the names of each others' family members—and who knew that if you gave no answer when asked how you were feeling, that meant they should ask again. The members told him that on one side of the farm, artists had arranged plants into a circular meditation labyrinth. On the edge of the cow pasture, wildflowers sprouted beside three rusty train cars like a message of *starting,* and a local boy with Asperger's climbed the boxcars to watch the sunset.

Though the man was still too new to know the quirks of the washing ma-chine or which shelf the honey belonged on, one of his roles was mentor to the two interns. Three hours each day of books on literature, books on relationships, sci-fi books (because one of the interns wanted to start reading again), magazine collages, long walks, talks about family, talks about careers and decisions and *What am I going to do with my life?* and what they would do after their summer ended, as if he were an expert on such things.

He was pruning tomato leaves when a hiker passed the field, and, thinking the hiker might be homeless, he chased after him and his backpack. He offered the hiker a meal in the house, and had a flash-thought of how lucky he was to live on this not-commune where the members' generosity was contagious. (This was early in his summer there.) But the hiker was only hiking back to his own house.

IV.

One summer was the summer of circles. He didn't know exactly when it began, but with time he noticed that seemingly every bookshelf in every bookstore featured Celtic spirit wheels or Karl Jung's mandalas. When thinking, he walked in circles. Maybe in the diner it wasn't coincidence, but something greater, that put the tune of *to turn, turn, will be our delight, 'til by turning, turning we come round right* in his brain—and then made him absentmindedly finger-draw circles in the air just before the overhead radio started playing *To everything turn, turn, turn*. And later, as he walked into a second diner, the same song. The TV happened to show a documentary on crop circles that speculated they were maps pointing to something.

That was when he realized that next month—while attending the French immersion school—he would live two hours from Chartres Cathedral, and the labyrinth on its medieval floor.

And if in the following weeks he read up on it excessively—"a miniature pilgrimage to Jerusalem," it was dubbed, people trudged it on their knees—; and if he expected the labyrinth to *balance* him the way that seems to happen only for characters of medieval literature, but never to anyone you know—he did not admit this to himself. (During French summers, the sun doesn't set until eleven.) He called the Cathedral, and the director told him he could walk the labyrinth if he came on a Friday. And that Friday when he made the trip alone—in the *I-hope-I'm-not-lost* kind of alone which had marked that summer—he arrived to see that the church's two towers were asymmetrical and that the labyrinth was covered in folding chairs.

V.

Sometimes the summers overlapped, scraping into each other like tectonic plates or kissing each other's cheeks as if Europeans. Sometimes he had two or three summers in one summer. Once he had a weeklong summer in the springtime. But despite all of the shape-shifting, there was one fact of solstice he could never outrun: the twenty-first day of June, the first day of summer, was the point all future days began getting shorter.

VI.

Even though the members of the not-commune had not asked him to give up his books or sneakers or money, it was difficult to know which of his belongings belonged to him. Time and energy, they all understood, were shared commodities.

Every week on the front porch, he discussed St. Augustine's *Confessions* with a high school student. But because he didn't have the hours both to read it and to farm, he would drop his spade in the dirt and sneak into the toolshed to snatch four pages at a time.

The yellow room was one of two makeshift bedrooms in the attic, which he thought would give privacy, but the door to it was only three-quarters tall, and anyone could see or hear into it from the staircase. It was summer, but to save money and the planet, those with downstairs bedrooms did not want to start the

Welcome to the Neighborhood

household air conditioner. Sometimes in the attic bedroom, he began sweating just standing still, so he avoided the room during the daytime. The members asked him too many questions but never the right ones. When he spoke sincerely on the phone to back-home friends, he did so in the secrecy of the pig barn.

For the members, he organized weekly, for-fun events—picnics, movie-themed dinners, a Christmas-in-July party. They were supposed to be the kind of activities people who were friends did together.

The members welcomed two dozen people for dinner on Tuesdays, studied philosophy together on Wednesdays, ran the soup kitchen on Fridays, taught volunteers about agriculture on Saturdays, made household decisions—by discussion rather than by vote—on Sundays, and for three separate weeks hosted youth groups who slept in the house and in tents on the front yard.

VII.

It was a mistake, he decided. Similar to locking yourself out of your car, but really, similar to somehow locking yourself *in* your car. He felt too tired—and too obligated—to like anyone in the farmhouse.

He wanted them to ask how he was doing and not refer to potatoes or mentoring interns. He wanted them to ask what his brother's name was. He wanted them to ask what he had thought the words *commune* and *intentional community* meant before he joined one.

And, sometime before he'd even moved in, they'd let the plant-made labyrinth get so overgrown with weeds that you couldn't make out the route anymore.

It was a mistake when he made an accusation about money, which turned out to be false. So he got into a vicious fight with the not-commune's not-leader— who shouted in the *don't-you-see-what-I've-done-for-you* way of a teenager's parent.

VIII.

One weeklong summer in the springtime he stayed at a Mennonite commune. The Mennonites were less cautious about the word *commune* than the members of the not-commune would turn out to be, but still they didn't use it. They lived mostly in duplexes and grew berries that they smashed, sugared, and canned together. He admired how they viewed time, how they said, "I'll meet you for canning tomorrow afternoon" without the pressure of a specific hour. Their life seemed like an experiment in something important—they thought aloud in groups, and volunteered at health clinics, and protested international war by apologizing when they offended the family in the next duplex. One family gave him their guest room, and because it was Lent, he knelt on their carpet each morning and whispered, "From the fear of being forgotten, deliver me."

It was from the Mennonites that he first learned of what was happening to the bees. (And the information bothered him for months, and soon he began interviewing old men at farmers' markets and calling biology professors.) Over biscuits, a pair of duplexmates told him that on their commune and across the country, farmers were finding their beehives completely empty. The whole swarm disappeared. But why?

The Mennonites kept asking why he was visiting. They said, "Lots of people might be *interested* in what we do, but they don't come and stay." He did not tell them that the previous year he'd printed off an application for their summer adult internship program, that he'd sat down to the desk with a pen, and then thrown the paper away.

In their bakery, he tried to prove himself useful, but he formed dinner rolls too lumpy and spared too much oil. The family upstairs invited him to dinner and their subsequent dishwashing ritual, which they had to rearrange so that he could scrub the forks and not feel left out. Their toddler put a diaper on her head, and her parents scolded her in front of him. The commune was a conversation he kept interrupting. And because one afternoon he was talking over biscuits about the bees, he was late to a berry-picking appointment, the starting time of which he'd thought was approximate. But when he reached the field, the perturbed lady called across it, "Didn't we say 2:30?"

And so, when, between the berry bushes he felt a virus rushing up to his head, he thought it might not be such a loss to end his visit early. And the next day, his symptoms sounded like lies when he said them aloud, but even so, he relied on them for his excuse and slipped out of the commune without saying good-bye to anyone but his hostess.

IX.

In the Sunday meeting, it was decided that the members would no longer keep breakfast cereal in the farmhouse, in solidarity with the world's poor.

Had it been cultish or extremist, it would have been easy to choose to leave, but this not-commune was a collection of kind people, the kind of kind people who struggle to meet their own high standards but somehow do.

X.

Though gone for only a wedding and a long weekend, he thought of the time as making a getaway from the not-commune. In their tuxedos, all the old friends jumped simultaneously so they would appear to float in the photographs. The groom gave him a T-shirt that seemed to stand for autonomy—it pictured a dog whose tail was really an arm and a hand holding a leash. It was walking itself. But the way back to the not-commune was packed with omens of another kind: two flat tires; and then he lost his wallet somewhere; and the needle on his gas gauge slid below *E*, and he couldn't find enough quarters on his car floor for even a gallon; and the gas station cashier wouldn't let him look at an atlas without buying it; and Triple A wouldn't come without the membership card, which was lost somewhere in his lost wallet; and when he finally returned to the not-commune, his bicycle tire was flat; and then his telephone broke and the store refused to replace it. All around him, bad choices were being made *to* him without his vote.

XI.

One summer he biked across the state. One summer he taught in China, and his students vowed to stay in touch once it ended, but he did not return the promise because he no longer believed it was a promise people kept. One summer he vowed to read every neglected book on his shelf—history textbooks, novels, the complete works of Shakespeare—and failed. One summer at the not-commune, a student on a research tour of intentional communities visited and said his next stop was the precise Mennonite commune where the man had once learned about the bees. He started to ask, then, that the student give the Mennonites his hello, but he stopped mid-request because he realized they must have forgotten him.

XII.

Because it was summer, there was nothing else. Because it was summer, he didn't think about winter—except when he did. And when he did, he thought of how— when the snow had turned black; and the iced twigs no longer captured light in a refreshing way; and pulling the front door closed behind him and covering the crack with a towel became a chore; and in the dark he left for work and in the dark he returned home, where he saw his breath in his living room; and each day felt like scribbling the same words atop the previous day's page—he had looked to summer in the way of easy daydreams and had thought it would save him.

XIII.

At a Sunday meeting toward the end, he told the long-standing members of the not-commune that, once the interns' summer mentorship program concluded, he would leave—ten months early—and move out of his room (out of the house, off the not-commune, away from the rusty boxcars, and the pig barn, and the three-quarter door, and the kitchen drawer of forgotten forks) and they nodded because it made sense to them too.

And besides, one of the interns had decided to stay a few extra months and would prefer to move upstairs.

The walls in the attic bedroom were still only one shade of yellow, and the floor was still a maze of cardboard boxes he'd never unpacked. He must have known all along that this summer would end like summers always did: he would avoid clocks at sunset, pretending the days were still long, and he'd refuse to bring the sweaters out of storage—until autumn arrived and made him feel guilty in the way only autumn can, and he regretted not improving himself, not accomplishing more with those weeks, and—even in this year of farming—not spending more time outdoors.

Some Rules for Foraging (excerpt)

Garlic Mustard Season (bright yellow turnip flowers; violets stitched through turf; day lilies fountain out of the earth):

1. Do not despise anything. This bitterness is your mother and this rampage is your father pervading everywhere.

2. The eye sees itself. When one hand meets another which is the one touching? Open your mouth to the possibility that you are this sound exploding across the universe, these white flowers, these seeds inevitably sown.

3. Imagine a clean world. Imagine Euclid. Imagine proof of the mind's architecture. Imagine the border. Imagine the present as the end of history. Imagined.

4. Eat this plant as if it was the rarest, most precious prize. Be voracious in your love for it. Hold nothing back.

5. Remember when harvesting this plant from the soil, roots and all, that the absence of one allows for the presence of another. Consider what your eventual absence will allow.

To the Fig Tree on 9th and Christian

Tumbling through the
city in my
mind without once
looking up
the racket in
the lugwork probably
rehearsing some
stupid thing I
said or did
some crime or
other the city they
say is a lonely
place until yes
the sound of sweeping
and a woman
yes with a
broom beneath
which you are now
too the canopy
of a fig its
arms pulling the
September sun to it
and she
has a hose too
and so works hard
rinsing and scrubbing
the walk
lest some poor sod
slip on the silk
of a fig
and break his hip
and not probably
reach over to gobble up

the perpetrator
the light catches
the veins in her hands
when I ask about
the tree they
flutter in the air and
she says *take*
as much as
you can
help me
so I load my
pockets and mouth
and she points
to the step-ladder against
the wall to
mean more but
I was without a
sack so my meager
plunder would have to
suffice and an old woman
whom gravity
was pulling into
the earth loosed one
from a low slung
branch and its eye
wept like hers
which she dabbed
with a kerchief as she
cleaved the fig with
what remained of her
teeth and soon there were
eight or nine
people gathered beneath
the tree looking into
it like a constellation pointing
do you see it
and I am tall and so
good for these things
and a bald man even

told me so
when I grabbed three
or four for
him reaching into the
giddy throngs of
wasps sugar
stoned which he only
pointed to smiling and
rubbing his stomach
I mean he was really rubbing his stomach
it was hot his
head shone while he
offered recipes to the
group using words which
I couldn't understand and besides
I was a little
tipsy on the dance
of the velvety heart rolling
in my mouth
pulling me down and
down into the
oldest countries of my
body where I ate my first fig
from the hand of a man who escaped his country
by swimming through the night
and maybe
never said more than
five words to me
at once but gave me
figs and a man on his way
to work hops twice
to reach at last his
fig which he smiles at and calls
baby, *c'mere baby,*
he says and blows a kiss
to the tree which everyone knows
cannot grow this far north
being Mediterranean
and favoring the rocky, sun-baked soils

of Jordan and Sicily
but no one told the fig tree
or the immigrants
there is a way
the fig tree grows
in groves it wants,
it seems, to hold us,
yes I am anthropomorphizing
goddammit I have twice
in the last thirty seconds
rubbed my sweaty
forearm into someone else's
sweaty shoulder
gleeful eating out of each other's hands
on Christian St.
in Philadelphia a city like most
which has murdered its own
people
this is true
we are feeding each other
from a tree
at the corner of Christian and 9th
strangers maybe
never again.

The Neighborhood Hawk

I pull another weed and catch
a glimpse of the hawk. It glides
above our home. I've seen it hunt
the Kwik Stop parking lot
and the little park on the corner.
Smart, this hawk—but lazy.

The neighborhood a buffet
of unhurried hares, five per yard
it seems. They feast on flowers
and unprotected gardens. The squirrels'
only worry—the occasional cat
and leashed dogs. The critters bury

their nuts under tire swings
and next to kiddie pools. Cars
are more fearsome than any talons.
My wife curses the rabbits that eat
the plants her mother gave her.
The hawk lands in the next-door neighbor's tree
and sits. My dog dances, prances, and hops

around the backyard on the lookout
for anything with legs. I do not know
the names of the weeds I pull—just
that they come back and that some
are so close to being flowers
that whoever decided what we plant,
what we keep and show off,
must have had a hard time deciding
whether or not to include them.
I pull up a plant that in another life

could have cost me eight dollars to buy
at the greenhouse. The dog stops—his
muscles rigid. He's in the corner of the yard
away. Suspicious of his stillness, I get up
and amble toward him. He's caught a rabbit

by the neck and clinches it tight.
I hope that I do not have to kill
for the second time in my life
a rabbit with my bare hands
to save it from the misery of becoming
a dog's plaything. I grab the dog's collar
and tug. He does not let go.
I say, "Let it go," the way I was trained

but the dog does not respond. I pull the collar
one more time. And the dog releases the rabbit.
Its eyes go from nothing to something
and it hops off, through the fence
to eat someone else's flowers. I check
the hawk to see if it's paying any attention,
but it's busy
cocking its head in a different direction.

Some Kind of Sisyphus

One plastic trowel shaped like a carrot. One teal galosh too small for my hand. A trio
    of bouncy balls after the snow melts, garish neon in dead grass. The hill between

our houses is a lesson he's learning: he must wait to get back whatever's hurled over his
    deck's high rim, into our garden beds, driveway, at our cat, at his cat,

at the roof of our car. And the hill between our houses is a lesson I'm learning: at least
    once a month, I can reach down to gather, walk back what's not mine, not mine, not

    mine, not mine, not yet.

Intimate Selenium

> " . . . *immensity in the intimate domain is intensity, an intensity of being,*
> *the intensity of a being evolving in a vast perspective of intimate immensity.*
> *It is the principle of 'correspondences' to receive the immensity of the*
> *world, which they transform into intensity of our intimate being.*"

—Gaston Bachelard, *The Poetics of Space,* p. 193

Metals concentrate in the breast/milk. The neighbors and their levels have/are a pattern not easily decipherable. We have/are interactions, become the sum of our interactions. Neighbors proliferate a map of readings.

There's the breastmilk and the garden soil; also the daycare and the glass factory's pink plume. Online comments like to remind you that you knew what you were getting into in such a neighborhood.

Some of us delivered some potentially compromised produce to the DEQ office and the organizers wanted the children up front. My toddler held an overgrown turnip. Later he nursed. I can't give you more than that. We played in the dirt and drank in the air.

Selenium is brain-protective from the milk. We might grow excess into our hair. It makes a ruby glass.

The Woman Who Was a House

There was a woman who was a house.

Not as big as. Was. A house. A vinyl-sided exterior coating her limbs, a sloped roof over her head. Her insides made of wood paneling, framed dusty pictures hanging on the wall of her chest cavity. Clinging to the back of her pelvis, a collection of Civil War–era spoons, family heirlooms.

A projector shone its light from her lungs, powered by her breath. The projector played home movies and vacation slides. Kodachrome past lives. A version of herself that she scarcely remembered, a clapboarded teenager ambling stiffly along the beach on a family vacation. Back in her cottage days. Now she stayed put, having grown into something closer to a Victorian.

Her attic brain stored forgotten things nobody wanted anymore. Wardrobes filled with her parents' mothballed clothes, decades of polyester and lamé. They'd taken the Civil War uniforms. Her little brother Abe's tricycle, unused for decades. Boxes upon boxes, black-markered "Memories" in her mother's scrawl, filled with photo albums, scrapbooks, and postcards. All the old newspaper clippings about her, with screamy, bold headlines.

All the lives lived in this house. Her family, sheltered for free and saving on mortgage payments, now come and gone, migrating to the Caribbean without her. "You can't exactly move a house," they said. "Here. Have these spoons."

She'd seen houses moved before: power lines lowered as a loaded flatbed trailer inched down the pike. She imagined the warm-belly feeling of a family still inside, a fire in the fireplace and smoke snaking up the chimney, though of course that would be unsafe. The family would be driving behind the flatbed in a station wagon. The fire would have been extinguished the night before. Her own family had burned many fires in her fireplace, esophageal soot that still rose up, now bitter.

Probably you could move a house on a boat, down to a Caribbean island. Maybe. "But how would we pay for that?" the family asked. "Be reasonable."

"We could sell the spoons," the woman suggested.

"Those spoons have been in the family for years! You should display them in your house with pride!"

And so she did. They clinked when she shifted and settled, reminding her that she was not particularly interested in Civil War history. Her family planned the first underwater reenactments; Abe had gotten SCUBA certified. The island had no reenactors, no connection to the Civil War, up until now. Which made the gifting of the spoons all the more poignant.

Home alone, she breathed and ran the projector. Her parents smiling beside the heavy artillery cannon, Mama in her petticoats and Papa in his blue uniform and cap. Abe as a baby, the tickle of him scooting across her wooden floorboards. She saw herself, growing taller each year, adding square footage alongside the flaming red maple. For years her house-proud parents had stepped outside to film her. Now she could only imagine the projector light pouring from her windows, which nobody filmed, nobody saw.

Exteriors

There was a woman
swallowing the cracked
sidewalk I used to go

home. When I explained
what she had done
to me she measured

the circumstance out
of my favor. I was the
only one who needed

that path, and she was
hungry. Without guilt and
between consumptions

a coarse and gritty
consolation issued
from behind her

shattered teeth:
"Suffering is just"—
more of the road

vanishing—"a surface."
Since that day I have
been without.

Vanquished

(Found Poem from Otsuka's The Buddha in the Attic
on Japanese internment)

Houses are boarded up.
Their newspapers and mail
litter sagging porches.
Abandoned cars sit in driveways.
Weeds sprout where tulips wilt,
laundry clinging to lines.
Telephones ring and ring.

    Perhaps they were sent to work sugar beet country,
    or marched single file across long wooden bridges
    to faraway cities, or sailed oceans zigzagging torpedoes,
    or crowded into windowless cattle cars to the camps.

Lights are left on.
Stray cats wander left in distress.
A listless canary sits in a front window,
koi dying in a pond. Everywhere
dogs whimper in sleep dreaming them.

    And by the first frost letters cease to arrive,
    their faces blur, their names elude memory.
    And they no longer linger in thoughts
    and we know that we shall not
    meet them again in this world.

Old

So as not to feel sorry for oneself,
one feels sorry for almost anything old
or used or overlooked or forgotten
—the rocking chair, a little broken,
not as pretty anymore, but not
broken enough to throw away,
the neighbor who drinks all the time,
who cries through the walls on weekends,
fights with his grown children:
"No one loves me."
"Why don't you love me?"
"Get out of my house. Get out of my house."
the coffee cup without handle, chip on the lip,
the old dog, almost blind, the blue
blankie, the pillow stained with sleep
—every one.

How to Get Back to Chester

I remember the greasy moon floating
like a tire over the highway, the last
stars flecked like dust on the window
of my father's garage. For years I've walked
away from the concrete fields of a lousy
childhood, the damp haze of life in Chester,

but now I've come back to follow the
moon through the toothed stacks of chimneys,
through the back alleys lit up by shabby
yellow lanterns. I've come here to stand
like a pilgrim before the tin shacks
holding their tin ears on the highway

while trucks roar by without stopping
and factories clack their fat tongues
together in wind. I've come here to listen
to strangers talk about football, to waitresses
talk to strangers. I've come to see myself
taking deep blasts from the old furnace.

Not much is changed here, yet
not much is left of childhood, either.
If you want to get back to Chester
you have to listen: you have to stand
like a penitent in your bare feet
and feel the air darken before a storm;

you have to stare at the one viny
plant waving on the family porch
until you feel your father's grimy palm
gripping your hand, until you finally taste
the words at the back of your own mouth, saying
Don't come back, son. And welcome.

Name & Address

When I call my father long-distance on a Saturday night,
                    he knows
my voice and doesn't need, as he did yesterday,

                    to ask me
my name. He says, "Don, I'm in a bit of a jam." I hear him
                    read from the creased

and greasy square of paper he folds and unfolds
                    in his trembling
hands. "99 South Canaan Road, Canaan, Connecticut? Son,

                    does that mean
anything to you?" "Yes, Dad, that's the address
                    of the nursing home

where you live now." "Oh, so that's my new house!
                    Well, I've got
to get on the road soon. Will there be anyone

                    to help me
out there on the road and tell me which way to go
                    to get back

home?" As I reassure him that his nurses will care
                    for him, I remember
my mother printing my name, address, and telephone number

                    on a scrap
of stationery and attaching it to my left breast pocket
                    with a safety pin

before my first school field trip. I forget
                    where we went.
I was a letter she sent out into the unknown. I feel again

                    like a child
blindfolded at a birthday party and spun around and around
                    by large, unseen

hands, then released, and told to stumble forward and pin a strip
                    of paper to whatever
my hand first touches. "I've got to get out of here

                    and start hitchhiking
now," my father says. "Wish me luck." Crazily, dizzily, I want
                    to pin my father's

name and address on his soft night-blue flannel bathrobe so that
                    whatever road he travels
strangers will know what word to call him by

                    and what place
he has come from on his long journey through light and shadow
                    to the country of the deaf and dumb,

which is our only home. As my mother did for me once so long ago, I want
                    to kiss him lightly
on the forehead and let him go. "Good-bye, Daddy," I say. "Good luck."

Late?

—for George Shelton

Sometimes everything feels like a trick.
Some days things seem to have been stolen from you.
Cash to pay the bills, your sense of humor, friendship.
You could almost believe those are what you look for
as you walk around your neighborhood. But, no, instead, you get
splashes of zinnias against stucco, cactus wrens,
a pack of kids who ignore the sodium amber streetlights
which just stuttered on, because it means their mothers
want them home right this minute. And, on the corner variety
store's wall, a crude, sun-washed mural of the angel Gabriel
defaced by thick black sideburns so he looks like a street punk,
a strutting cholo, so he seems the only creature on earth
who hasn't heard the news that everything can be lost.
His strong upper arms curving naked and graceful
as the tan thighs of a slender, athletic girl.
A girl he's after, though she's gotten bored waiting
on the stoop and watching the sun set behind the foothills.
Sky reddening until it slams into a blue that blesses
anyone oblivious to all the negations,
including the one, pal, where you think it's possible
to step out of your heart and leave it empty as
an egg shell or a cardboard box.

When you finally return home
the tint of sky more or less matches the flash
of a thrush as it swoops from limb to branch,
acacia to willow. Standing at the kitchen counter,
you pick through a carton of strawberries.
Good juicy ones from the moldy and over-ripe.
Choices that are easy. What do you trust anymore?
The aproned man in the mercado said California strawberries,

they're the best this time of year. In bed, later,
you remember the grocer, round belly under his apron,
but as you start, nearly asleep, to tell your wife about him,
how he talked about his deals, she starts
reading aloud from a tattered bird guide, that the wood thrush
is "essentially useful and worthwhile."
What is worthwhile?   Now, remember.

Animals

On Raymond Street, across from the park
where the Christmas lights stay up
all year, a girl says to her mother
that the piece of cake she ate with a scoop
of ice cream on top was as big
as the Great Wall of China.

How do you know about the Great Wall of China?
the mother asks, turning
her bicycle around, not a young mother
but healthy, she takes care
of herself, she has her own bike for training,
not just for riding with her daughter.

The girl does not think
this is a real question. You can tell by her face,
in the middle of what comes next so completely.
She says, with enthusiasm, *we pinned
the tail on the donkey.*
I understand the love for the donkey,

like you could love it without thinking
of being pinned, like the pinning the tail part
and the donkey part stayed separate.
Not even that reality and make-believe
stayed separate, but that pinning
wasn't the only way to touch the donkey.

When I was that girl's age, I played
an easier game. At school, on someone's birthday,
we got to write on the chalkboard.
The competition was to list

as many animals as we could name
inside a minute.

I knew *cat* and *dog*. Then I wrote *jackal*.
How did you know that,
my teacher said. She wasn't satisfied
with the *World Book*
being the answer. She wanted to know
who let me understand what I had found.

The mother and the daughter ride off together,
into the world behind the park, where the daughter
can't go alone, under the lights,
through a corridor of maples. They have trouble
hearing each other because of their helmets.
But they look forward, they've done this

before, I am watching them
from the four-way stop where no one stops
completely but strangers.
The four-way stop, oracle of accidents,
something concrete to obey,
equal distributor of delay.

The Street

Streaked and fretted with effort, the thick vine
Of the world, red nervelets coiled at its tips.
All roads lead from it. All night   upholsterers

And wainwrights work to complete the wheeled coffin
Of the Emperor's dead favorite, the child's corpse
Propped on brocade cushions. Frankincense, rouge,

Kohl on the stiff lids. Slaves spread rose petals
On the street for the cortege. Our mortal faces
Flowers that shoot from blisters on the one same vine,

Ramifying to streets. On mine, Rockwell Avenue,
It was embarrassing: Trouble—fights, the police,
Sickness—seemed never to come for anybody

When they were fully dressed. It was always
Underwear or soiled pajamas, unseemly stretches
Of skin livid through a torn housecoat. Once,

A stranger drove off in a car   with somebody's wife
And he ran after them in his undershirt, to throw
His shoe at the car. It bounced into the street

Harmlessly and we carried it back to him, but
The man had too much dignity   to put it back on,
So he accepted and held it, weeping in the street:

"He's breaking up my home," he said,   "The son
Of a bitch bastard is breaking up my home."
The street rose undulant in black, road-cracking coils

And still holding his shoe he rode those waves,
Upright like a trick rider in the circus parade
That marched full-force down Rockwell every August.

Dragon-like humps of road swelled and plunged, him
Atop them, cursing and ready to throw his shoe—
Woven into the fabulous   flesh of the vine,

Carried with bears and clowns along the tendril
From Flock's Mortuary Home at Rockwell and Broadway
To Flanagan's Field. . . . It was a seedy place

And off the center, and so much a place to itself
I felt like a prince or aspirant squire. I knew
Ivanhoe was about race. The Saxons were Jews,

Or even Coloreds, with their low, sour-smelling houses
Down by the docks. Every thing was written
Or woven, ivory and pink and emerald. Nothing

Was too ugly or petty or terrible to be weighed
In the great scales of the dead, the silver balances
Looming on the live, shifting surface of our street.

Reading Celan in a Subway Station

I can't say whether the other commuters stand arrested
　　　by this music—the accordion player
near the vendor's hutch—but it comes toward me, world-
　　　sorrow drafting through the hyaline
shell of myself in thought. Reconstruction-delays,
　　　the stench of piss & nothing
weather shaped, nothing ocean spun. Steam hammers
　　　& dynamite tunneled out
a labyrinth, this inner ear where eros doesn't linger.
　　　Unbeautiful in its volts & watt-hours,
its generations of mice. The wall is dinged & saccharine-
　　　glazed where he plays in a suit.
I follow his fingers' minuscule work over a column of keys,
　　　drawing out & in the melody

of that pleated lung. It lifts away from us climbing the stairs
　　　past horse patrols & jewelry hawks,
past scaffolding & saplings blown like tonophants,
　　　past fruit stands, placards & idle
Greyhounds, the corridors of silver buildings, the thunder
　　　with silver veins—it lifts away
because it seeks the high, lone sun. Admit his music,
　　　cause-of-all, it is handmade.

Fire Island

(for Karen and Alan)

Duneless beach; moonless night—
swimming, I forgot the land, forgot
the mist, forgot the sea.
Time passed, I guess. Came to; no Pete;
must've gone in. On shore someone held

a lantern in his hand.
Where were you, he asked (with an edge).
Who the hell was *he?* Look, he said, pointing.

For two miles down the beach
people stood with lanterns, calling *Frank!* That's me.
        Each lantern was haloed by mist.

Frank . . . Frank, they all called—
irregular as wind-chimes; patient;
fainter down the line. At the lacy edge of ocean
people stood to call me home.

And I had thought heaven
was swimming at night!

Gay Marriage Poem

We could promise to elope
like my grandmother did
if a football team won

on homecoming night.
We could be good queers?
An oxymoron we never

longed for. We could
become wed -*locked*
as the suffix was once intended:

laiko, Common Teutonic for play,
not *loc,* Old English for a cave,
an enclosure. Instead

of a suit, I could wear my T-shirt
that avows, "Support Your Right
to Arm Bears!" Or we could

wed in bear suits
just as I saw people do
one summer in San Francisco

standing amid a grassy median
during rush hour.
They were so personally

anonymously political
blocking the ocean breeze
in acrylic fur.

Forget such solemnities!
I want to run through streets
shouting up to all my beloveds' windows:

"Friends! In sickness and in health
I refuse to forsake you!"
on Charlotte Street, Home,

Euclid, Decatur, Union,
Straubs, Rebecca, Bennett Ave.,
38th, Woolslayer Way.

In the only wedding I was a part of
I was the flower girl
who held up the ceremony

kneeling to drop equal dividends of
petals beside every pew,
refusing to leave anyone out.

Let us speak without occasion
of relations of our choosing!
Tied intricately

as the warps and wefts
amid mats of moss,
without competing for sunlight

our hairy caps are forever
lodging in spaces
that myopic travelers can't see.

Of such loves unwrit, at the boundary layer
between earth and air,
I feel most clear.

Marriage

It is difficult to speak of marriage.
The tree in the far room twinkles,
and beneath it, wrapped things,
and the trees outside are bare,
and as a girl, there was a willow
I lay under the only time I remember
really wanting to die. But what did
I know then of wanting to die,
any more than I know now, any less?
In Oklahoma, my mother cut all her
trees down—to let the sun in, she said—
but here, up north, we have planted
a whole row of arborvitaes so that,
if they grow the way we hope,
the neighbors won't even know we're home.

Forest Ridge Farms Nocturne

'Twas eleven hours in the cube today,
and Fran and the kids look cooked when you
get home, rapt in the flash of a high-def
Rembrandt three group in the great room
while you quickly warm your dinner. The vinyl's
falling off the house next door, you say.
She throws a sexy smile the kids can't read.

Eleven trips she made today, she says,
from school to home, to lunch, to home,
to school, to home to change their clothes,
to softball, grocery, softball, home, and last
a walk out to the drive, to meet you all alone,
a kiss because she missed you, and also
cause she's lonely, so what is she to do?

Tonight, you say, we'll find the good urge
to close the door with minutes to spare
and while we lie, we'll talk out our days,
the Blankman account, Em's ankle sprain,
sun rays and the warm grass smell. Tell me,
darling, how you pushed the window open
and stood staring, waist down naked.

How did you know? she asks. It was around
midday. The lonely quiet turned me on,
so I stared out at the vacancy, the vast
empty chain-link silence of it, 'til I, close-eyed,
crosslegged underneath, shivered myself,
then napped on the made bed an hour.
Work, I think, would fill the void, she says.

It fills the time, but not the space, it makes
the day go quickly by, and that's what's got *me*

scared these days, you say. The girls are asleep,
she says. A humid waft slips in the window.
That cut grass smell? You smell that? she says,
That's what got me going. I love you, you say.
This love, these thin walls can't contain it.

Welcome to the Neighborhood

Pornograph, with Americana

Don't move to Calgary, Apna,
have sex! possibly even with me
if you're willing, not even in wedlock,
possibly backwards with one knee
on the vanity, the shower heaving steam
to the Big Band webcast out of KCEA,
Atherton, my mother napping downstairs
in the great room, she won't know you
scaled the carport, ducked an eave
with a joint and a sixer of Stroh's,
my kurta in ribbons now, your lengha
undone, I put every part of you
inside my mouth and bite down
a little as if I'm a rototiller in heat,
you the churning earth, and I love you,
honest injun! while the sun slinks
behind the Fitch's Big Boy across
the interstate, fireflies make erratic
synapses above the drainage ditches,
the fir trees sway like frat boys at a kegger,
and the neighbors who watch us framed
in the naked window, who wish us
deported into a darker corner of the duplex,
they can clench their hymnals, Apna,
and glare, we won't go anywhere
till we're finished, Waheguru!
Waheguru! we won't go.

Doorstep

after T

there is yet another
official at my door

wanting to know
where I stand

waiting to check
the depth of

my commitment
my legal

rights
to land

you see
I don't police

my protection
don't put those

wooden fences
around

until I feel
safe to

you see obedience
comes easy

for those wedded
like me

who haven't banned
committed actions

but have held
on tight

who haven't
banded together

but flickered
blankly, our

latent invest-
igation of

skin on the
doorstep

kin at my back
sirens hinging

just to own
forty acres

to be cool
with the humans

at the scene
you see

me listening
but I am

carried at night
bolstered

on a tankard
of brutal patrolmen

only in light of
recent officers' events

can I say power
is the fog

I live in, my
blind chief

Upon Hearing about the Student Arrested at the Gun Shop

If he'd shot up the school
it would've been in March or April
because, contrary to popular belief,
spring is the time it's hardest
to be human. The psyche
rises back to the surface—
a sinking woman, not yet
done struggling—never quite
breaches, but floats there with
all winter hatreds intact.

This
while I examine
the inside of my Kleenex
for sinus infection—snot
clear as a bell, so why do I
feel so bad?—, thrash around
in bed, ask my boyfriend over
and over to kiss my forehead
for fever (there is none).
What's going on out there?
I mean besides the birds
and the breezes, the insensitive
crocuses and that certain light
that imparts something like
significance—

It's this that's convincing.
That new light touches everything
and turns it into
cipher, everywhere hidden meanings.
He, the searcher, excels at finding
messages—makes a broken system

of the shadows crossing
the brief span
of his patio,
of the birds that lift
or refuse to lift,
of that particular cloud settling
stupidly on this or that particular
stretch of sky.

Free Variation on "Saturday Night in the Village"

Blinds up on the clarity and social club
drinkers of Mythos and black coffee
and watchers of white marble soccer legs.
Sometimes, the lovers look at each other
and two words pop into their basic heads:
       L E O N S P I N K S,
because his teeth. It's Friday.

Sometimes, from a passing car, "Black Dog"
or the Steve Miller Band on the way
to Luau Night at the church gym,
a K through 8 chicken dance
Maryologists all around
down the broken step
past the third grade teacher
in his actual neck brace.

In a room behind the pizza ovens
and the white wooden walk-in cooler,
the busboy feeds loaf after quartered loaf
of mozzarella to the cheese grinder,
bin after bin of cheese
in the pure dairy air of love.

Down on the avenue,
the bands are unloading
their black-cased amps and instruments
from their open vans
in the sunlight of evening
that begins the night,
empty tables in the bar,
trees over the alley
in green twilight.

No railings on a wooden flight of steps
to the back apartment on
the second floor
overlooking garages
under catalpa tree flowers,
to go up that way and then down.

All this pushes an immense longing.

The Population

One of the feelings which returns so often:
I mean the way that winter afternoons

call back those childhood sulks at the window.
That incessant need to sketch in the people

behind the lichened shingle of facing houses.
Now, when evening gathers, the walls conceal

no lion tamers lounging with the lions,
no divers plunging inside an aquarium.

Just a catch in the stomach like falling:
sweet emptiness . . . which others must also feel.

Even hours after, mothers and children
crossing the bright street by the supermarket

cut such vivid profiles. And they have a fierceness:
like ravenous hummingbirds who couldn't care

about the thorns they thrust through to devour
the little beads of honey in the flower.

Or like themselves . . . Lucent apartments shelve
into the hills, the whole volume of sky

falls on the spaces between, and passing strangers
move with the urgency that darkness

lends them: their skins much brighter against the expanse
of towers, suburbs, and fields they pull behind.

Neighborhood

I was away for a long time.
Houses weathered drop
by drop, shingles punctured
and swollen with plastic.

Fenced rocks, the burnt stumps,
floods took over the groves.
Roadways and bridges divided,
streams crowded under by driftwood.

I looked for hickories and tricycles,
slats from flaking trellises.
Who jimmied those windows?
Sometimes the things people say

are so tangled, I have
to pretend they're right.
I remember bonfires and spills,
the violent rescues of wildflowers.

The motel cabins mildewed
under rain clouds and pollen.
The vacant lot grew weeds
and teenagers and disease.

Sometimes all that's left
are the doorways,
a crooked window frame.
It never felt like a long time.

I don't always understand
when people speak.

I can't always remain there
when they shut up.

What's visible in forgetting?
The locals know the difference
but I couldn't see the change.
I can't sit anymore in these fields.

Song for the Festival

At the May Day parade, my mask made of moss
and bark, my hair full of flowers, my friend beside me,
her pretty red mouth under the hawk's beak
of her mask of green sage.

At the children's pageant, music
died in the speakers. The shadow
of a crow passed over. My hair a crown
of flowers, yellow and red roses large as fists,
flowers on which I'd spent my last $20
at the mercado.

But beauty wasn't enough. Being admired
by strangers was not enough.

I saw a girl, wandering, looking for her mother.
I knelt down, lowered my mask, showed her
my face. She's looking for you too, I say.
She tries to spot her mother's yellow dress.
A gold dog passes, happy and white-faced,
wearing pink nylon fairy wings. The girl points
and laughs; the hard part of her day
is over.

The people I'm looking for—I don't know where they are.
I don't know the color of their clothing. From across the park
I see the dark windows of my apartment.

Spring has arrived.
Let me not despair.

The Heater Repair Woman

The heater repair woman takes the stairs
two at a time as she enters my apartment,
her belt heavy with surprises.

She drops to her knees, pulls the wall unit apart,
and with a tube in her mouth blows
into the cavity.

She taps the small pipes with a wrench,
wakes up the entire neighborhood.
She does not have the tools she needs

to look inside and I think of the mysteries
of my own body. I lie back in bed and she shouts
to me from the hallway

that she's seen heaters in worse shape,
but these chambers are choked
with white ash. I drowse

and her voice holds me
between sleep and wakefulness. It
is the wakefulness I love.

Blizzard Poem

For the Boston Yeti

Neighbors and a Yeti emerge
when all else is hidden. Newly we see

our shovels rise together
as children dive daringly on the drifts.

Time to thaw out verbs like *romp* and *hunker down,*
sing *Snow Day, Snow Day—like no day, I know.*

Newly we play, and thar he *plows:*
our wild Yeti id, reminding us how to chill

and go with the snow. He was here all along,
but we needed blindness to find this

layer of track. We follow. Sometimes
it takes a blizzard; sometimes Mother Nature

gives us all a timeout. Kids,
this is how it feels to submit

with Irish coffee. This is how it feels
under the white flag. Blissfully bundled,

we help each other dig out again.
Not unlike a lockdown,

we meet each other
in absence.

Not unlike a forgot sound:
when we played King of the Mountain

not to win, but to fall
fearlessly on snow like forgiveness.

City Morning

The monkey house wakes up
the neighborhood with a call and response

not unlike the whoops of homecoming night:
hollow, incessant, hard to decipher the edge

between joy and lament. The other team has scored
a point. The zookeeper is out of bananas.

They have no species in the early morning hours
from blocks away. How could I have confused

an orangutan and a lemur? A gorilla and a macaque?
We walk closer and they have names

their parents never chose. Their extended
families have fallen out of touch.

The children are placing their hands on the glass.
The monkey's breath fogs it up in return.

They're silent when we circle them.
They chew and stare.

Later, they, too, will hear the neighborhood—
dusk's calls for children, nightfall's moans and fights.

We're each other's misplaced habitats.
Calling out into the city's rising and falling light,

hoping someone will hear. Each thinking
we've made them just like us.

Middle Class Love Song

When some know-it-all on public radio insists income
       is more hereditary than height or weight, and some other

dour economist agrees we're on the fast track back to serfdom,
       we shrug, so yeah, maybe everybody's broke, but not too broke

to catch a matinee at Miracle 8 or grab a venti from Starbucks,
       and okay, our rental looks kinda trashy, the jasmine vine dying

on the chain-link in a gothic brown tangle—poisoned, we think,
       by our duplex neighbor's latest crazy ex—but we're rich in

monkey grass, which spreads so wildly that the neighbor's kid
       just mows it down in a verdant stubble, and we may not have

tidy box hedges or a golf cart to tootle around the block in,
       like the doctor in the McMansion next door, his yellow

labs loping in the wake of his cigar smoke, but we also don't
       have his patients suing us for urethral surgery mishaps,

and we can hear the jazz from the Bose speakers of his gazebo on dusky
       Sunday evenings, and we dance on our front stoop,

just hugging really, a long swaying hug, and at least we have
       this cement stoop, right?, and this fenced yard our dog patrols

with full-hearted devotion, as if she's guarding the Taj Mahal,
       and Coltrane on a humid breeze and our hug dances and our glossy

textbook of crazy exes and the medieval tapestry of our jealousies—
       not to mention the pleasure of knowing our children

and our children's children will have ever-increasing latte options
       and even richer neighbors and even crazier, more creative exes.

Announcement: The Theme of Tonight's Party Has Been Changed

We switched the theme
     of the party
from Tropical
     Night to
Old Dog Vestibular
     Disease but
didn't have time
     to get the
word out so
     Porter, Eric,
and a couple
     of students
came in straw hats and
     board shorts, sunglasses
propped on their wiry
     heads.
Willa had a
     grass skirt. The
sick dog was featured
     in a cage
up near the
     front door. She
had finished
     seizing. I saw
to that with
     an "injectable"
of dexamethasone
     wheedled from
Dr. Stroud that
     afternoon. But
she was
     still panting
and listing and

not allowed
to stand. The guests
        had to maneuver
around her
        to get to
the San Pellegrino, wine,
        and beer. She
barked once,
        sharply, seeing
a person thieving
        from the
cooler.

        The ailment is sometimes
        less pejoratively
called
        Canine Vestibular
Disease. I loved
        her for refusing
to be stashed
        in the back
seat of the Volvo
        as she
usually is
        for Don's visiting
writer parties. (Many
        times, ignored,
I've wished
        to hang there
with her.) For
        tonight, insisting
on putting her (mostly)
        mute self
front and center.

        Two
people
buttonholed me
        drunk. It

took me a minute
        to figure
out that their
        confidently
delivered
        statements
were nonsense. They
        were sentences,
they were on
        topic. With Helene,
it was the light
        gleam of sweat
on her forehead
        her upper lip
her erotic slit-eyed gaze at
        our guest of
honor, which could
        not have been
more inappropriate—
        but this
is the only thing
        some people can
think of in terms
        of poetic
"intensity." While
        she drank
him in seductively
        tilting her
chin up slightly
        she made
an utterly insipid
        statement
about his use
        of tetrameter (which
he'd already explained
        was deeply
personal—*the man*
        writes poems
to God!) and
        hers of the

sonnet. SNORE. And
      her students'
resistance to
      the use of form.
Double snore.
           The other
      person nailed
me by the mirror,
      kept repeating,
Sally looks so young!,
      referring to
the dog. I said,
      Yeah, well,
she's not, and then,
      finally,
I don't think
      we have
much time left
      with her.
I wanted
      to say she
was recently groomed
      at the kennel. That
she was simply
      clean, not
young. I wanted
      to say,
Look in
      her eyes. There's
a film, like
      iridescence on
a puddle. She's practically
      blind. Look
at her hind
      legs. They're
sticks, constantly
      flying akimbo.

I've been those
      people. Helene, with

her head thrown back
        to imbibe
the honoree.
        During
my high-slut
        phase, I had
scant knowledge of
        poetry and certainly
wasn't teaching
        a class. That
was the only
        difference. I hated
her avaricious
        sweaty sexual
moon face
        though.
                Paul, by
the mirror,
        a Crate and Barrel
special, improbably
        decorated
with coat hooks,
        going on about
Sally's "youthful
        appearance," wasn't I *him?*
Recently? Complaining
        he'd been
passed over for a
        job by
an inside candidate
        who *had*
no pubs—and then was
        never
notified. I joined in,
        loudly exclaiming
I'd been on unemployment
        a year and
a half, and was

now, at this point,
an honorary canine.

                        I wanted
        to think
of something else, seeing
        Willa in her
grass skirt, besides
        the times
she insulted me
        that year
I held the "visiting
        position." I blocked
out the day
        she kind of
tried to make
        it up to me
in the Marsh
        parking lot. Telling
me about her
        sister, sick
in Ireland, and her recent
        trip to
Cambodia. Without a
        direct apology,
it didn't
        count.
                        She
stuck her foot
        out once at
some reception, in
        front of
a bunch
        of people,
and giggled maliciously
        when I nearly
tripped. Another
        time, she sighed

loudly when
		I turned up
in front of her in
		an auditorium,
as if my height
		was going to be
some kind
		of insurmountable
barrier to her
		view (I kept
thinking, I'm not
		even tall
from the waist up).

				The afternoon
		before the party
I crawled into
		the cage
with Sally
		when she
was violently
		shaking.
I started
		giving orders.
First I got
		Don to go
get the oral
		prednisone, and when,
after a couple
		of hours, she still
did not
		improve, and Don
was no longer
		there to help,
I called around
		for the needle. I had
to leave her at home
		in the crate
for about 15 minutes

to go pick it
up. Every
        second, I thought
of my ill
        father, at
a similar
        stage, with his
Parkinson's tremor
        and disequilibrium.
His Sally-like
        determination,
valor, courtesy.

                We haven't
        had to use
the ramp to get
        her up and
down the front
        porch steps
since the
        night of the
party, the night
        of the last
attack. It had been
        hours and I knew
she had to
        pee. I lured
her down the retractable
        ramp with
half a dog
        biscuit in
my free hand and my
        daughter Lucy
guiding her
        feeble rear
end walking down
        the steps at
her side. A few people
        were arriving

and squeezing through
        on what was
left of the stairs—
        to get into
the party where
        the real thing,
whatever that was—
        the greasy
overtures, the
        florid missing-the-
mark red-in-the-face
        remarks,
snubbing
        and being snubbed,
intricate status
        updates
and assessments—
        was going on.
                        My
daughter had laid
        out the platters.
Alternating
        leaves of radicchio
and endive around
        the rim of
one, with the bleu cheese
        dip forming
the hub cap. Bowls of
        tortilla chips, mounds
of Milanos. Such
        are the reliable
forms. A white-frosted
        cake with our
visiting poet's name
        written in
blue script between
        red rose blossoms
on the top. All
        things

requiring a higher
        intelligence
than Sally's. I walked her
        down the street,
farther and farther from
        the house lights,
into the dampness,
        her spirit
steady, her corporeal
        self swinging
uncertainly
        from side
to side.

My Neighbors: I Know Them

As you suggest, I will have the nettle tea
to calm my conscience. It is terrible to have to tell you
where I've been. This morning, I sat several hours
in the city courtroom. I felt so out of place—
exposed, I mean. Since the policeman pulled me over,
I've asked friends repeatedly for pointers.
Whatever they advise, I repeat into the bathroom
mirror: *No, your Honor. Yes, your Honor.* As you see,
I wore my best black pants and the boots
you always praise. Last night I washed my face,
extracting all the filth. At 8 AM at the city court,
I hardly found a space to park; cars wedged
like star points in a crowded constellation.
In the lobby, straightened folding chairs. I studied
only limbs—observing hands, but never faces.
A woman hurried past. No one moved as thumps
and screams soaked through the bathroom wall.
Whatever crime it was, she could not unmake it.
I sat, folding and finger-pressing my unease.
My number flashed. They sent me down the hall.
Inside the courtroom, a defendant swallowed
hope too loudly, waiting for release. A clock played
its repeating sounds, the weighted helpless seconds.
The judge called through the docket, and didn't
ask for many reasons. All was done with great dispatch.
I gave my ears to the click-click of the surly clerk,
typing fees and failures, as I filled with half-
knowledge and sudden knowledge of the law,
of how to measure angles, how to lie explicitly
and estimate each outcome. Nothing else to do;
I prepared a face. When I heard my name, I stood,
carrying silent oscillations with my body.
What I'd done was hardly worthy of such worry,

but we each discount the bristles of our dangers.
At the podium, I nodded and looked down to trace
the carpet pattern. Anyway, she pardoned me.
You were kind to ask about my morning,
but this is rude, my going on so long. And why
this matters now? A piece of me was matched
with every person, every consequence, with each
acknowledged break of margin.

Fireflies

A painter came to Papertown and built a house there. She worked in oils on canvas, or made her own paper and folded it into origami whales or horses. But when she first arrived and they heard at the Farm and Fleet that here had come a painter, several people nodded optimistically and said, "It's about time. My house has so dulled from the sun and needs a going-over."

Chaos itself aspired to become the artist's house. She had no sense of boundary it seemed, no idea that the neighborhood covenants had the cosmic bearing they had. Everyone else knew down in the bones that only the laws of commerce kept Papertown from popping at the seams, springing leaks, opening up the throttle until there went the gaskets. It was too much really to even think about, what lay beneath the surface of the things they wrote down as a group and signed and stamped in order to put a hard clear seal on matters of unpredictability. In this way the artist started off on the wrong foot. The people of Papertown gave her a wide berth.

Some of the other houses were painted, but always in accordance with the palette chosen by the town council to keep to a minimum any anxiety caused by brightness and saturation. When a couple walked their dog in the evening along the broad asphalt track that circled the town, and the bean fields stretched out summer green away from them, a plume of dust from a car receding down the dirt road and out toward the melon light of a small house, and then in flickering celebration of the misty heat over the field a half a million fireflies in semaphore blinking *magic* and *sweetie* and *mira,* well then, okay. Then they thought that maybe there was something to this business of color and beauty and untidy nature, whether or not they attributed all this to some conscious invisible painter of the whole scene back in time immemorial, the same entity as before cave people, the same painter of lava flows and ice floes. They thought, although they seldom used the word, of art.

The dog would pee on a hydrangea. The dog would look up lovingly and trade evenly the leash for the scents of rabbit and juniper and the air on his own happy tongue. The issue, the dog seemed to indicate in his pure simplicity as he stared quite humanly at the walls of the artist's house, is whether or not you can put a paisley door into a fleur-de-lis wall and make it work.

Unbelievable, this house. Indescribable, since the people of Papertown didn't do very well with the art of description. They loved to say, "Words cannot express." They loved to say, "I'm speechless." They collected apps on their phones and tapped away frantically but seldom spoke into them. For some time they were upset about this derring-do, this ridiculous carnival of a house on their street. But if boredom and pleasant weather conspired, a dozen or so of them would congregate in front of the artist's house like carolers. When she hung Moroccan windows, with their teardrop tops and their indigo tile frames and plum lattice work, into that deep navy wall with the gold fleur-de-lis—my lord. She suspended swag lamps in a line along the eave that gave off a gel of light, but never lit them until just before most people had gone to bed, rather than right after dinner, the way of those who thought of porch light being only for safety.

Drifting to sleep, or watching the spastic garish screens of their plasma televisions, some of the neighbors would suddenly feel a tranquility as if they'd breathed a sweet tobacco. They would sense a whispering correction from outside their rooms. They might even turn off the TV, sit for a moment in the darkness lapping around them like a warm bath in order to figure it out. Most suddenly realized how tired they'd been for hours, the television keeping them from knowing this, and let themselves drift to the deep sea of rest. But some were the inquisitive types, the ones with words for art right on the tips of their tongues, and they traced the source to their bedroom windows, looked out, and saw the burgundy wash from the lighted baubles muting the whirling patterns of her walls to a kind of filigree that included the fronds of palms she'd planted. They knew then that the artist was sleeping, knew it from the smell of her watered herb garden that timed its aromas with the passing of light, that her house was sending out a tonic of peace. And the designs on the artist's outer walls—the palm shadows, the golden spades, the aquarian paisleys—were all so intertwined and seamlessly integrated that the building itself seemed to be something organic and imbued with gnosis, drinking from the well of the moon like a leopard at a jungle pool.

She rose early, her house velvet dark inside before the sun's own glow, and she painted. She put the smell of her strong cinnamon coffee into a painting of the spruce line on the mountain. She breathed the fur of the dog on the brick floor and painted his dreaming smile into a sky. She painted the kisses of her long-dead lover from her girlhood into an abstract expression five feet tall, a life-sized embrace. The aromas of linseed and turpentine filled the room. She socialized some chickadees and a tufted titmouse. A wren couple like two little doddering octogenarians started coming around in the afternoons, perching in the hazel. She watched them fondly and scratched a tattoo of a mandala on the inside of her forearm.

She began a painting of the town circle, but found the people of Papertown difficult to depict. Her agitation in the evenings came from these efforts, and once she understood this, she soaked in a turpentine bath the canvases that portrayed human subjects, and switched to painting still lifes of clothing. Winter coats on pegs. Umbrellas in a stand with bright yellow rubber boots on a pine floor. She concentrated on the drape of an unoccupied cloak, the curve of a hat brim empty of a head. She supported herself by illustrating children's books that were sold in other countries, painting in alphabets with umlauts and carats, languages written with long sweeping calligraphy in letters that were themselves art. In time this course of work, the empathy woven into children's stories, along with her general and unrequited gregariousness, led her to consider trying people again. The birds that visited her just were not quite enough, but she wrestled with trepidation, doubt, at the thought of portraiture. She knew not to paint a crowd of this town—something about their anger and the way they seemed to be fading in the cloudy light of their century—but maybe one face, some gateway to an empathy she hoped to find.

One day with her dog, on the lawn near the university to which she always turned her back while enjoying the grass with her feet, she saw a child with a model rocket. No adult in sight. On his back he wore a small grubby neon green backpack like a deflated balloon, and she thought that the child might be from somewhere else, like her. She asked him. He said that no, he lived right over there, but he didn't come to this park very often, only when he wanted to get away. He said that his father was gone a lot and when he was home he beat up on him, and the artist saw that the child favored his right leg and had two fingers splinted together with black electrical tape. The boy said that he found the rocket kit in a trunk at his friend's house, and that his friend's mother gave it to him. He scratched at the back of his neck, which was brown from the sun and speckled with dirt. The boy petted the dog, who sat obediently and looked up with his cool blue eyes, and the boy said, very tenderly, "Good dog." He pointed at a wire stand on the ground and explained that the balance was off. He was trying to fix it so that the rocket wouldn't rip off at any old angle and land too far away to find. The C-pack engines were expensive. He didn't want to lose the rocket before he'd used up the five engines he had.

The rocket was a tight white roll of paper, about a foot high, with a ceramic cone for a head, painted blue with a yellow lightning bolt. The stabilizers on the bottom matched the lightning bolt. The boy's favorite part of the rocket was the parachute, which was a candy-red plastic, thin as a doll's raincoat. He said he liked packing the chute into the rocket. "Without this," he said, "if you do it wrong and then if you're over a sidewalk or a parking lot or something and you come down, you just break into pieces and everybody inside dies. Can't have that." He said, "I'd like to get a motorized boat and do a water landing and rescue the guys with the boat, like the way the astronauts did it way back before the shuttles. Talked about that in history."

Welcome to the Neighborhood

He set up the rocket, showing her each step, backed up a few feet with two wires in his hands, and touched their copper ends together. The rocket thumped, hissed, and flew off of the long metal rod, higher than she had thought it would, and its trajectory took it against the wind, so that it blew back toward them again and landed only fifty yards away, near the backyard of a house. The dog ran to it.

Smart kid. She smiled. He ran for the rocket and called the dog to him and then brought them both back, both of their faces happy in the waning light. He showed her again how to do it. He let her burn one of his engines, which he kept in a Quaker Oats container in his backpack, and her rocket flew well. The boy said so.

Twilight began to saturate them and all around them, and the rocket's last flight reached its apex with the fuselage a black silhouette against the pink sky under a cloud, the chute a bloom of rose, the falling angle hard and straight, following an invisible guy wire down. She could feel that the boy did not want the rocket to land. When it did, he didn't run after it. He tugged his ankle sock up from out of the back of his tennis shoe and held the oats container under his arm, tapped the top with his bandaged fingers in a nervous tattoo. He looked up at the sky and said, "I can see some stars. The sky's still blue up high, but there are stars out. Isn't it weird when that happens? Like when the moon and sun are out at the same time."

"Venus," she said. "That one is Venus, so it's a planet." She gave him a scrap of the blue and gold fleur-de-lis origami paper for the fuselage of his next rocket. The boy smiled and held it up against the sky, into which its background disappeared and there for a moment the span of the coming night was patterned with golden spearheads.

She wanted to say, "Maybe tomorrow we should try to get your rocket to make it to Venus." That seemed too youngish for him. She could see him now as he would be when he was a man, and he looked at her as if he were about to ask an old hard question. Afraid for him, she wanted to say, "Tomorrow let's go get some more engines and also some blue jeans, and you can smell shampoos until you find one that smells like a guy. Let's have pancakes and I'll show you the birds that eat from my hand now. It takes patience, but you can get them to go from a tree to a perch to your hand in about three weeks." She wanted to say those things.

The boy rubbed his leg above the knee. He looked into the face of the dog, and the dog met his gaze and did not shy, and cocked his head, then thumped his long heavy tail on the ground. Three weeks seems like nothing to you now, the artist thought. And so in her mind she completed his portrait, and would paint it that night, into the morning's warming radiance, and between the small comforts of her life.

What she said was, "That was fun."

And he said, "Yep," and nodded, and put the paper in his pocket, rested one hand on top of the dog's head, and with the other pointed out at the fireflies beginning to pop out over the lawns and said, "Look. More stars."

As I Wander

Four hours after burying Gene and Judy no longer knew what to do with herself.

She fingered the elongated leaves of her Wandering Jew plant, knowing she'd pay for it later. Touching the plants always made her itch, yet she couldn't keep away from their pointed leaves. These plants were the only things she had never killed. They grew wildly, recklessly, regardless of her tending. Despite her lack of devotion, they managed—somehow—to thrive. Sitting on a high perch above her kitchen sink, their leaves trailed over the corners of the wooden ledge. They would grow anywhere. With a bit of guidance, they'd entwine their enduring selves around anything that would let them. She took comfort in touching the hardy, invasive plant considered by all but her to be a nuisance.

Outside, it turned abruptly dark, the way it did when the season began to change. Judy could barely see the patch of yard and street beyond her window. Then, in unison, the lampposts in each home's yard flickered on, their dim lights revealing the yellow stripe in the road that divided the street in half. Old man Sampson was out there sweeping dead leaves from his stoop when a young man turned into his gate. The two spoke briefly, then went inside. Sampson left the broom by the railing and the leaves unbagged. His house was directly across the street from hers and Judy worried about his leaves blowing across and ruining her yard, which seemed more of a possibility than that the guests in her home would leave anytime soon.

She sought refuge from them in the kitchen, having been driven from all of the other rooms of her home by Gene's preying relatives. With the exception of his daughter Phoebe, Judy had never met any of them before. Gene drove them away when he first became sick, carefully and effectively cutting himself off from all of his near relatives. Now they were here, meeting her for the first time and treating her more like the hostess of a party than a bereaved wife. Some had come as mourners, others as poachers. Phoebe, who had not been over in four years, would periodically materialize at Judy's shoulder, holding a highly prized knick-knack. Judy tried to avoid her, having seen the way Phoebe's eyes lingered on the china cabinet, the mirror mounted on the wall behind the sofa. She was counting, tallying up everything, quietly assessing. "When did Dad buy this?" she'd ask, suddenly appearing, fingering the costly item. She dragged her little boy all over the house, pointing out all of the possessions she assumed would soon be theirs. The four-year-old boy seemed remarkably strong and hale. Judy couldn't keep from scrutinizing him—this handsome boy that Gene had never met—wondering at Phoebe's selfishness in carrying him to term when she knew the risks, wondering how Phoebe dared.

"So this is where you disappeared to."

It was only Hank. Their neighbor and Gene's buddy, Hank had been nearby for as long as Judy could remember. Dressed in a checkered shirt, a pair of faded dungarees, and work boots, he looked like a man who made a living with his hands, which he was. He held a bag of ice in each hand. "What're you doing in here all by yourself?" he asked.

"Need something?"

"Everyone's looking for you," he said.

"Like who?"

"Your daughter, for one."

"Not *my* daughter," she said.

Hank stood quietly, adopting a silence that made her feel petty. "I'm being unfair," she said.

"That's not for me to say." He hefted the bags of ice onto the counter, dropping each one hard enough to break the ice into chunks. Hank put his hand on her waist and nudged her to the side. He reached around her, opened the silverware drawer, and pulled out a butter knife. He drove the handle of it into the belly of the ice bag. "Think about it this way," he said, pounding the ice with the base of the knife. "Tomorrow you can be anything you like."

"That's what it's all about, isn't it? Getting through this night. Fine," she said, breathing deeply. The more air she tried to take in, the tighter her chest became. "Does she have to touch everything?"

"Jude, what are you talking about?" Hank pulled a large bowl from the cupboard over the refrigerator and filled it with broken ice.

"I just can't watch her, going all over the house, touching everything. Don't you see the way her hands go all over everything?"

Phoebe was the worst of them all, but just now Judy couldn't bear to be near any of them. For hours she had listened to the memories of people she knew Gene had detested in life, yet decorum dictated she make welcome in her home. Listened as they swapped stories of a Gene she didn't know. They painted a picture of a man far different from the one she'd lived with. A man she wished she could have known. Their memories, numerous and weighty, obliterated hers.

When the bowl was filled, Hank turned back to her. "Jude. You crying?" He pulled her into an awkward hug, rubbing his cold thumbs across her upper arms.

"I'm fine. I just have to make it through tonight," she said, wiping her eyes. "But then there's tomorrow, and after that, another tomorrow. What then?"

JUDY AWOKE to the sounds of garbage trucks approaching. She threw on a robe and ran outside. The trucks were half a block away at the corner of 43rd and Spruce. She rolled the cans to the curb, noticing all of the cans lining the fronts of all of the other homes. It was eight AM and she had not seen any cans on the curb the night before. When, she wondered, had everyone else come out with their trash?

If she had let him, Hank would have put her garbage out for her. When she returned home at daybreak, she'd heard his voice message offering to do just that. Because Gene could no longer do it, Hank had taken over performing the small odd jobs necessary for maintaining a home. For the past four years, he'd sprayed weed killer on the lawn during the spring and summer. In the winter he'd bled the radiators and shoveled the snow. Each year, Judy watched him take what looked like an old roller-skate key and move among all of their old radiators, letting out air and steam. While each radiator hissed and sputtered, Judy would look at Hank, resplendent in health and heartiness and wonder why Gene had not been spared instead. She resented his ministrations—the way he hefted bags of ice and pounded them to shards against the counter, the familiarity he had with his own body, the way he could walk without jerking, the ease of his well-meaning smile—simple things over which Gene had long ago lost mastery.

She'd been out when Hank called about the garbage. In the month since Gene's death, Judy had taken to wandering the neighborhood whenever the mood took her. Though she'd lived in the University City/West Philadelphia area since her marriage, she'd never really seen it. She'd given up her apartment in Rittenhouse Square when she'd married Gene and she had never spent much time in West Philadelphia prior to dating him. Gene began a progressive decline shortly after their marriage five years ago and most of her time had been spent visiting him in the hospital or providing full-time care for him inside their home. The neighborhood was not a place she associated with him. They'd taken no strolls past the University of Pennsylvania and visited none of the restaurants that surrounded it on Sansom, Walnut, and Chestnut. They had watched no movies at the *Cinemagic* or the new theater, *The Bridge*. None of these places reminded her of Gene. Unlike home, they held no memories for her, so she frequented them. Wandering kept her away from home, freeing her from condolence cards, visits, and phone calls, the wounding sympathy of others.

After hearing Phoebe's voice message asking if she could come by, Judy had left the house and gone to Clark Park. She had no desire to see Gene's daughter. She went to the park in only a black fleece; she'd taken no jacket. She'd ordered the fleece for him from an online catalogue. Gene liked the way it fit across his shoulders and took to wearing it constantly. Even when it was stained and dirty, he took no notice of the offending dirt or odor and wore it blithely. Eventually, it became too baggy for him and hung from his thinning frame and still he wore it.

She'd sat on a bench in the park until the sun came up. During the day, people brought their dogs to the park, and on the weekends it became one giant flea market, but late at night it was a place for transients. Judy sat there until the last owners took their dogs home, until the last grad students headed back to their apartments, until the last families bundled up their children and took them away, until the last couples stopped kissing, and waited. She watched them all leave, some getting into their cars, some boarding the trolleys on Baltimore and Chester Avenues, and some simply walking. Then she made her way deeper into the large park. West Philadelphia's homeless buried themselves in the park's recesses, away from the vigilance of campus security bike patrollers who swarmed the park's perimeters, bent on protecting students who lived off campus. Judy selected a bench among them and huddled. She had lost her ability to find anything disgusting in mingling among those whom she would have normally avoided. Most, she guessed, were addicts or mentally ill, but she made no distinction between herself and them. Life had stolen something from them, robbed them, made them crazy and despairing so that they cared only for something to distract them. The park had become a depository for the unwanted, forgotten, and discarded. Sitting there in Gene's extra-large fleece, Judy pulled her arms deep within the sleeves and laid herself down among them, wrapped in the fleece full of Gene's funk.

Gene had said he would not leave her before it was his time to go and she had believed him.

The next morning, when she made it the few blocks back home, there had been no garbage cans on the curbs, yet now here they were. Across the street, Old Man Sampson bumped a shopping cart down his front steps. Haphazardly thrown into the cart were hardback books without covers, institutional copies. She assumed he was going to campus to return them. Why he did not pack them into bags, she did not know. The books, jumbled as they were, poked through the spaces in his cart. With every bump of the wheel against the concrete steps, the pile jostled and tomes threatened to slip out.

No garbage cans lined Sampson's curb. After he pushed his cart down the street and crossed it, Judy thought how neighborly it would have been of her to remind him of garbage day.

LATER THAT day, Judy brought out a folding chair and placed it on her top step. From her vantage point, she'd be able to see Sampson's return. She would apologize for not reminding him about the garbage and assume responsibility for him suffering the inconvenience of keeping his trash around an extra week. Judy knew little of him, only that he was a retired professor, that he lived alone, and that he had an abundance of young male visitors. Gene had not liked him. Since she'd taken to wandering, she'd seen the parade of young black boys going in and out of the old man's house at all hours of the night. To Judy, they seemed impossibly young and thuggish, arrogantly rough. Small and wiry, they were none of them over six feet tall. Judy was no fool. She knew Sampson's preferences, but it was not her place to judge.

The 42 bus was at the top of the hill inching its way down Spruce when a young man jogged up Sampson's steps, rang the bell and waited.

"He's not home!" Judy yelled.

The boy looked for the voice. She stood and waved until he noticed her.

He crossed the street. "You say something to me?"

"Sampson's not home."

"He always home."

"I saw him leave earlier," she said. "He had a cart full of books."

"Oh," the boy said, as if that explained everything. He was standing at the edge of her steps.

"Are you his nephew?"

"Nah," he said. "I ain't related to that boy." In his mouth *boy* sounded like *ball.*

"Do you work for him, then?" she asked.

He wore a du-rag on his head and was dressed in a long plain white T-shirt that came down to his knees, and a pair of baggy jeans barely visible beneath the T-shirt, looking like so many other young boys she had seen all over West Philadelphia, indistinct and indistinguishable. His youth clung to him, a mixture of freshness, arrogance, and bravado. He smirked. "Work for him? Yeah. You could say that."

Judy had seen the old man a scant number of times and had spoken to him but once. His voice had been gravelly, reminding her of Louis Armstrong's. On the rare occasions she did see him, he made her think of a turtle with his shy and slow ways, his heavy-lidded eyes and wide wide mouth. She could not picture him and this insolent youth together.

"He forgot to take out his trash today," she said.

The youth shrugged. "I don't do garbage. How long ago you say he left?"

"About two hours, I guess."

"Shit."

"I guess he'll be back soon," Judy said.

The boy looked at his watch. "He ain't coming back for hours." He turned to go. Judy didn't want him to. He was the first person, other than Hank, that she'd spoken with in all of the days that made up the month it had been since Gene's passing.

"You ever read any Baldwin?" she asked.

"Nah. Who's that?"

"I would imagine that Sampson has a lot of interesting books."

"I don't read when I'm over there." He smirked again and hitched his pants, giving Judy what she supposed was meant to be a belligerently knowing stare. She saw only the awkward patch of dark hairs above the bridge of his nose where his brows connected. The boy held a toothpick between teeth that were strong and white. She guessed he'd wanted to make her uncomfortable, but she felt only a rush of desire for the arrogant and impervious youth.

"You can wait in here for him if you'd like."

HE FOLLOWED her in and moved through her house as if he'd been in it a hundred times, making a circuit through her enclosed porch, living room, and dining room, picking up things and looking at them as he went.

"Does Sampson's house look like this?" she asked.

"Kind of, but he's got more junk and shit than you," he said. "He never clean up. There be like papers everywhere. I gotta step all over them. I try to be careful, but sometimes it's like too many and I step on one and then he get all crazy—be like 'That's my conference paper from 1992!' and I be like damn nigga if it's that important why you got it lying all on the floor and shit? Pick that shit up, then!" He stopped abruptly, as if realizing he'd said too much. He patted the couch and sat down. "Nah, this here is real clean," he said. "Real nice." He picked up the universal remote control and turned on the TV without asking. He skipped through the channels before finally settling on some sort of reality show. From what Judy could tell, the premise of the show was for young and uncouth women to attend a version of charm school in order to compete for the hand of a former rapper who lacked charm himself.

"So, where your husband at?" he asked.

"I buried him last month."

"My bad," he said, not looking away from the TV screen. "You ain't got no pictures of him up nowhere."

The sicker Gene had become, the more he'd refused to take pictures with her since he could not be sure to smile. His face seemed to settle into a permanent grimace he could neither feel nor control. "Remember me the way I was when I met you," he would say whenever Judy tried to change his mind. She had only two pictures with Gene, their wedding photo and a picture that had been taken of them on the *Spirit of Philadelphia*. She'd removed those pictures from the living room before the wake and had put them upstairs in her bedroom. In both pictures, Gene had been smiling.

"I don't like taking pictures," Judy said.

The youth shrugged and put his feet on the coffee table.

Judy waited for him to ask what Gene had died of and thought of how to answer, but the boy flipped to another reality show about students at a historically black college and became engrossed.

She asked how much Sampson paid him, and it was very little. She removed the money from her wallet and laid it on the table by his feet. He looked at her until she began to feel she had erred. Then he crushed the bills in his hands and shoved them deep into his pocket.

She gestured for him to remove the black nylon stocking cap tied around his head. Beneath the du-rag, his long hair was braided in a complex pattern with two whorls on either side that reminded her of ram's horns. Judy lightly touched his hair, finding it as soft and downy as a child's.

He pulled her hand away. "Don't touch me," he said. "And no marks either."

"Okay," Judy said. She thought of stipulating her own conditions for protection, then decided she had nothing to lose.

After taking off his du-rag, he removed the rest of his clothing, revealing a lanky frame. His legs were long, his calves small hard knobs protruding from the backs of bony legs. She pulled his face to her and kissed him hard and tasting. His lips were soft and fleshy, unlike the rest of him. He was surprisingly gentle and silent within her. She'd expected the inadequacy of youth, the exaggerated violence of the disadvantaged. She'd wanted to be an outlet for his unleashed anger, had prepared for it, hoped it would cleanse her of her own.

If she was angry, she had no one to blame for it but herself.

Though she'd married late in life, their marriage had been her first. It had been Gene's second. By the time they'd met, Judy had convinced herself she was bored with the formalities of dating and she cared more for companionship than courting. She and Gene had dated a mere three months. She had not been deceived. She had known what she was getting into. She knew Gene was getting sick, knew she loved him, knew he hadn't wanted to die alone. Three months or three years of dating would not have changed her feelings or her decision. Some called it selfish and calculating. His family accused her of lying in wait, marrying him just because he was dying. Once he'd gotten sick, they'd wanted to lock him away in a nursing home and wait for him to die. They behaved as if he were a nuisance. Judy was his protection, his shield against a lonely death.

She had not thought of needing her own protection. Of course she had known that Gene would die before her, but she had not known how it would feel once the empty days came. She'd thought that she could prepare for it, keep it from touching her as deeply as she'd suspected it was able.

The boy's eyes, liquid black, were focused on something just over her shoulder. His body seemed to move of its own accord. He seemed oddly untouched, detached from the manipulations of his body, as if sex were something one did rather than something one had. Somewhere, in his own neighborhood, he had a girlfriend whom he did not think of at times like this. Somewhere, he had a separate life that he kept intact. Like her, he foolishly believed he had an impenetrable core that defined him, shielded him from his outward self, kept him from being touched.

In minutes he was asleep, his legs carelessly anchoring her. Judy touched his face, finding it remarkably smooth. She'd loved all the lines on Gene's face. Summers spent down on the beaches of the Jersey shore had not been kind to Gene, but she'd loved the deep creases of the premature wrinkling that had given his face character.

It was unfair, Gene had said, meeting her at a time like that. He'd said he wished he had the proper time to court her, said they shouldn't lose a single day together. The man that had finally taken his own life rather than continue to waste away was not her husband. Gene had promised not to so long as Judy didn't put him away. She'd kept her word, relying upon the tenuous love of the dying man who had taken all of their remaining days, all of their tomorrows, and left her with only promises, fragile as strands of hair.

The boy jerked under her hand, and Judy touched his hair lightly, soothingly, her fingers wandering over his intricately patterned cornrows, following their winding paths along the contour of his head to the base of his skull where they curled under at the ends. Once he quieted, Judy grasped the soft and tenuous braids, undoing the plaited strands.

JAROD ROSELLÓ

THE NEIGHBOR

Welcome to the Neighborhood

IT WAS LAST WEDNESDAY WHEN I FOUND THE HOLE IN THE BACKYARD.

I THOUGHT, SOMETHING MUST HAVE DONE THIS DURING THE NIGHT.
I WAS CERTAIN IT HADN'T BEEN THERE THE DAY BEFORE.

I MENTIONED THE HOLE TO THE NEIGHBOR, BUT HE SEEMED
DISINTERESTED OR DISTRACTED, AS THOUGH HE HAD BETTER THINGS
TO WORRY ABOUT THAN A HOLE IN MY BACKYARD.

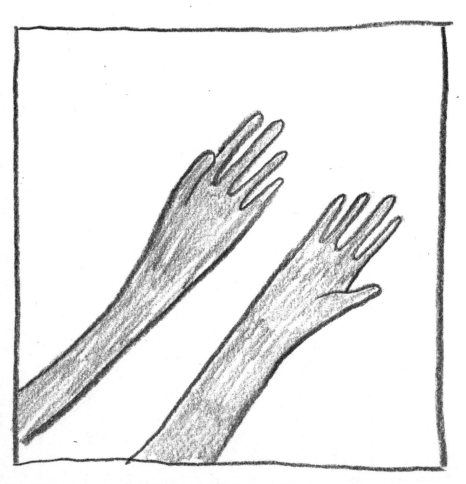

I ASKED IF I MIGHT BORROW HIS SHOVEL TO FILL THE HOLE. HE
HESITATED, THEN AGREED, AND HANDED IT TO ME OVER THE FENCE.

I THINK THIS WAS WHEN HE WALKED BACK INTO HIS HOME. I DIDN'T
SEE HIM, BUT I HEARD THE SWOOSHING OF THE SLIDING GLASS DOOR,
AND THEN A SILENCE I ASSOCIATE WITH ABSENCE.

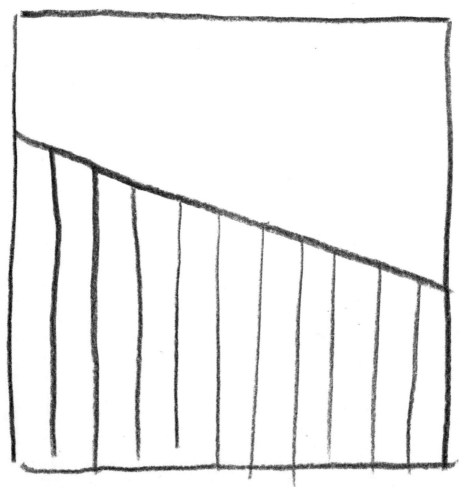

BUT THIS IS THE STORY OF THE HOLE, NOT THE NEIGHBOR.

THE HOLE WAS PERFECTLY ROUND. AT FIRST I BELIEVED SOMETHING HAD FALLEN FROM THE SKY, OR BEEN SHOOTING THROUGH SPACE AND HIT HERE WITH SUCH VELOCITY IT DUG ITSELF STRAIGHT INTO THE GROUND, COMPACTING THE DIRT BENEATH IT.

AND BECAUSE THE GRASS AROUND THE HOLE APPEARED TO BE BURNED,
IT MUST HAVE BEEN MOVING WITH GREAT SPEED.

SOMETHING SMALL THAT FELL FROM A TREMENDOUS HEIGHT.

BUT IT DIDN'T MATTER WHAT CAUSED IT, ONLY THAT IT WAS HERE
AND THAT I NEEDED TO DO SOMETHING ABOUT IT. SO I USED THE
NEIGHBOR'S SHOVEL TO FILL THE HOLE WITH LOOSE SOIL AND ROCKS
FROM AROUND THE FENCE THAT SEPARATED OUR PROPERTIES.

AFTER AN HOUR, AND ONCE I'D DEPLETED MY OWN SOIL AND ROCKS
AND LOOSE PLANT MATTER, I CAREFULLY SCOOPED SOME FROM THE
NEIGHBOR'S YARD JUST UNDERNEATH THE FENCE, BUT IT STILL
WASN'T ENOUGH TO COMPLETELY FILL THE HOLE.

WHILE CONTEMPLATING WHAT TO DO NEXT, A GUST OF WIND BRUSHED
AGAINST MY LEG.

STARTLED, I SHIFTED MY BODY AND THE SHOVEL SLIPPED FROM MY HAND, FALLING INTO THE HOLE.

I SCRAMBLED TO RETRIEVE IT, BUT I WAS NOT QUICK ENOUGH.

I SAT DOWN BESIDE THE HOLE AND TRIED TO THINK OF A NEW PLAN.
THE SHOVEL WAS LOST. THE NEIGHBOR WOULD BE ANGRY. I COULD
THINK OF NOTHING ELSE TO DO.

JUST BEFORE THE SUN SET, I WENT TO THE NEIGHBOR'S HOUSE TO
TELL HIM ABOUT THE FATE OF HIS SHOVEL, BUT BEFORE I COULD
KNOCK ON HIS DOOR, I HEARD THE SOUND OF A PERSON CRYING: A
DEEP, LOW SOBBING.

I PLACED MY HAND ON THE HOT WOOD OF THE NEIGHBOR'S DOOR
AND WAITED.

THERE ARE TIMES WHEN IT IS APPROPRIATE TO INTERRUPT
SOMEONE WHILE THEY ARE CRYING, AND THOUGH I DID NOT KNOW
THE REASON THE NEIGHBOR WAS CRYING, THE MANNER, DURATION,
AND INTENSITY ALLOWED ME TO DEDUCE THAT THIS WAS NOT A
CRYING THAT CAME FROM THE MOMENTARY PAIN OF INJURY.

Welcome to the Neighborhood

IT WAS NOT A SADNESS ASSOCIATED WITH A HEARTBREAKING
COMMERCIAL OR THE PENULTIMATE SCENE OF A FAMILY DRAMA.

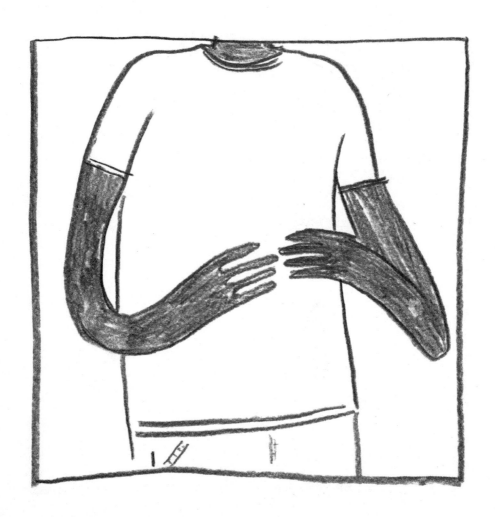

INSTEAD, IT WAS THE KIND OF CRYING THAT COMES ONLY WITH
DEEP, ENDURING SADNESS: THE KIND THAT COURSES ITS WAY
THROUGH ONE'S ENTIRE BODY, TINGLING THE FINGERTIPS,
WARMING THE FACE, AND TWISTING THE STOMACH.

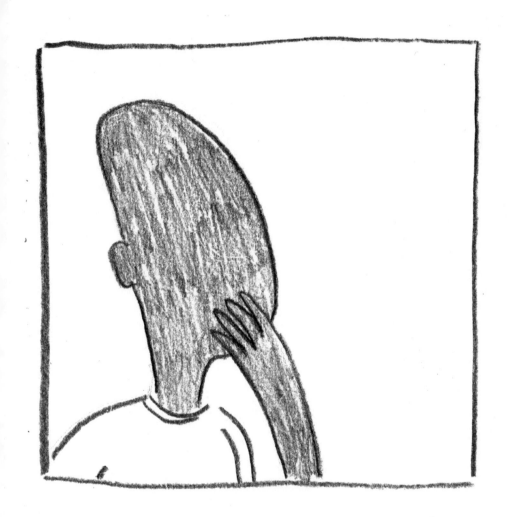

THIS, I BELIEVED, WAS THE KIND OF GRIEF THAT REROUTED
ENTIRE LIVES, ALTERED TRAJECTORIES OF ONE'S EXISTENCE. OR
ELSE, THIS WAS THE KIND OF SADNESS THAT MADE IT IMPOSSIBLE
TO CONTINUE ON: THE PAIN THAT RENDERS A LIFE UNLIVABLE.

AT A LULL, I KNOCKED ON THE DOOR AND WAITED.

THE TREES ABOVE MY HEAD RUSTLED IN A GENTLE WIND.

SOMEWHERE A CAT HISSED.

A SIREN DISSOLVED WITH DISTANCE.

I TAPPED MY FOOT ON THE GROUND, THEN KNOCKED AGAIN.

Welcome to the Neighborhood

THE DOOR OPENED AND MY NEIGHBOR APPEARED: EYES BLOODSHOT,
FACE RED, FISTS CLENCHED.

FOR A FEW SECONDS WE STARED AT ONE ANOTHER AND THEN I
SAID, "SOMETHING'S HAPPENED TO YOUR SHOVEL."

AND HE SAID, "I KNOW."

Welcome to the Neighborhood

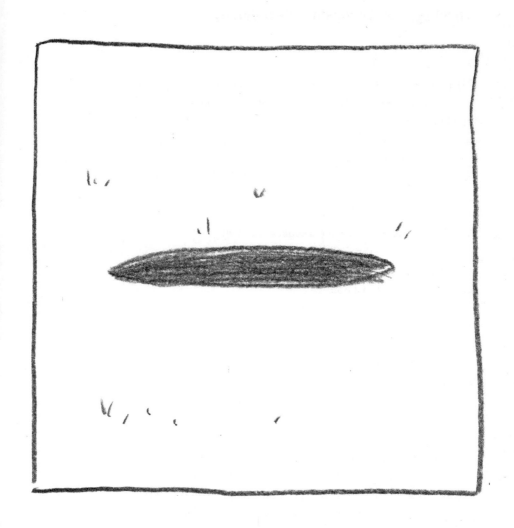

AND LIKE THAT, THE HOLE WAS NEVER FILLED.

Thanksgiving: Livingston, New Jersey

My grandmother had gold chairs. In her small house, wallpaper
grew in soft green stripes, like moss, which you could pet,
and her magnificent and certainly objectionable fur coat
lived inside the closet like a civilized animal without a head.
And the cast-metal boy forever whistling at the base of a lamp.
And bowls of raisins and walnuts, like in a Yiddish song. Curtains you could hide
behind, yellow chiffon. Upstairs, an artificial fern and silvery chaise longue.

We played outside where like a shot of mercury
the brook plunged through the woods. In the luscious deep piles every leaf
was chased with copper foil. And inside, always, grown-ups' aromatic
coffee just coming to a boil.

Were we Jewish? Well, Jew-*ish*. In that house of crowded
oil paintings, not one much bigger than the span
of, two up, two down, four ordinary grown-up's hands. The farmer
plowing by his blooming tree, and the one she always
said she'd one day give to me: a Primitive, kids with balloons,
a sky of birds that looked like fish.

In the kitchen with its friendly wallpaper of stylish orange flowers,
I smelled dill and chicken broth and schmalz. Papa's brick- or lilac-
colored vitamins sat beside his breakfast cup. You could kneel
next to the dishwasher and see the pattern (houses, wagons,
horses) that had long ago been covered up. We never had apple pie

or cornbread or anything, besides a turkey, that the Pilgrims ate,
but lemon meringue, and dark sweet chocolate Bundt cake
Aunt Roz baked reliably, each year. And in the morning,
always, bagels and a schmear. I slept dreamless nights
in my father's bronze-colored childhood bed. Or lay beneath
the dining table, where you could look up through the glass

just like the dead. November now means all of it is gone.
Those strange Thanksgivings, which I never can get back:

No pumpkin pie, no green beans, no Mayflower,
but gilt-legged chairs and late dark minty hours,
powdered sugar topping cakes like swirls of stars,
and on the mantel, Yahrzeit candles burning in glass jars.
The leisure, glitter, silkiness of those old days
are nothing I can find now in simple flat American ways.

You Know How It Is

Some months before we married, Raegan and I were walking in L.A.'s Fairfax district, where we lived. A Jewish part of town. Hasidics, even, who, since it's Saturday, have set aside the keys to their Mercedes and are out and about, roaming the streets in silent gangs, all bearded and wooly.

I crack a joke loud enough for even the devout to hear:
—Looks like 'unflattering' is all the rage *again* this season!!
Raegan doesn't laugh. That's Raegan for you. A tough room when she's uncomfortable. I love her for her almond eyes, her hellfire curls, and her smothering bosom. But oh what to do about her stubborn head, filled to bursting with misguided, archaic notions like: "Are we not all of us equal in the eyes of God?" and "We should love each other exactly as we love ourselves."

Anyway, so we're walking. Holding hands. Headed to Rite-Aid for a refill of Ventolin. It's mid-morning. In six hours we'll be flying to Boston, my hometown.

Up ahead, an old woman is sitting in the middle of the sidewalk in a wheel-chair. She is the spitting image of my paternal grandmother, Yetta, the very woman we're heading home to see. Recent surgery has left her delusional, paranoid Nazis are landing choppers on the Hebrew Rehab roof. She is no longer herself.

As we pass, the woman stops us with a practiced gesture:

Old Woman: You look like a very nice couple.
Nice Couple: Thank you very much.
Old, Prying Woman: Have you voted?
Nice, Lying Couple: Yes, we have.
Old, Prying, but Easily Conciliated Woman: Good. It's important. Have a good day, now.
Nice Couple: You too. Enjoy the weather.

Old Woman: I will. I am. But those poor Hassidim! Ach, look at those poor dears—children, too. All in black on such a hot day as this. And the men with the long coats and the furry hats? It's a wonder they're not having heat stroke all the time. And the women . . .

She motioned us closer.

Old Woman: Did you know? The women, they wear wigs. On top of it all. What is that? Our own hair isn't good enough? Now God wants us buy artificial hair to cover over our own hair? There's just no pleasing Him, is there.
Nice Couple: Are you sure they don't shave their heads? I think I read somewhere that they shave their heads maybe.
Old Woman: Those are the—what do you call them—Krishnas you're thinking about. Talk about crazy! Well, I'm glad you voted and you look very nice, you two. Nice young couple.

And that was that.

It may be hard to imagine a daylong argument arising out of a conversation so banal, but like many things in life, all it took was one misplaced word.

—Ten bucks says if we'd stuck around she would've asked if you were Jewish.

It seemed an innocuous comment. After all, I knew the type: elderly yentas with nothing better to do than pass judgment on the happy relationships of perfect strangers. Generally speaking, they sit by the Frigidaire, making good use of their genetic pull by instilling guilt in shy grandchildren over long-distance lines with the precision of a neurosurgeon and the delicacy of a meteorite. I thought, therefore, that I was on pretty solid ground.

Then there was a pause and Raegan released my hand.

—Why do you have to do that?
—Do what?
—Ruin everything.
—All I said was if we'd stuck around any . . .
—I know what you said. Why do you assume everyone's like that?
—Believe me. They are.

—Maybe you're like that. Maybe that's why you said it.

—I don't think so.

—Maybe you need to find a nice Jewish woman.

—I'm pretty sure I'm okay.

—I don't know why you have to be such a dick, then.

—You don't know these people! These are not good people.

—She was very nice!

—That's how they get you. They rope you in with the nice bit and before you know it . . . WHAM! They hit you with the Jewish thing.

—That old lady was right. You are crazy.

A gray pall settled over the remainder of our erranding. We chored through the hours awkward as newlywed Muslims. She didn't want to be with me and I didn't want to be with her, she not wanting to be with me but we've got this flight thing coming up and my parents at the end of it, so we're kind of stuck with each other.

As we wander down Ralphs' frozen foods, Raegan resigns herself to this fate, sets her discontent aside and graciously resumes cordial relations. Nevertheless, I postpone further discussion and mentally set aside any new indecencies for use at a later date.

Things are looking up. In the supermarket I manage to engage her in some funny shtick involving new rice cake flavors, to whit: Strawberries and Cream, Bavarian Chocolate Mousse.

—They sure are getting ambitious with these rice cakes.

—Uh-huh.

—Look at these crazy flavors! What's next, I wonder, Salisbury Steak?

There's a pause. She's coming around, thinking flavors. She can't refuse the bait:

—Borscht.

—Good one. I mean, really. What kind of technology have they got? A rice cake's a rice cake.

—Hm.

Oh no. A regression. I've been too frivolous too soon. She's slipping back.

—And a Jew's a Jew.

—I didn't say . . . !

—I just don't know if I want to be with someone who's so prejudiced all the time.

—Not all the time! Just around old Jewish ladies who feel it's their personal responsibility to keep the race pure for Jumanity.

We're back to the silent treatment. And this time, no manner of abrupt stutterings or frustrated ejaculations will bring her around. But I know I'm right. And I'm not saying it doesn't go both ways, that I haven't received preferential treatment, too, for being Jewish. My landlady in Milwaukee for instance, an old half-batty curmudgeon who lived below us. We were three guys, all of us med. students, living up there but I was the only Jew and as such I was her favorite. She never asked me to take out her trash or shovel the sidewalk or anything the way she did my roommates. And she confided in me, talking about my house-mates as though she and I had grown up together:

—That Bill, he's nice and all, but you know. He's not like us. Know what I'm saying?

—So true. So true. Poor old Bill.

—So, do you have a girlfriend?

—Not at the moment, no.

—You need to meet a nice Jewish girl.

—Sure I do.

—Trust me. It makes a difference.

—Why do you live here alone? What happened to your husband?

—He's dead.

—I'm sorry.

—Oh, no. We divorced thirty years ago. Just couldn't get along.

For the rest of the day, any discourse that passed between Raegan and me was purely functional in nature. As in this Fluff & Fold interchange:

—Did you bring the soap? Don't tell me you forgot the soap.

—So I'll buy more soap.

It's five hours later. We have shopped, laundered, packed, and showered. We have made it to the airport and parked the car. We are boarding the flight. Things have smoothed out considerably between us, time being nature's great elixir.

An elderly woman is seated next to me on the plane. Now, were I to suggest that this woman is an old Jewish fussbudget about to inquire into my dating habits and question my allegiance to the faith, I understand it would come off as the worst sort of contrived fictional device. But this isn't fiction. This is real life.
Here's how it happened. For most of the flight, the old lady and I mutually ignored each other. She had her reading and her grandchildren across the aisle, and I had Raegan. At some point, she called her daughter over. There was a pain rising from her feet. She needed to walk a little, maybe. Then the woman stopped speaking English and her words took on a funny, familiar sound. A timbre I hadn't heard from my grandmother in a while. I grasped a word here and there: Shlump. Mishpacha. Goyishe. I had to ask:

—Excuse me, is that Yiddish?
—You speak?
—My grandparents did. My father a little. I just recognized the rhythm.
—Not so many speak it anymore. Where do you live—L.A.?
—I do now, near Fairfax.
—Wonderful! You have a girlfriend?

Here's the funny part. Raegan was sitting right beside me. And this lady had been next to us the whole flight, had seen us hold hands, exchange niceties.

—Yes, I do.
And then she said it.
—Is she Jewish?
The daughter butted in:
—You don't have to answer that.
—I'm just asking . . .
—Ma.
—Nevermind "Ma."
—Ma, what is the matter with you?
—It's important. These things are important. My whole family, you understand? I lost my husband to them. You never know when is going to be the next time. You think we had warning? Nobody could believe it. Even we ourselves couldn't believe such a thing.

—Ma, the restroom's vacant. Take a walk. Do yourself some good.

She turned to Raegan:
—She can't help it. It's a thing with them. They grew up with it.

She turned to me:
—You know how it is.

Meteor Dreams

At least once a week, homeless men and stray dogs broke open the bags of curbside trash in front of our East New York diner. It was my job to sweep up and repack the garbage neatly by the curb before the police issued a summons. Throughout grammar school, I spent long mornings with a push broom, chasing after Styrofoam cups, flattened milk cartons, and balled-up napkins. Sometimes, the garbage trail extended out onto the road, and during breaks in the traffic, I scurried out to sweep stray items back toward the gutter.

I always rushed through the task, dreading that someone from school would see me ankle deep in trash. At St. Basileus' Elementary, I maintained a manageable and predictable routine of humiliation. In 1982, I was the only Korean girl in a class filled with mostly black and Hispanic students. Almost daily, some school-yard boys formed a ring around me, miming martial arts moves, dancing to a soundtrack of high-pitched whining they associated with some Asian language. Their show usually ended with the lunch toss—the pitching of my cheese sand-wich over the schoolyard fence.

Even at ten years old, I sensed that it was sometimes a good thing not to fit in. Most of my classmates were rooted in East New York, where the public schools were flanked with barbed wire, and storekeepers were shot dead for three rolls of quarters. For me, East New York was only a temporary stopover until my family saved up enough to leave. I went to bed each night thinking I didn't belong here. This place was not for me.

Embracing my outsider status, I was most comfortable observing the neigh-borhood activities from a single, narrow window on the second floor of my house. It was the only window that wasn't strapped with iron bars because it was inaccessible to intruders. If I crouched down low enough and stared upward, I saw only sky and could imagine myself anywhere—a fancy hotel in France or a beachside resort in Florida. At night, I caught faint glimpses of three or four stars, and secretly wished one of them would fall right into our backyard and deposit good aliens like ET or Superman.

Directly below this window sat a thin strip of our side yard, but the real activity played to the left of my view. The corner entrance of Hugo's Auto Repair Shop set the stage for rattling cars that scraped up the driveway, some of them needing a last-minute shoulder push from their owners. Thrilling curbside dramas unfolded when husbands and wives fought openly about some car accident; their shouts and insults carried clearly throughout the neighborhood. I once saw an aggravated woman kick off one high-heeled shoe and use it to hammer at a man's head. The squabble stopped four lanes of traffic, and some drivers honked and cheered until a couple of local firefighters pulled them apart.

On the opposite corner from Hugo's stood the only brick building that sat in full view of my little perch. Mickey's Flooring and Carpet Store was owned and run by Mrs. Haley, and other than my own mother, she was the only female business owner I knew. Her gray-streaked white hair was always pleated in a single, long braid that reached down to her lower back. The marbled whiteness of her hair looked neon against her olive complexion, and her freckled cheeks helped prop up the thick, plastic-framed glasses. Whenever I walked past her store, she waved through the window, and I waved back. But when we didn't have that pane of glass between us, I never knew what to say.

She lived above the store with her two, grown sons, Crane and Joseph. Actually, no one confirmed whether these were her actual kids or her nephews or even grandchildren. Everyone had different theories. I was convinced that Crane in particular had to belong to Mrs. Haley based on his laugh. That's when he looked exactly like her. But the resemblance ended there. On bad days, when Crane sat stoic and somber, chain-smoking on the cement stoop, his expression was his own, attached to no one.

According to my parents, Crane was the reason why Mrs. Haley had so much white hair. He didn't work hard enough and was always running off with his lazy friends. My mother said in her broken English, "Troublemaker son make too much stress. Make mother old."

To me, Crane seemed exceptionally kind without any of the wildness I'd heard about. Like his mother, he always greeted me with an easygoing smile. Whenever I stood nearby, he flicked away his cigarette or fanned the smoke in the opposite direction. His small talk was always complimentary and encouraging. And after a long morning spent picking up damp, rank trash, he was the first one ready with a morale boost.

"How's Brooklyn's hardest-working lady today?" he often called out when I passed by. My shyness prevented me from responding with anything more than a quick wave and a mumble. And I always regretted my sparse comments, feeling as if I'd rushed along too quickly in the tightly reserved manner instilled by my parents. But my timidity didn't discourage him in the least.

In addition to his cheerful words, he regularly tucked a quarter into my palm so I could buy some of my favorite candies. He'd always flip the coin high in the air first, and catch it with a swipe, as if he was plucking a moving creature out of the air, capturing it just for me. "Lady, stop looking so serious all the time," he said. "Go buy some sweets and put a smile on that face." Those quarters felt cool and fresh, like they had indeed dropped out of the sky.

I always smiled and pocketed the coin, thinking about the chocolate and penny candies I would buy at the corner store. I was supposed to say, "No thank you," and return the money. That's what my parents had taught me, and usually I followed those rules, except with him.

When my sister, Lon, found out about Crane she said, "It's bad money. Don't take it."

But I didn't understand the concept of bad money. Wasn't all money good? I secretly compared Crane's coins with the ones in the cash drawer at my father's hardware store, and I was hard pressed to notice the difference. I decided to ask Crane about it, but the next time I passed his stoop it was empty that day and for many days thereafter. This was nothing new; he had a way of disappearing for weeks at a time. Then he'd return one day, cutting carpet and driving the family van as if he'd never been away.

He was absent for nearly two months that spring, much longer than usual, and I regularly perched by my favorite window on the lookout for some glimpse of him. And when he finally showed up, smoking on his stoop as usual, I had completely forgotten about the money. It was already after dark when I first spotted him, so I had to wait until the next day. But the following morning, his friends had gathered around him. Crane milled about the sidewalk among the group, and seeing him play-punch and clown with his peers reminded me that he was much younger than I'd thought. Through him, I began to understand the ranges within grown-up society, the difference between adult and young adult.

Among his friends, Crane ignored me completely, and I didn't acknowledge him either. We both followed this unspoken rule. This arrangement didn't feel the least bit unnatural. As silly as it sounded, I felt that I knew the real Crane. Around others, he was just pretending.

As one of the many black men in East New York, Crane should have blended with the crowd, but I could always tell him apart, even from behind. He wore only three colors—T-shirts in solid khaki, white, or black. In winter, he threw on a leather or sheepskin jacket, but he never closed up the front, exposing the thin shirt underneath. And he always kept his hair neatly sculpted, a perfectly round, half-inch depth of hair. While other men started experimenting with various styles—long, braided, twisted, and capped—Crane's hair remained constant. He must have gone to the barber religiously once a week to keep it so uniformly tame. While his friends habitually combed their hair in public, pulling out afro picks and small brushes for a quick grooming, Crane never fussed. He stood aloof, hands in his pockets. To me, it was the epitome of confidence and class, and I enjoyed being his secret friend.

When I caught up with him a few days afterward, back on his usual stoop, he seemed to be in a particularly good mood. He called me over and handed me two quarters instead of one. "For your birthday," he said.

"But it's not my birthday," I said.

"I know," he said. "It's an advance, Lady. You never heard of that? It means you get your treats early."

"Oh," I said, closing my hand around the quarters. "Okay. Thank you."

"And if you're lucky, when your birthday comes 'round, I'll forget I gave you that, and you'll get another quarter out of me."

"Oh, that's okay," I said. "I'll remind you."

He laughed, holding his cigarette-free hand to his belly. "Now why you want to do a thing like that for?" He waved me away, still chuckling.

Giddy with my new windfall, I decided I couldn't wait to get to my usual bodega to buy the candy. Toward the end of the block, I ducked into the first store on my route. I'd passed this place a thousand times but never entered because it looked a little run-down compared to the others. The storefront glass was soaped over in some spots, and in other places, faded boxes of laundry detergent and baking soda were stacked so high it was impossible to see inside. But since most stores in the neighborhood were in various states of disrepair, it wasn't too far from the norm.

Two men with knit caps stood on either side of the door, both smoking strong, sweet-smelling cigarettes. I stepped between them through the main entrance and realized that this was not a typical shop.

The room was largely empty except for a short counter, two tables, and mismatched chairs. About eight men loitered against the back and side walls, and they all stopped and turned toward me. The man behind the counter said, "What you want here?"

"Candy," I said, holding out my quarters to prove I was a real customer.

After a two-beat pause, the room broke open with laughter as thick as the smoky haze. Some of the men pounded their palms on the table or leaned against the walls.

"*Candy?*" the counter man said, doubling over. "Man, this girl wants some *candy.*"

He stressed the word *candy* each time, as if it I had asked for plutonium or vampire blood. Another round of cackling pulsed through the room. I felt my face flush even though I couldn't place my embarrassment. I just knew I was saying something really wrong.

"Oh, we got lots of *candy,*" the man said. "What kind you be wanting?"

I was about to name a few brands when I heard Crane's voice behind me. "Girl, get out here!"

I whipped out of the store toward him, hearing one last roll of laughter behind me. Crane guided me by the arm at a brisk pace down the street.

"What you doing in there?" He said through his teeth. "Don't you know what that is?"

"A store? A candy store?" I muttered.

We turned the block out of sight of the store's gatekeepers.

"You listen," he said. "You don't want nothing from there. You got me?"

I nodded.

"That place is not for you," he said. "Not never."

I suddenly knew what he meant. It was a bad place. They sold bad things—their candy wasn't for me.

He walked me to my father's store. Although Dad thanked him for the kind escort, when Crane was gone, he quickly turned on me.

"Who is that?" he asked in Korean.

"Mrs. Haley's son," I said, hoping he would not ask whether it was Crane or Joseph.

"That's the bad one, right? The troublemaker."

"He's not so bad," I said. "He—"

I was about to explain how Crane had saved me, but then I would have had to admit my own stupidity and shame. "He's not bad," I said weakly.

"Not bad?" Dad said in English. "Not so good either."

I felt guilty for not defending Crane more staunchly, but at the time I didn't know how. To my parents, and the rest of the neighborhood, he was just another boy gone awry, someone who stomped out his mother's hopes and made her hair go white. When people talked about young men like Crane, they used words like "lifer," someone who belonged in dead-end places like East New York.

It seemed unfair to judge him so severely. Like my science teacher said, even the moon had two faces. One side was ugly and beat up from surface flaws and meteor strikes; the other side looked more smooth and serene from a distance, like an eggshell. From that moment on, I resolved to help Crane show his positive side. I would be his ambassador, his assistant. If people understood him more, maybe he wouldn't have to go away so often.

But Crane disappeared again through most of the summer. He returned toward the middle of August, but he didn't work. He sat on his front stoop or on the curb, chain-smoking. Every time I happened to glance out the window, he was there.

A couple of times, I thought of going out to him. Maybe I would bring him a corn muffin from my mother's diner, but each time I changed my mind. What would I say? Besides, I didn't want to admit that I'd been watching him, that I sensed there was something wrong.

The next Saturday, on my way to the hardware store, Mickey's stoop looked empty until Crane stumbled out from its shadows and fell in step with me. He threw a paper bag into the gutter, and I heard glass breaking as it hit the ground. I had never seen him litter, particularly in front of his own house, and I could tell by his sluggish shuffle and his loose gestures that something was off. We walked for nearly a full block without speaking. I glanced up at his face once, but he was staring straight ahead, his jaws clenched, his neck muscles taut.

When we got to the corner, he slumped onto the steps of the public school. I didn't know whether I should walk on or sit with him. So I stood a few feet off to the side, waiting. A more socially adept girl would have asked if he was all right, but I stood quietly for several minutes before he spoke first.

"You got any brothers?" he said, keeping his eyes on the patch of sidewalk between his feet.

I shook my head. Everyone in the neighborhood knew I didn't have any brothers. He raised his head and looked at me full in the face. His eyes were watery and bloodshot. "Me neither," he muttered. "I got no brothers neither."

He shot up to his feet faster than I thought possible, and he staggered back from where we came. I looked after him a long time, wondering what to do. I could have used someone's advice but that was the tough part about being someone's secret friend: I had no one to tell. After this puzzling exchange, he vanished again.

A couple of weeks later, on a Sunday after dinner, I was working in the kitchen on a summer reading report when I heard a familiar *pop-pop pop-pop* followed by the screech of tires. I ducked lower to the ground, listening for more. When we heard these sounds, we were trained to stay away from windows and doors, and stick close to the center of the room, but this time I sidled up to the edge of my favorite window sill and peeked over.

Across the street, in front of the carpet store lay a man, face down with one arm outstretched. He was still for a moment, but then his head lifted a little. He groaned and said, "Help me." The narrow streets carried that whisper a lot farther than I thought possible. It was both a murmur and a reverberation.

I gripped the window ledge. The man began to drag himself forward, although it wasn't clear where he was going. He managed to move a few feet, and I began to see an uneven smear on the pavement. From a distance, it had the same glint and sheen as pancake syrup.

The man was a few feet short of the corner when he turned his head, grimacing. It looked a lot like a forced smile, and that's when I gasped. Even from fifty feet away, I knew.

Hearing my yelp, my father joined me by the window, and I stepped back, letting him block most of my view. I rushed over to the phone. "We have to help him," I said.

My father put his finger to his lips, hushing me. In East New York, you didn't advertise a call to the police. Snitching was punishable by death. He shut off the lights and pulled down the shade almost all the way. By that time, my mother also joined us. It was clear that neither one of them had made my recognition.

"It's Crane," I whispered. "Mrs. Haley's son."

My mother squinted through the side of the roller shade. "You sure?"

"I'm sure," I said.

"Crane," my father murmured. "The troublemaker?"

"No," I said, my voice a shaky whine.

My parents stood off to the side, discussing in hushed undertones how we could call the police without getting it traced back to our house. We couldn't use the corner payphone because that required going outside. If we used the house phone it could be traced. Back then, we didn't have cell phones.

Crane had stopped moving forward, but he still lifted his head and moved his arm slightly every few minutes. Mom gave me a nod of permission. She said in Korean, "Make sure you don't tell them our names."

I was about to dial when I heard another muffled commotion outside. Peeking through the side of the shade, I saw a brown Lincoln Town Car with dark, tinted windows. I caught a glimpse of a man stepping into the backseat and slamming the door shut. The car pulled away quickly but without burning rubber. As it passed out of view, I noticed that the sidewalk was empty.

"He's gone!" I said.

My parents stepped in front of me and quickly looked as far back and forth as the narrow view would allow.

"A car came," I said. "They must have taken him to the hospital. Maybe those were his friends." I hung up the phone, excited at this fresh bit of luck. His friends would know where to take him. They would get him some help.

My father looked at me; then looked away. "Not friend," he said in English.

I stood confused, struggling to consider why anyone else would be interested in carting off a bleeding man. My parents left the kitchen, somber and stunned.

I called after them. "Then who were they?"

"Doesn't matter," Dad said. "It's finish."

They left me standing there alone, straining to piece together what I was missing.

Usually, there was a neighborhood funeral or memorial service for the fallen, but we never heard about one for Crane. Mrs. Haley never brought it up; although she, too, disappeared for a few weeks. Several times, I wanted to tell her about what I'd seen, but I knew it would cause her too much pain. Some things you can never say.

It took a few days of eavesdropping for me to realize who had taken Crane away, and for the first time, I experienced a quiet rage inside. It seemed that there was a lot I didn't know, and no one seemed eager to tell me.

For the short remainder of the summer we suffered through a heat wave with temperatures reaching one hundred degrees during the day and only cooling down to about eighty-five at night. The weather matched the boiling pitch of my mood. I spoke less and less in the days leading up to the new school year, and I spent my free time reading and watching television. I no longer gazed from my favorite window. Any time someone rolled up the shade, I pulled it back down with such diligence the rest of the family eventually left it closed.

Late one afternoon, as I washed the rice for dinner, the radio weather report closed out with a quick mention of a meteor shower that would pass through the skies later that night. The reporter predicted favorable viewing conditions with clear skies and only a slight possibility of some cloud cover.

After quickly rinsing my hands, I hunted through the closet for a picnic blanket. Despite the unrelenting slog of heat, I felt a brisk forward momentum. I wanted to catch a glimpse of the fiery meteors streaking by, to witness something supernatural, something bigger than all of us. Maybe an alien creature was folded up inside one of the rocks; a creature who was inherently good and generous— someone powerful enough to fix things.

The meteors were supposed to start streaking at around 11 p.m. and last until about three in the morning. At half past ten, I was camped outside on the hood of the car. Lon spotted me from the kitchen window. "Get off there," she said. "You'll dent something."

"I don't care," I said, still gazing up at the sky.

Unlike the weatherman's report, it was cloudy and overcast. The sky was a luminous lavender rather than the deep purple necessary for star watchers. I waited, convinced that the skies would clear at any moment. Even the occasional spatter of raindrops didn't deter me from my vigil.

A little after midnight, Lon joined me outside and looked up for a while. "You won't be able to see anything," she said.

"How do you know?" I asked.

"It's too cloudy."

"Meteors are really bright," I said.

"It's hard to see stuff like that in the city," she said. "You have to go way out and drive somewhere else."

"What about stars? If we can see them why can't we see meteors? Aren't they even bigger than regular stars?"

She shrugged. "Plus it's too cloudy," she added.

"Go away," I said, keeping my eyes fixed toward the hazy skies. I only needed to see one meteor—just one.

She stood there for a few minutes, as if she wanted to say more, but she didn't. She walked around the car once and looked up a couple of times; then she went inside. Although the air was heavy and hot, I felt a chill. I stayed there most of the night, scanning the sky—waiting, waiting.

I spent those hours going over the image of Crane crawling on the pavement as I peered out the window through a closed shade. If I ever got the chance to go back to that night, I promised that I would collect enough courage and run out to him. I would gently turn him over so he could at least look up at the sky instead of the concrete. And as we waited for help together, I would tell him what we both knew all along: "You never belonged here. This place was not for you."

DINTY W. MOORE : fiction

Racism in America: The Official Report

INTRODUCTION

Adolph Baltz is in his window, watching twelve inches of snow bury his marginal, crumbling neighborhood. He is thinking, "Go ahead, Big Guy. Cover it all."

About Adolph

He is old with a large, veined nose and thin white hair. No moustache. He was a machinist for forty years, ever since coming to this country. A machinist in a factory that made machinery for other factories. He is quite tall. He remembers when people ate regular food and painted their fences.

Some Background

This is happening in West Philadelphia, in December.

SECTION ONE: Contributing Factors

Adolph watches Toto

He looks out and sees a small man across the street, a man with black eyes and a shabby, ill-fitting suit. The man moves quickly and nervously, reminding Adolph of the little dog from *The Wizard of Oz*. Adolph watches the young man (he calls him Toto) hurry toward a big car, a maroon Buick.

Toto uses his hand to clear snow from the lock. Then he opens the door.
The Buick starts up—Adolph can tell from the exhaust.
Toto guns the engine—Adolph knows because the white wall tires spin furiously. The car doesn't move.
Adolph thinks:
If you spin you build up friction, the friction creates heat, the heat melts the snow, and, at ten degrees above zero, the melted snow turns to pure ice.
It makes Adolph feel good to know this.

Adolph meets Toto

Three weeks back: Adolph is shoveling out from an earlier overnight snow and the young man sprints up to him. The young man's skin is more or less the color of a paper grocery bag, but shiny, and he's looking at Adolph's shovel, red plastic with an aluminum handle. Martha made Adolph buy the shovel because his old one was getting too heavy.

"That is good," Toto says, pointing at the shovel. "No?" Toto's smile is yellow, and wide, like a banana.

"What?" Adolph says.

"That is good for moving snow?"

"It's the general idea."

"What do you call it?" Toto is still grinning. He can talk and grin at the same time.

"It's a shovel," Adolph says. "ShoveEl!"

Toto pulls his head back, considering this. "Where do you buy one of these shoveels?"

"Sears," Adolph tells him.

Now, Martha

Adolph and Martha used to talk about foreigners a lot, before her heart stopped in 1983. Adolph blames Martha's death on the fact that the new wave of immigrants brought home stray dogs but didn't take care of them. Martha often worried that one of the strays was going to bite her. Adolph used to say, "Martha, when are you going to ever stop this fretting?"

Then she died.

SECTION TWO: How Racism Proliferates

Lack of Vision

Adolph is in the window, watching Toto gun his engine. The tires spin. Toto gets discouraged, stands on the cold sidewalk scratching his head, then walks across the street and onto Adolph's porch just as if Adolph had invited him to share breakfast. Adolph can't see because of the way the window is set, but he can hear Toto stomping the snow off his low black shoes. The doorbell rings.

Lack of Understanding

Adolph is curious. So the next moment, he is holding open his front door. Toto is smiling as if Adolph was about to take his picture.

"I am sorry to be bothering you," the young man says. "But I knew you were awake. You are always the first one awake."

That bothers Adolph. Does Toto have nothing better to do than watch to see when Adolph gets up in the morning? Adolph feels the anger moving around in his head, like something small and furry looking for a place to lie down.

"I cannot move my car," Toto says, pointing to the large, maroon Buick still idling across the street. "I thought you would know how to help." He folds his hands, as if praying. "You see, I teach at the University and I am late for class."

Adolph thinks:

Why should I help this creep? He's one of the idiots who killed my wife. Just like the old neighbors, the ones who left that Scotty dog barking in the snow all day.

So Adolph asks:

"Where's the pooch?"

Toto looks at Adolph and says nothing.

"Out with it," Adolph says. "What kind of dog do you have?"

"No dog," Toto says. "It is my car."

"I fought the Nazis," Adolph says.

"My car is stuck."

Adolph, nearly a foot taller than the young man, slowly lifts an arm and places it on Toto's shoulder. Adolph has arthritis and this is not easy. Toto appears to sweat along his upper lip, but doesn't move.

"The Nazis," Adolph says, his voice rising involuntarily, "were everywhere I looked."

Adolph sees that his anger makes Toto's eyes dart across the street. He likes that, so he raises his voice even more:

"I fought the Nazis so people like you could move into my neighborhood and turn it into a pile of dog-doo. Dog-doo. Dog-doo. Do you understand this? Do you understand what I'm telling you?"

Toto still doesn't move.

"What I'm saying," Adolph continues, shouting now, "is that I can't help you unless you've fought the Nazis too!"

The young man opens his mouth then closes it slowly. He reaches up and runs two fingers along his upper lip. Finally, he turns and races back to the Buick.

Like Butter

Adolph is ecstatic. Seventy-two, and he's just scared a strange young man off his porch. Wouldn't Martha be proud? You have to draw the line somewhere, with foreign dictators emptying their jails, and Adolph's government holding the door wide open like it was relatives coming for Sunday dinner.

SECTION THREE: Impediments to a Lasting Solution

Economic Factors

Adolph marches back inside to turn the thermostat down. It's cold and Adolph can't afford to be burning oil on a machinist's pension. If he and Martha had been able to have children, maybe now one of them would help Adolph meet expenses. Maybe the child would have bought his parents a new home, away from stray, homicidal canines. Martha would never have had her heart attack. But they had no children. Martha always blamed the war for that.

Local Government

Adolph knows there are two things Toto could do. He could put something under the tires to get some traction. Adolph keeps a bag of sand in his front hallway for that purpose. Or he could shovel the snow from behind his car, clear a bare patch of asphalt, and back up. An automobile has more traction going in reverse.

While Adolph is thinking, Toto gets out of the Buick and stands shivering on the sidewalk. An agent of the Philadelphia Streets Department comes along with flashing yellow lights and plows a four-foot wall of gray slush up against each and every car on Toto's side of the block. Toto's Buick is completely trapped, the wheel wells packed with ice.

Religion

Adolph knows not to park along a snow route during a blizzard, but he figures Toto never gave it a thought.

Foreigners don't plan ahead, he thinks. Their religion forbids it.

SECTION FOUR: Can Racism Be Stopped?

Yes

A moment later Toto is back on the porch, ringing Adolph's doorbell. Adolph is amazed. This time he opens the door quickly.

"My friend," Toto says. "Sorry to bother you again."

Adolph tries to stand as tall as he can, and says nothing.

"Please, can I borrow your shoveel? For a few minutes."

"What for?" Adolph asks, even though he knows. It's a test. For honesty.

"I must go soon or I will not make it to class at all."

"So what good's a damn shovel going to do you? You shovel your car out, you're still stuck on the ice."

Toto's smile sags. "Do you know how to get my car free? I could pay you to tell me?"

"No," Adolph tells him. "I haven't a clue."

No

"Well, can I just borrow your shoveel, then?" Toto says, running his fingers along his lip.

Adolph doesn't want to lend the man anything, but he can't pretend he doesn't have a shovel because he knows that Toto has seen it. So Adolph says, "Go ahead," and reaches behind the door where the shovel is kept. He hands the shovel to Toto and says, "But you're wasting your time. No one's going to show for your class."

Toto takes one step back, and says, "Maybe not." Then he leaps across the street so quickly that it reminds Adolph of Allied soldiers storming a Nazi bunker.

Adolph feels weak in the heart. He stumbles back to his window and watches Toto toss enormous clods of snow over his shoulder, into the center of the street, a clod every ten seconds. Then he notices the flakes. Within five minutes it is a blizzard outside and Adolph is having trouble even seeing across the street. He can no longer spot Toto, but he can hear the shovel scraping against the asphalt.

Adolph remembers the plow.

Even then, it takes Adolph a while to get into his big coat and big hat. The arthritis. He still wears black rubber boots with metal buckles. They take a while to snap on. Adolph doesn't know why everybody doesn't wear them. He has tried, but he really doesn't understand.

By the time he gets out on the porch, boots buckled, the snow is swirling like smoke and the visibility is about to the end of Adolph's veined nose. Adolph thinks he hears the scrape of the shovel, but it is hard to tell. The snow muffles all sound.

The Streets Department plow is going to turn around at Woodside and start back, and Adolph doesn't think Toto knows that, and he doesn't really want to see his neighbor crushed. Not right out front, at least. He doesn't know if Toto will hear the plow, and he is sure the plow operator won't see Toto. He heads to where he imagines Toto to be, but carefully so he doesn't stumble over the trolley tracks.

He remembers the last time it snowed this hard: 1954. Martha got stuck coming back from her sister's house in Norristown and had to sleep in a motel outside of the city. She couldn't call because the snow had collapsed the lines, and for about a day and a half Adolph had no idea if she was dead or alive.

Adolph reaches the middle of the street and yells:

"Toto! Hey, fellow." Toto is the only name Adolph knows for the young man, and he hopes no one's feelings get hurt.

There is no response. Instead, Adolph hears the dampened sound of an ignition, the screech and slap of windshield wipers, and he sees the Buick's headlights snap on. He moves toward them and spots the dim outline of Toto sitting in the driver's seat, leaning forward, trying to see. Adolph gets close enough to rap on the window, thinking he might warn the young man that the plow is coming, but Toto yanks the Buick into gear and shoots out into the street like a tank rushing a low hill. It nearly knocks Adolph down.

Perhaps

The classroom will be empty, for sure. And Adolph can't imagine what the man could possibly have to teach anyone—the professor not even smart enough to stay home in a blizzard. Adolph turns and heads back for the house, barely able to see his way, but aware of the flashing yellow lights advancing slowly up the street. He finds his way inside just as the plow passes, roaring like a jumbo jet. He takes off his coat and bends over, his fingers frozen and the boot buckles crusted with snow.

He wishes Martha were there to take his boots off for him. But she isn't, so he works each buckle loose, slowly and painfully. This takes ten minutes. Then Adolph hears the doorbell.

SECTION FIVE: If Happy Little Bluebirds Fly

Beyond the Rainbow

The doorbell. For a confused minute, Adolph thinks it might be his wife, and his heart pumps with gaiety. He feels a flutter in his antique chest, like little wings beating a song. But then he remembers what year it is. He remembers the little grave on Woodland. He opens the door a crack and sees Toto grinning from one frozen ear to the other, holding the shovel like a gun.

"I moved the car," Toto says.

"It's snowing," Adolph says back. "It's a damn blizzard."

"Thank you for your shove-el."

Toto smiles and drips snow onto the porch. Adolph looks at the young man and it is at that moment he realizes Toto has proven himself to be a true American. A fighter. One of the guys.

And then Toto makes his announcement: "We fought the Nazis too. I wanted to tell you. We fought them in Africa. We were not afraid."

Adolph decides that perhaps he knew this all along. Perhaps he sensed it, and that is why he had tried to help. He pushes the door open wide. "Come in then," he shouts. "What's your name?"

Toto says something that Adolph cannot understand, something that sounds like 'Kickball.'

"Well never mind," Adolph says. "I'll make us some cocoa."

Kickball cocks his head to one side, surprised, then extends his hand and gives the shovel back to Adolph. "Cocoa," Kickball says, "would be very nice."

Why, Oh, Why?

Adolph moves away from the door to allow his neighbor to enter, but Kickball hesitates. "You don't have a dog?" he asks, peering past Adolph and into the house. "A biter?"

"There is nothing in this house but you and I," Adolph says, pointing at Kickball's chest and then his own. "No dogs. No Nazis. Just men like us."

"You like that?" Kickball takes a tentative step inside.

Adolph shuts the door. He leads the dripping foreigner across the living room carpet, swaggering his arthritic hips as best he can. "Like it? Why I love every damn minute of it."

Can't I?

Kickball sloshes into the kitchen and seats himself at the table. "But you must get forlorn?"

"Sure," Adolph says, his spine aching from the effort of standing tall and proud. "We all do. But no one ever said this war would be easy."

Kickball laughs and begins to unzip his jacket, but Adolph is weeping. He knows now exactly what his foreign neighbor has been through. Adolph knows the horror of battle. He knows what it is to be alone and afraid.

"My God," Adolph chokes, focusing on the thick crust of snow coating Kickball's lean shoulders. "My God, look what they've done to you."

Kickball shrugs, scattering bits of the snow.

"No," Adolph says. "We won't let them get away with it. There's just the two of us now, but by God in heaven, somehow we'll find a way to stop them."

American Valentine

When a flag is wounded, worn,
or simply unwanted, and its owner can't burn it,
or won't, it arrives in the Dead Flag Office
where a man too young to look so old
logs it, but not before he buries his nose
in the stars and stripes
as he's done with every flag
he's ever carefully pulled out of its envelope
as if it were a love note.
At first the sniffing was a game,
this "nasal immersion,"
as his doctor called it, a game to identify
a flag's home by its smell: citrus
was Florida, or California, white salt
and fish could be New England, and so on,
only, recently the game became a ritual
as so many games do
because this man with the forgettable face
and nimble hands, this lover of Marvin Gaye
and Sinatra and anyone who ever sang of loving love
hadn't left the portable building
that is the Dead Flag Office
in five years and so his parsing
of the subtle odors masked
by the native scent of each region
became a way to know
the history of each flag's family: grease
was bowls of fried chicken and asparagus
on Sundays, while exhaust and hot dogs
were a bank on a busy street corner, and moths,
moths were always a soldier
with no one left to air the three-point keepsake
his memory had soured in.

When a flag arrived carrying the light scent
of petunia and sap and wind
heavy with pine, he knew
this was the flag from his porch,
the one that had flown on a cruiser
in the Pacific during the war,
knew he had to leave, had to go home.
Because his clothes had long since turned to rags
he dismantled what he loved best,
but since he couldn't sew his new red,
white, and blue clothes had no real shape
to speak of, nor did his pants have hems
nor his sleeves cuffs and so long
were they that his hands were not visible
and so it was in this way he stepped
into the chill of a late afternoon in fall
and walked once more
the eight blocks through the old neighborhood,
down the streets
where he had been called Old Gory and Betsy Ross,
had been mocked as the Dork of July
every month of the year until the day
the courage to cross the door of his office had died.

The sun was gone behind the hills now
and so he walked faster,
ignoring the questions of his neighbors, the shocked faces
of those who had given him up
for dead. Faster and farther,
his feet bruised, he ran up the sidewalk
and onto the pile of rubble
where his house had once been
and stood there, looking
like a cut-out heart, a wild
thing panting on a bed of ice
for a new dark to wrap it up again.

A Map of the World

When I was in ninth grade, my father ran away from home. One frostbitten New England morning, he climbed into his gray Toyota and drove toward Guatemala. He left a letter for us written in blue pen on a single sheet of my school notebook paper. Somewhere around DC, he turned back. I have always wondered how his life, and mine, would be different had he kept driving. His longing has haunted me ever since. It is why I am here in Guatemala, living day to day, page to page. I want to understand how my father could possibly love a country more than his family.

I am sitting in a library in the Western Highlands. Tattered spines of paperbacks line the locked doors of the glass wooden bookshelves. Paulo Freire. Rigoberta Menchú. John Updike's Rabbit Run. The library is one room with three square wooden tables and, posted on the white wall, a map of the world. It is an upside-down map: North America is in the southern hemisphere; Australia trades places with Europe. A window the size of a door places afternoon light in clean strips across the cool tiles. Outside, clouds cast shadows over the mountains.

The one librarian's name is Aracelis. She is rosy-cheeked and wears a pearl-white sweater with a fur collar. Her black hair is thick and long like mine. She hovers over my desk, examines the black marks I have scribbled between the thin tan lines in my leather-bound journal. She leans in. My shoulders tense. I have seen her before. I return to this library like I return to this country, over and over. But today, it's as if my face has a sign that reads: Tell me your story.

"My father lives in the United States, in Arkansas City, and when I was three he left Guatemala to work, but he always called and said he had gifts for us—my mother, my sister, and well . . . my father, for me, he was just everything, hope, a hero, until one day when it was my sister's birthday and we had the cake ready, the food, everything, and the telephone rings and it's him."

All this she tells me in one long black hair of a sentence. She talks with her hands and her eyes dart left to right. She speaks as if we'd penciled this conversation into our calendar weeks ago, like she'd been practicing it while twisting along the narrow, cracked sidewalks in the pink light of sunrise, the orange light of sunset.

"So he says, look, I'm only calling to say that I have another family now. I don't love you anymore and I'm never returning."

We both nod. Me, side to side, and she, up and down.

"I didn't want to say anything to my sister. So I waited until my mother asked me what was wrong. I had to tell her. My mother sat down and she cried. Then my grandparents. My sister. And me."

"Maybe he was lying," I say. "Sometimes life is hard in the U.S. People can't find work. A man can feel like a failure."

"No." She pulls down her sweater. "After that I didn't want to have anything to do with him. Yo sufrí. I even had to go to the hospital . . . yes."

In the window I spot an old man pushing a rickety wagon full of empty gas tanks. The shade from his cowboy hat hides his face. The high sun has moved its attention to another latitude, another longitude. Seated at the wooden table, I want to cry, not for Aracelis, not for her father, but for mine. He could not do what other men did, my father, who has been homesick for forty years. And yet a feeling of gratitude swarms me. Thank God he didn't have the guts. Thank God my father came back, and that I, his daughter, can relish the warmth of both suns. That is what I felt as I listened to Aracelis that afternoon in the library, when I stared long and hard at the upside-down map.

Path to Nowhere

My neighbor stands on her back stoop, watches me stamp
on shovels, me sweat, me tug up trash trees in my yard.

This yard was all packed dirt, a crap-ass lack of grading.
One old syringe, a hundred broken bottles. She watches me

work. She *loves* to watch me work on my knees, digging, lifting,
flipping Goshen stone from pallets into pathways, raised

bed for the cherry, its silken iridescent bark. She sighs, *Whew!*
A lot of work! I smile the way that means *shut the fuck up,* get back

to, yes, a lot of work. When I finish settling flagstones, pat
their sun-warmed little backs, their gorgeous curves

a mica-gleaming weight from gate to barbecue, she brays
A path to nowhere!, a line I keep, use again and again. All

that work: a path to nowhere. A lush backyard: what's
the point? Poetry: a path to nowhere, outsiders not knowing

where we are. Here we are! I found us! On our paths, each
ambling along. Sometimes I cried, taught seven classes, cleaned

houses, painted them, waited tables, tended bar. Not true, not
really: I tended bar so badly, and for just a second—ask Misty,

anyone. I made gorgeous garnishes, achingly slow cocktails.
A path to nowhere, those cocktails. Like poetry, they got so

much nothing done. A path, though, a way, a way forward:
a way to think through our lives. Our lives, what we want

to do with them. Even my bitch-ass neighbor a gift,
a punchline, each piece a glinting, sun-warmed stone.

Not Trash Day

The holiday pushed it back.
I drag my crates out anyway. I threw away
my roommate's rotten produce to liberate the crisper,
but I did it a day too early. On the street, the only other
trash bins are empty, left from last week.
I put a teakettle on the curb and it filled
with rain water and then somebody took it.
I've started putting water out for my neighbors'
cats, who seem to live on my porch.
Does this mean I don't trust my neighbors? Yes.
But I don't trust most people to take care
of animals, not even myself—that's why I don't
have a cat and have to steal my neighbors'.
It's not trash day. One crow says "no no
no no no no" and two others say
"nuh-uh" "nuh-uh." They sound like a family
on vacation, nothing left to talk about,
just sitting at a restaurant booth commenting
on the local color. Once at IHOP there was a wood stork
walking past the window and we watched the cook
out the back door give it kitchen scraps.
Was it being taken care of? If the volunteer
cactus in the side yard suddenly
has yellow flowers, so thin they could be made
out of crepe paper, does that mean it doesn't need me?
And the dog at night off leash, running after a shirtless
running man who stopped and let it catch up and lie down
under the streetlight, tail wagging, and the man hit
it slowly, heavily, rhythmically, on the stomach
with the flat of his palm, were they playing?
The two disappearing around the corner, the dog's tail
still wagging, me startled alone in the dark,
like I was somewhere I wasn't supposed to be.

A Small Guest

Alan Kurdî (2013–2015)

Seaweed followed the law

        It released you to waves bussing

                your small body

down, down dark currents

        silver minnow tunnel. Your red

                shirt swallowed

the Aegean, billowed

        and swelled, but your shoes stayed on

                By them the sea

knew your refuge dream

        restored you to shore so your father

                Abdullah could find

you, a guest of the sea

        Without guests all houses would be a grave

                the poet wrote

making a worm from mist

        a bird from sand. What prayer

                transforms this empty

castle guards watch

        ignorant of the gift to shelter each other?

                Who will help

close, open, close

        your velcro laces for the journey

                your father dares

for your sake? You a gift

                loved with milk cake and honey. You

                                practice the names

to keep you safe—

                not Mohammed, Jesus. Not Muslim

                                Christian. Hush—

don't bother now

                as tourists gather and multiply your image

                                on their tiny screens

You are not their orphan

                of beach foam, Alan *flag bearer,* watching

                                from the lap of God

C. E. FORT : poetry

Arrest Dance, Oakland, CA

put your hands in the air, step out;

put your hands in the air, don't move—

now lower your body to the ground,

lower, keep your hands up, *lower,*

now put your hands

away from your body, away

from your body, palms out—

wrong way—put your palms out

War Game, America

The war scenario has: [vegetable stalls], [roaming animals],
and [people] in it. The people speak

the language of the country we
are trying to make into a kinder country.
Some of the people over there are good
others evil others circumstantially

bad some only want cash some
just want their family to not
die. The game says figure

out which
are which.

Steel Valley Songbook, Volume I

Praise dead-end signs peppered with buckshot.
Praise shop windows shattered by rocks.
Praise the beige Pinto up on blocks. Praise playing chicken on Butcher Road.
The matte black Camaro praise, and praise the '71 Chevelle:
blessed be the boy who swerves first.
Praise pig wrestling, cow tipping, cock fighting, arm wrestling, and barn loft
    boxing.
Praise and praise the prom queen's ass.
Sweet corn, rhubarb, apple butter, pumpkin bread, and blackberry jam, praise.
Praise the 606-pound squash at the county fair.
Praise bingo, scratch-off lotto, and bagging the limit.
Praise the twelve-point buck strapped to Jimmy Jones' truck, friends
in orange caps gathered around, beer can in every hand.
Praise Iron City Beer. Praise Red, White, and Blue. Praise Everclear.
Praise sniffing and huffing whatever is slapped with a warning label or without:
    whip-its, whiteout, model glue, copy toner, paint thinner, gasoline, and fat,
    black markers.
Praise the view at night—200 feet above the town's steeples and oaks—from
the highest rung of the water tower.
Praise the urge to jump and praise the harvest moon.
Praise flat light falling on flat land.
Praise and praise the Cuyahoga caught fire. Blessed be the man who keeps his
    bobber in the water.
Praise the closed mill.
Praise the abandoned strip mine.
Praise the sign that reads DANGER: DO NOT WADE, SWIM, OR FISH HERE!
    Praise, in jeans shorts and ripped concert T-shirts,
the girls who swim anyway.
Praise the jackknife, gainer, cannonball, psycho, Zeeko, and belly flop.
Praise first sex in a wood-paneled station wagon.
Praise the dirt bike and turnpike. Praise the taxidermied pike—44 inches long and
    open-jawed—hung above the bar at Penn Grill.
Praise the Gin Mill, Side Door, and Hooker's Barbershop.

Praise the butch, fade, mullet, Caesar, flattop, and buzz cut.

Praise the Steel Valley. Praise the Rust Belt.

Praise the Mistake on the Lake. Praise the City on Seven Hills. Praise the Land of Drive-Thru Liquor Stores.

Praise the home of the Fighting Quakers, Potters, Bulldogs, Warriors, Indians, Dukes, Cardinals, and Mighty Clippers.

Praise and praise, forever and ever, the Rubber Capital of the World!

Assembly

While the bombers were playing basketball
or smoking weed and powering up a level on Xbox, I was falling a little out of my tube top

down the street from them at Christina's Ice Cream, dropping my sunglasses, trying free
spoonfuls: rose, cucumber, chocolate, green tea.

Last summer, I still hoped a certain man might change his mind.
I swam. I watched *The Bachelorette.* The loudest noise was my neighbor once a week

at the fire hydrant setting a blue bin full of rinsed-out bottles down. Next door, all three triple-
decker porches glowed at 6 PM from solar lanterns. The bombers were not bombers

yet, just brothers, both younger than me, wrestling. I had some things on my mind, like
which sandwich to buy—while I waited, a very old waitress put up her feet.

She was wearing compression stockings. Last summer, the younger brother decided to grow out
his hair because girls liked it. The right lung of one of my friends showed a dark spot,

another friend called me in tears about a pregnancy she didn't want, I cried
when a third friend called, finally pregnant. I was happy for her. I traipsed in flip-flops

for some peach muffins, some iced coffee. Men asked did I need help carrying groceries? Men
argued, loud, outside the mechanic's, about Red Sox trades. We were all very alive—

all of us and the brothers. *Who cares?* the bombers began to say, I guess, and then believe.

Sometimes You Know before You Know

The neighbor who never smiles steps out
of his dress shoes in a parking space, leaves

their velvet mouths to soak, tongues still
lapping the milk-round bellies of clouds.

There are no clues, only pennies pressed
in fresh asphalt, smell of burn, black windows

reflecting the same sunken face, until one day
I see through—she's surrounded by stacks

of folders to be filed. Destroyed. *Sometimes*
you never know. I wait for his bus to corner,

but in every dream I have he isn't on it.
He's always in the field they found. Sting

of a needle lost. The fruit he asked me
to name, there, rotting on the ground, grass

rippling with flies. I watch the creep
of vine on picket. *Or maybe you become*

the ghost you're looking for. If only we
were home now it'd be summer yet, but no—

the dandelion spores keep morphing into snow.

SARAH C. HARWELL ⦂ poetry

God Speaks through the Seals

The seals returned from near extinction
to rest and brood on a J-shaped brooch,
fastened, a mile long and a few feet wide, to nothing stable,
a breach that interrupts the sea,
that ceaseless and unworried sloshing—
if you wear your glasses underneath
you can see what the sea is wearing—
claws and weird blooming things
and tiny fish flurrying like exploded flowers—
giving rise to words like marl and bight and others
that you rarely say, unsure of meanings—
but under there you understand you don't belong
to that which causes light to split
into streams, a fish out of water, and so retreat
to shore to watch the seals who slip in and out
mooing, grunting, clapping their flippers,
hundreds of their black, wetted heads popping
out of the water, staring at us, friend and foe,
the landed daughters and sons of amoebas
who chose the trees and air and breeze
and walked away from that which isn't solid
and when it rains, as it did today,
feel closed in and snug and cared for.

There is something to be said for seeing
that which can kill you—
unlike a seal who slides in and out of danger,
unaware of the shark who, with no warning music,
no crunch or rustle or baying, rises from so deep
a place you didn't know it existed—
and when it strikes the seal deflates—
gallons of blubber oil becalm the water
and seagulls pick at the tasty bits,

Welcome to the Neighborhood

while half the time the seal slides out
of that toothy darkness—too fat and slippery
for the jaws to pierce—and swims off bleeding into the sea
which turns all our excretions back into sea.

Staring at them staring at us, we who trekked
the mile on sand—years ago we wanted them
dead, called them thieves—and even now grumblings
have begun, you stink, you bring the shark,
you're greedy, stealing down our cod.
But to see you plopped down on sand, odd
amalgams of grace and gracelessness,
gives the sundown sky a lighter color,
and we watch in confusion—
are you a pest or is it true you're part us
as in the old legends—your faces appear so kind—
your eyes so curious—we feel, yes, feel
you're one of our children—
rocks, sea, seals, sand,
the turnings of what we love, we hate,
and the short cycles between them.

Heidelberg Beach, October

1.

Lake Erie stretched out and shining
and once again, the sunset,
leaving me speechless.

2.

I know, it isn't the sun setting,
it's the earth turning away,
neither of them worried
by the details of their intimacy.

3.

The heron on the dock
turns its head slowly
as if to remind me
we're gifted, both, to be part of it:
the traveling light,
traveling light.

Winchendon

The bus rocks gently into some town
at 5 p.m. I sort of look at the houses and stores
the way you do from a bus just passing through:
happen to notice
                            a paperboy and his pal
in small-town America
on a forgettable side street back of the hardware store
down from the brick Methodist church—
the friend wobbling his bicycle to go slow,
the paperboy fiddling with the red strap on his sack of
evening news . . .

What evening news could there be? In Winchendon . . .
The bus thrums and I'm so okay on it.
The bus thrums and I'm thinking Winesburg, Ohio,
while in Winchendon the paperboy and friend are
already way out of sight,
                            discussing a girl named
Mary Jane,
daughter of Ned of Ned's Used Cars and Parts,
how she says one thing and means the other;
the paperboy thinking of her hair as beauty itself,
conscious that he can't explain this logically.

Up by Ned's, near where some twenty Holsteins
graze stolidly all facing away from the highway,
there's a sign BLIND PERSON
                            and I think "That's me"
and the bus thrums
into gathering dusk
and I ride thinking "gathering dusk"
away from all that other life I meant to think of
in Winchendon:

methods of local survivors—
who's making peanut waffles for dinner,
who's playing Patience over the oil-rag wilderness of the garage,
who's singing "Hit the Road, Jack"
and who's walking fast out to the darkening Common
in the hope of some personal and effective encounter.

Neighbors

The apparition of these faces in the crowd—
Petals on a wet, black bough.

Boston's MBTA Red Line used to end at Porter Square, until recently the town-gown divide in Cambridge, with working people living north of Porter and east into Somerville's Davis Square and Powderhouse neighborhoods. Now it continues to Davis Square, and then on to Alewife Station with its tiered parking garage for commuters from the suburbs. All this change, along with the repeal of rent-control, has transformed the neighborhoods so that Cambridge now has the greatest number of homes worth over a million dollars of any city in the US, and Somerville's Davis Square is going through the familiar transition from workers to artists to money.

Outside Porter Station, a 46-foot-tall red steel sculpture, *Gift of the Wind* by Susumu Shingu, makes its benefactor visible in a mesmerizing and graceful kinesis above the plaza. A remarkable work, it seems to allude to a weathervane and Ferris wheel and sail and horseshoe crab and lobster all at once while it swivels and dips and turns like a prayer wheel or thurible, its blessings quintessentially New England.

I love the Red Line's public art. Over at the Davis stop are life-size statues by James Tyler of people he recruited from the neighborhood, and people from out of town are always having their pictures taken with them. The sculptor's given them masks. Tourists pose with them so that their postures blend, to see if they can fool the folks back home, if only for a moment: *Who are those people with you? Why are they wearing masks? Oh.* Elsewhere the art is themed to the stop; at Kendall/M.I.T., for example, the walls chronicle the history of scientific and technological discovery, and a button on the wall activates a series of colliding chimes between the inbound and outbound tracks.

On this particular rainy day, just inside the door of Porter station, the flower vendor has her ephemeral inventory arranged in buckets on risers, but it seems futile: who buys flowers on their way *to* work? At the top of the escalator a man hands each commuter a Metro, a mere outline of a newspaper, little more than headlines and advertising. I take mine and step onto the moving stairs down.

The escalators plunge deep into the earth, the first long ride down bringing you from street level to a plaza with a snack bar, an ATM machine, and a vendor whose cart, depending on the season, is loaded with baseball caps, sweaters, scarves, gloves, battery-operated fans, and of course incense and prepaid telephone cards. Both vendors, the man with the cart and the man at the snack bar, are clearly Arab, and I have wanted to ask each where he is from but worry the question would seem an affront, my sociable curiosity freighted as it is with history and politics and fear. Everyone is fully aware of the changed context for all our interactions since the bombing in the London tube, but even to talk about that fear openly would brand you a suspicious character. Next to the vendor's cart, a man is selling *Spare Change,* "The Newspaper By For And About The Homeless." He is always there lately, standing with his stack of papers under one arm, holding out a copy to us as we debark the stairs. His left eye may be glass; it stares up and to the left so that the one eye that is fixed on you seems ferocious and accusative. And why should he not be angry? Or his fierce gaze may be serving him as a disguise, a mask suggesting danger, covering his otherwise naked vulnerability. No doubt he is homeless himself, and he seems surrounded by unasked questions about how he came to be here glaring at us and importuning us to buy for a dollar what we wish not to know.

Just ahead of me on the escalator down, a woman is rummaging in a huge purse hanging from her shoulder while her child, a girl about four or five, holds onto the moving black handrail with both hands. This is the next chapter of the descent, an additional hundred and fifty feet or so to the inbound train platform; there's still another level down after that, to the outbound trains. And here's more art: the bronzed gloves of the workers who dug and tunneled and blasted and laid track and tiled and otherwise carved this now taken-for-granted place out of earth and rock not so long ago; there are pairs of them at intervals along the aluminum console that separates the UP and DOWN escalators. The artist, Mags Harries, calls them "narrative sculpture," presumably because they allude to the story of the building of this station, but also because one is led from one glove or pair of gloves to the next as one moves through the narrative of one's own journey. The little girl in front of me notices the first pair and cranes her neck to keep looking as the stairs take her away, and then another pair comes into her view; now she realizes there must be others, too, and she looks both up and down to see where they are. She pulls at her mother's sleeve to show her and her mother says, yes, yes, I see, I see, but she is deep in her bag and isn't looking. Watching this child, I think I understand something; I see that art, this art anyway, can serve to direct our gaze, to somehow help us manage our attention. Art gives us something to do with our voracious eyes; it occupies our thoughts, tempers our anxieties, soothes our discomforts. At

Welcome to the Neighborhood

least until we get to the platform itself, where commercial space begins, with ads for booze, for dating services, for Christian Fellowship and deodorant.

In some situations, the subway being one of them, it is important to "keep custody of the eyes" as the nuns used to teach my classmates and me in talking about temptations of the flesh. When we were in third or fourth grade we were curious to understand this phrase but still too young to grasp its meaning; later we weren't at all interested. I always figured it meant, sort of, "mind your own business." Once, not long ago, I heard a woman on the street yell at a man, "You keep your goddamned eyes to yourself!" and I couldn't decide whether she was crazy or if the man, who of course gave me an exaggerated innocent shocked look, had been leering at her.

Today the music is provided by a young woman playing the violin, a Bach partita interrupted by a recorded announcement reminding us that for our safety we should report any unattended packages or suspicious persons to the station manager. Her music is on a stand before her, case open on the floor with a few coins and a couple of bills in it. A few other people have distributed themselves here and there on the platform, some students, an older Asian couple who are both wearing white surgical masks, two mothers with babies in strollers. One of the people looks remarkably like my brother Joe who lives in Pennsylvania and whom I see too seldom. I've been seeing this guy around the neighborhood for years; once when my daughter Veronica was small she grabbed my arm and pulled me down to her to ask, in a hot little whisper, cupping both hands around my ear, "Is that Uncle Joe?" and I had to look hard to assure myself he wasn't my brother. The guy's a dead ringer. Over the years Veronica would tell me now and then that she had seen "the Uncle Joe guy" again.

A few feet away from me on the platform, the woman with the heavy purse—sliding down her arm—grabs the little girl by the wrist and yanks her arm and slaps at her bottom all at once but the little girl, practiced, I guess, in these matters, goes limp and twists herself away from the blow. The mother yanks her back to her feet, "Stand up!" she says. Then she spits on a handkerchief and wipes the child's face with it. "I'm not going to tell you again. You hear me?" The little girl seems far from crying. She doesn't look like she's ever cried in her whole short life. I can see she is watching her mother's hands. Suddenly the mother is looking at me, a glaring challenge: What*chew* lookin' at? As I turn my gaze away I register for the briefest moment that the child is giving me the same look: I've witnessed her shame and now she hates me from behind her mother's leg.

You can feel the train approaching before you hear it or see its light in the tunnel because it pushes air ahead of it into the station. I take out my iPod, put in my earbuds, choose some Thelonious Monk for the ride, and as the train pulls into the station, I check my watch, which is always set ten minutes fast, a strategy that depends on my fooling myself all day long.

I GENERALLY look for that single seat in the corner of the car, and it was free, not many people on the train yet since Porter is only the third stop. Monk was laying down a deep melodic and harmonic framework, a starting point for his explorations, and I took out my paperback of *The Idiot,* settled my half-lenses on my nose, and looked forward to picking up the story of Prince Myshkin where I'd left off the day before. Of course as we entered the tunnel I checked myself out in the dark mirror of the window across from me, a ritual of self-consciousness I try to keep in check. And then I looked around at the others, wearing the most unthreatening look I could muster. To my left was a young man, well-dressed, with a leather briefcase flat on his lap. Across from me was a man sprawled across three or four seats, sleeping, I supposed. Among the other thirty or forty people in the car there seemed to be four or five different uniforms, depending on race, class, and occupation. Though some people dress to call attention to themselves, to stand out, most people dress to blend in, to become invisible. In the middle of the car was a man impeccably outfitted and assiduously groomed but whose hair was clearly not his own; in fact, it didn't much look like hair at all. The way he was glaring at himself in the window, brushing at his coif with his hand, made him seem mercilessly impatient with himself, a miserable sort of narcissism I thought, as if his attempts to make himself blend in and become acceptably invisible had backfired and he wondered why it wasn't working, why everyone was still, well, giving him those *looks.* He caught me gazing at him, looked away, reached under the seat for a discarded newspaper to read.

Can a person *feel* a look? Of course he can. In situations like this, when we are together not by choice but by necessity, we get nervous, we get on one another's nerves, and our sense of personal boundaries becomes acute. Decorum requires nearly absolute self-containment, and the lack of privacy feels threatening. Both observer and observed are caught in a double bind. We're not supposed to stare; in fact, our stolen looks, like shots made with a secret camera, prove our implacable desire, our utter fascination with one another. Fortunately, there's art. What else could possibly aid us in averting our gaze, brimming with curiosity, judgment, desire, and fear, but art? What else is more interesting than other human beings except, perhaps, the things human beings make to look at, touch, read, hear? Thelonious Monk was just unravelling the melody like taking apart an elegant theorem while pleasurably demonstrating how the parts might be reconfigured to create a different mood, even a different set of premises from which to start over. Without entirely intending to, I looked at myself in the window again. I assessed what I saw there: not an unpleasant face, better from the left because my nose is crooked, beard needs a trim, hairline receded but in a way that seemed all right to me, forehead high and shiny, smart, mature. I was wearing my nobody's fool expression, and trying, I think, to avoid the image just behind the image of myself, the blackness roaring there. Maybe that roaring is behind every image we have of ourselves. One thing is for certain: anyone who thinks his reflection in a piece of glass is what other people see when they look at him is even a bigger fool than he is a narcissist.

I tried to return to the story of Myshkin; I was just picking up at the part when Roghozin attempts to murder him, but we were slowing down and soon had pulled into Harvard Station. As people came through the door, they looked at the seats across from me where the man was sprawled, and moved away to find seats elsewhere. I think this was what first got my attention, and I noticed that the man sprawled across from me seemed not to be merely sleeping. For one thing, his posture wasn't that of someone trying to make himself comfortable—one arm was hooked behind the seats at an angle that made me wince to see it, and his other arm was folded behind him. His head was lolled back, mouth open, the whites of his eyes visible under half-shut lids. His skin had the color and granular look of the inside of a baked potato, and his lips were chalky white. All in all there was an alarming rigidity about him. About a dozen people came into the car, people with shopping bags, with newspapers folded just-so to the articles they were reading, students with backpacks, a mother with a child in a stroller. I watched each register discomfort with the ghastly body angled across the seats as they moved away.

As the doors closed, I looked to my left at the young man with the leather briefcase in his lap who had been watching me take in the scene, and now he gave me a conspiratorial smirk, a look that said, "It takes all kinds . . . ," a look that asked for reassurance that whatever kind we were we were different from whatever kind he was over there across from us looking like a broken puppet. I looked from the young man to others around us. A smirk from a young woman, clearly a student, who went back to highlighting her spiral-bound text. A dark-skinned woman, her hair in cornrows and with enormous rings on several of her fingers, avoided eye contact with me and was moving her lips, perhaps praying, maybe in another language. I thought the unconscious man was breathing, that I could see his chest rise and fall. But then I wasn't sure if it wasn't simply the rocking of the train. A man in business attire except for a Red Sox cap caught my eye; he raised his eyebrows, gave me a tight-lipped smile, looked over at the sprawled man, back at me, and shook his head.

I HAVE never been especially squeamish. Even in school, back in the first grade, I was the one—along with my friend Patrick McFadden—who the nun would send to the janitor's closet for the bag of sawdust and the spaghetti mop and the wheeled pail with wooden rollers whenever one of my classmates threw up. And in college, for a time I worked as an ambulance attendant in the Bronx, back in the days when the only certification you needed was a card from the Red Cross and a strong stomach. No, the force-field around this man was an entirely different kind of fear.

Somehow, with more of us in the car, the looks that went around began to take on a multiplicity of meanings, shot through with distaste, disapproval, annoyance, and a little panic, as if to say, "Isn't there somebody here who can take care of this?" Monk by now had the melody in pieces spread out like an exploded diagram so that if you hadn't listened from the beginning it would be nothing but chaos, noise. We all wanted someone official, someone who worked for the transit authority, maybe a cop, to clear up the question of whether the broken man was alive or dead and to remove the offending item of his contorted body and slack-jawed awful face. The train continued on its way. I looked and looked. I turned off Monk who was by then raging against the rules of harmony, asking if they were for real, and put the earbuds and my book in my bag. I was already in motion, I can see now, even though I didn't really know what I was going to do, or even that I was going to do anything at all. The situation was simply intolerable. An ad above the inanimate man read DO YOU SUFFER FROM DEPRESSION? with an 800 number to call, and on a larger placard beside him, next to the window, a school promised to change one's career prospects but there were none of the paper tear-off applications left. The man did not appear drunk to me. I thought that he might be an addict overdosed on heroin. Or an Oxycontin casualty. He was dressed in clothing sensible for winter, with none of the signs of one who lives on the streets.

I got up and lurched the few steps across the car; holding onto the horizontal pole above him I leaned over. "Sir? Sir! Are you okay?" I chided myself, *Oh yeah, he's great. Never felt better.* I looked at his sallow skin and his slack jaw; his eyes rolled back in his head, little crescents of white visible where the lids were not quite shut. The last guy I saw who looked this bad was dead, I thought, and it was true. A woman in the Bronx had called for an ambulance after coming home from work to find her husband dead in his BarcaLounger, evidently for several hours. He had stiffened in the shape of a shallow Z. We couldn't use the stretcher and had to take him down by making a seat of our clasped arms.

This close I was able to see that the man was breathing. I looked up and everyone was watching us. Now there was drama. The young man with the briefcase made a face at me that I took to mean, "Don't bother. He's a doper. Let him sleep it off." Others gave me that sneer and shake of the head that seems to accompany the attitude of superiority. A tall man came toward me, clearly a workman, with plaster-spattered, rust-colored clothing and molded kneepads now slipped down to his calves, his leather tool bag slung over one shoulder. "Is he breathing?"

"Barely. But I can't get any response from him. Sir!" I barked at him again.

"Let's try and sit him up. Hey buddy. Hey, come on now, let's try to sit you up." I managed to free the arm from behind the seat. The hand was cold and the arm was stiff. The workman was holding the man's head straight and tapped him, gently, on his clean-shaven cheek. His eyelids twitched just slightly. "Hey buddy, you with us? Can you hear me?" The man seemed to be trying unsuccessfully to regain consciousness.

At the next station, Central Square, I stepped out onto the platform; there's always a brakeman somewhere midway in the train who sticks his head out and looks up and down the platform before closing the doors, and when I was sure he saw me, I waved my arms and pointed into the car with both hands. I waved and waved at him, but I wasn't sure he was going to do anything; he pulled his head back into the car. The workman, still holding the other man upright, looked to me for information and I shrugged. I felt prissy in my sport jacket and topcoat, stupid and ineffectual. Then I noticed the callbox a few steps away, next to the door between cars: three louvred slots above a red button. I pressed it and heard a crackling sound. I wasn't sure it was working, and I also found myself wordless: I didn't want to say that someone was sick in our car; that would sound like somebody'd puked and I didn't think that would be taken very seriously. I said, "Excuse me. Someone is very ill here. We have a medical emergency in our car." There was no answer.

I sat next to the unconscious man to help prop him up. Although the man had not regained consciousness, the workman kept talking to him in a warm and soothing voice. "You just hang in there, buddy. It's gonna be all right. Just hang in there, okay?" The callbox crackled and a voice said, "Hello? Hello? Can I help you?" just as a uniformed man I recognized as the brakeman I'd been waving at entered the car. "What's the trouble here?"

I happened to see, behind him, a look of exasperated disgust on the face of a man who, exhaling loudly through his nose, made a big fuss of looking at his watch.

"I'm not sure," I said. "This man's not well."

The brakeman's face had a strangely skeptical look on it, as if we might all be playing a joke on him. Finally he spoke into his walkie-talkie: "Yes. This is seven nine. We have a situation here. Central Station. Caucasian male, unconscious, appears to be sick or intoxicated. Requesting medical assistance."

The unconscious man seemed to stiffen and his head rolled back. The workman opened the man's jacket and loosened his collar. "No no. Stay with us, buddy.

Stay with us," the workman said, and he held the man's head upright, his face between his hands as if he meant to kiss him, his thumb moving on the man's cheek below his eye, for reassurance.

The callbox beside the door was crackling, "Hello? Did you call for assistance? Hello?" The brakeman ignored it, so I pressed the red button and said that help had arrived. In fact, it was another ten minutes or so before three EMTs lugging boxes, oxygen, a folding stretcher, arrived. The leader of the group proceeded to take his futile turn at rousing the man, and he almost managed, too; there seemed something in his voice that was calling the man forth from wherever he was up there where his eyeballs had rolled. To me, the man's voice made questions sound like commands, an assertive concern asking, in a deep baritone, for help in solving a problem he and the patient had in common, and I could see the man trying to open his eyes. Then, softly but clearly, he said, "Gerald," though his eyes remained closed.

"Is that your name, sir? Gerald? Gerald? Can you hear me? Do you take any medications, Gerald? Any medicine? Gerald?"

The man shook his head from side to side and said, "No," in what was somehow only half a syllable. One of the EMTs already had Gerald's coat off and sleeve rolled up, caressing his forearm as if to rub the circulation back into it. I thought he was looking for heroin tracks. "Gerald, we're going to start an IV. Gerald. Try and stay with us, Gerald." He called the brakeman over and they conferred. Then the brakeman turned to us, "Let's give these men the room they need to work, okay? Move back everyone. Give them room." A number of people, already impatient, hoping no doubt the EMTs would carry the man off the train so we could be on our way, groaned at the implication we would be stuck there for a while, and the man I'd noticed looking at his watch harumphed off the train, flashing me a glare and muttering he would try to find a cab. Most of us moved away, to the other end of the car, including the tall workman with the kneepads. I only moved a step or two away myself. I felt a little proprietary; after all, I was the one who had set this all in motion. I thought that maybe the EMTs would have some questions for me. When the brakeman took a step toward me and said, "Sir, we need you to move away and give these men room to work," I felt insulted. How dare he talk to me as if I were an obstacle? Wasn't I the one who'd summoned him? Didn't I earn the right to learn the outcome of this situation?

As I moved away, one of the EMTs was looking in Gerald's wallet. He pulled out a card. "There it is," he said. "Diabetic."

"I'm already on it," said the man on one knee by the first-aid box. "Gerald, we've started an IV. Gerald, can you hear me? Hang on, pal. We're going to get you through this."

As I walked deeper into the car, people looked at me and then away into newspapers, books, puzzles. Maybe three or four minutes later, the brakeman instructed us to evacuate and move to one of the adjoining cars. I met eyes for a moment with the tall workman, and though I cannot explain it, his look managed to communicate to me what these new instructions must have meant: either there had been a sudden crisis, a heart attack or stroke, or Gerald was dead. Once again, we were momentarily co-conspirators, savvy, in-the-know, and I wanted to cut through the crowd and talk to him, but the look he'd given me had also somehow put that off limits.

At Kendall the platform was quite full; the train was late and as it slowed to a stop I could see the impatience and anxiety in people's faces and postures. The car filled.

Soon we were rising into the light and over the Longfellow Bridge, its four stone towers giving it character beyond its function. An Anglo-American bridge, unlike the bridges of Paris, say, or Prague, it makes no promises of angelic protection. It was a gray day but the rain turned the river to a beautiful infinity of intersecting rings. When the recorded voice intoned "Charles MGH. Mass. General Hospital" and we pulled alongside the crowded, elevated platform, I wondered if the EMTs would have taken Gerald off the train back at Central, or continued until now, which seemed to me to be a faster, surer route to the hospital than an ambulance through city streets.

When you leave Charles MGH you accelerate past a brick apartment building very close to the tracks, and just when you are about to get a glimpse of somebody's kitchen, you're plunged into darkness and your own reflection again and the train descends on its way to Park Street. By the time our tightly packed train pulled into the crowded station, passengers were readying to debark in a hurry. The doors first open on one side and then on the other, and I moved with the crowd onto the center platform, making our way through the reluctantly parting throng of passengers waiting to board. A man behind me bumped me, hard, as he went past, in a way that may well have been deliberate. I moved away from the train and turned to look back at the car still emptying like a burst pod, the new passengers beginning to surge forward, and I noticed that the next car back, the one on which I'd started my commute, was still closed to riders, and I wondered what that meant. Above the track, a great bronze hand, one of a pair comprising Ralph Helmick's sculpture *Benedictions,* in the unmistakable sign of blessing, bestowed its peace on every single one of us. I looked at my watch, but I knew the time was wrong.

The Kindest

When I was dying, people were nicer to me. Nurses washed my hair. Old teach-
ers and old roommates and total randoms came to see me, kissing my bandaged
hand. Bao brought me underwear and slept beside me on a chair. Mom drove
from Malden, Dad up from Quincy, and Sui from Xian, all the way across the
planet. The flowers! The questions! *What hurts? How much?* I was scared and
they wanted to hear all about it. No one said *Why?* or *How come?* or *How could
you?* No one rolled their eyes or said *Well, I'd better get going.* They didn't let me
smoke, but I saw them mull it over, as if to say *Well, it isn't going to kill her.* They
leaned forward. They were riveted. They were hungry and I was their food.

Getting born must be like that. If you could remember. But you can't.

Then along came my Angel. A real one, too: no accident of her own, no
sudden onset anything. She wasn't dead, and she wasn't even doing a chain thing,
aimed ultimately at saving her husband or her sister or her very best bud.

It was just that she had two kidneys and she only needed one. And on top of
that, grinned the surgeon: we matched.

We rushed to Boston Medical. That night a thin tube dripped cold dreams
into my elbow. Bao squeezed my fingers and kissed the cross around his neck. "It's
happening," he said.

It's happening? I tried to speak but my throat felt stuffed with rags. Beyond my
eyelids Bao stammered mutely, like a face in a flipbook. I counted backwards and
drifted down a valley of misty waterfalls.

Fingers snapped. It was over. I woke to the sight of my husband crying into
his hands, overwhelmed like I've never seen him. "Bao?" said my voice.

"Baby!" He leapt from his chair and wedged his eager arms underneath me,
and we were laughing and the laughter felt strange traveling up my lungs, like a
language I was remembering only now. Even the ceiling looked new: large tiles
sprayed freely with black dots of so many shapes and sizes. I could see in them
intricate patterns, like constellations in stars.

Bao looked up too, but his eyes were somewhere else. "How can we ever
thank her?" he said, so joyful he was enraged. "How? How?"

The people gathered around me. They shook the surgeon's hand, clinked
champagne over my bed. It spilled on the sheet, it spilled on me.

Night came. The people left. They said *Thank God* this was behind us. They
said *It's time we got some rest.* Bao pried my fingers off his arm as nurses wheeled

me behind curtains, putting a tube in my hand with a button for trouble. Lights went dark, fans slowed to a stop. A janitor wheeled a bucket down a hall. And there was me: blinking fool, alone in my anger just like they've always wanted. At 3:13 I started buzzing on the tube—listening for echoes, for shouts, for footsteps come running. I buzzed and buzzed. I jammed it with my thumb. I wanted to know didn't anybody give a shit.

⋮

I got better. They brought me home. I learned to angle my wheelchair, then stand, take a step. Weeks went by—four long months—strength creeping into my neck, my arms, my back. Bao whirred loose the screws of the handrails. Little dark holes remained in the walls, damp with stray fibers, and when I touched them I remembered where the smooth cold metal had been. I found our I ♥ Sullivan Square coffee mug, rolled behind the washing machine and miraculously intact. Even my hands hardened with muscle: I was a superhero discovering her powers. On my pelvis a new scar stretched in a cracked smile. I poked it when I sat on the toilet, the pain underneath still tender. Who's in there? I thought. Who are you?

Okay. So we no longer had a car. But Bao didn't seem angry. Instead he was grateful, dutiful, the person he used to be. He poured me my Froot Loops. He signed up for Hubway and used those bikes. I was still sleeping on the rollaway, worried that somehow I'd now be bad at sex. But Bao didn't seem to mind. Instead he looked at me each day like I was worth something immeasurable. After a while I started getting the hang of that too.

Little things amazed me. The smooth curves of the teakettle, dotted with moisture. Tree needles, sprayed out and brushing the window in a breeze.

More and more the hospital seemed far away: its shiny boxes, relentlessly clean.

From the basement Bao brought up Grandmah's zitan chair. He slid off the sheet, eased it to the table, smoothed its legs with a damp silver cloth. I lowered myself onto the bony cushion, thumbing the grooves of dragon tails that curled down the armrests. Suddenly the chair seemed too big for me, too grand. But that was ridiculous—when Grandmah was alive she would fart all over this thing. I scooched my butt, got comfy. Bao folded up the wheelchair. To the curb went the crutches, the walker, both canes. We could have recycled them or given them away, but we liked watching the garbage men hurl them into the truck, those grimy walls descending to slurp them up for good.

Right about then is when the letter showed up.

Bao was at work. It was a sunny, ignorant day.

It came in the mailbox: real envelope and paper and gold sticker sealing the flap. It was wrapped in a second letter from the surgeon himself, his boxy handwriting rushed with loops of fervor. So awestruck was he by the selflessness that he just had to chaperone the missive himself. I looked at his letter. I thought that doctors couldn't write at all, not even their own names.

Then came hers. She had used a notepad shaped like a daisy. Blue gel pen.

Dear Friend,

By now you are likely wondering just who this person—your kidney donor—could possibly be. Today I reach out to share a warm hello. It is me.

I am a thirty-eight-year-old white female, and I live in Newton, Massachusetts (born and raised). Last year, while lost in a difficult period, I saw a documentary about altruistic kidney donation. As the credits rolled, I felt shocked by the daily hardship of so many people in need. Equipped with this new awareness, I set forth on a journey to offer a great gift, to do my part in bettering a fellow human's life.

I shook open the letter. Six whole daisy pages. Stuff about her surgery, the prep, the PT. It went on.

I'm so grateful to the MGH transplant team, who held my hand from my very first blood test. I myself know something of suffering, but from those experiences I've learned courage and perseverance. Whatever you've endured, remember that you are never alone.

A few things about me: I like sailing, camping, jewelry, and cats.

My journey to you has entailed immense time, money, and yes—pain. But throughout it all I found a profound sense of purpose, knowing that your life depended on my gift.

I stared at the YOUR LIFE, underlined three times.

Now I smile at the thought that you are enjoying renewed health. I hope—with all my heart—that you feel emboldened with a new sense of hope.

Naturally, I am curious about your healing, and perspective on our shared experience. Perhaps we could meet. If you'd rather not, that's fine, but I'll leave my number here regardless. Consider it token of my affection—a lifeline, should you ever need reminding that you are loved.

Kindly,
Rose M. Rothario

THERE WAS a photograph. She was tall, slender, a bursting ponytail harnessed to one side. Scissors had cut away the image near her shoulder, as if to remove a person who'd been standing beside her. I held it to my nose but it just smelled like a photograph: paper and faint glue, with no whiff of a particular person. She was at some county fair. She was around my age. She was standing by a Tilt-A-Whirl, surrounded by blurry feet, holding a rainbow-swirled lollipop in her fist.

So her name was Rose.

I wanted a cigarette.

But I didn't have one. Bao was at work. Sui was in Xian, obviously asleep. Mom out cleaning and Dad at the shop, but they had never been any help at all.

I hobbled to the kitchen, opened the cupboard. A stupid move—what did I expect? No car and no booze. I looked for the mouthwash, the vanilla extract, that vial of Estée Lauder. But Bao had done a full sweep.

I sat on the couch. I breathed in and out.

At some point Bao came home. I woke to see him scanning the letter sprayed across the table, wearing red bike shorts circled with sweat. Bao in bike shorts! He looked like no one I knew. Just a stranger pausing to examine a map. He read the whole thing standing up, helmet still on. "Wow," he said, blinking at the wall.

"I know," I said.

"Where did she come from?"

"How should I know?" I said, sounding ugly. But Bao didn't seem to hear; he was glancing frantically around our house.

"We need to do something," he said. "We need to show our thanks."

"Of course," I said, though that wasn't what I'd been thinking at all. But all of this gratitude: it shut me up.

There was some debate over who should make the call. "Can you do it?" I said. "Can you say I'm still recovering?"

Bao frowned and unclicked his helmet. He pulled at the Velcro straps on his gloves. Okay: I could see that he didn't want to. But when I was dying he'd stopped saying No, and the habit—for now—was sticking. I saw indecision worming under his face. I let it. Finally he went to the kitchen and beeped forcefully at the microwave.

We washed the dishes. We dried them. Then Bao called her up. He was nervous, chewing rapidly on a wedge of Big Red that I could smell from the couch. I could see that he wanted a drink. I hugged my knees, bending to suck the wet collar of my sweatshirt.

Bao's voice twisted to a whole new register, leaping to each sentence like he was competing for enthusiasm. "We would love, love, love to have you," he said. I held still. Bao never love, love, loved anything. "Her name is Chuntao. That's Shun, tow-oo. No, no. It would be an honor for *us*."

Arrangements were made. She would come on Thursday.

Suddenly the whole house looked barbarically disarrayed—the faded curtains, outdated carpet, objects that made no sense, revealing our vulgarities. That old panicky feeling. I imagined her perched on this sagging couch, tanned legs too long to fold under the coffee table. It was too late to change the cabinets, too late to paint the trims. This wasn't a place where we chummed out with guests. This wasn't a place where people wanted to hang.

She would come at eleven a.m. "What do we get her?" said Bao, shaking his head. He laughed in choked bursts. "Your other kidney? Your spleen?"

I wanted to be sick, to hide under the table. I said that I'd better get going—there's this yoga thing at seven. "There is?" Bao smiled, startled, like someone slapped across the face. "That's great, baby. Good for you." He hurried his gloves back on. "I'd better get a haircut. And something we can cook."

"Okay," I said, and stood as he left like I was about to put on my shoes.

But I didn't. Instead I dropped to the couch, scanned my phone. *Did you take your Xyletenol?* Mom had written. *U ok?* said Sui. *Where did u go?* I ignored them all and played Angry Birds. They weren't writing to check in. They were writing to *check.*

.

In the morning I went to the basement. Looked for something sentimental. On some boxes were a wine decanter, a stereo system, scratched roller blades, a jar of batteries. A ceramic Christmas tree that lit up, a velvet painting of John Wayne. An exercise ball with some wind chimes slumped on top. I thought about the wind chimes. They were nice, I could dust them off. But all these things had to do with me, not my Angel. She needed something that meant something. Like a pint of my own blood.

I figured out the bus. I went to Target. And oh my god: the white floor tiles: so shiny! They reflected the fluorescents gleaming overhead, as if the whole place was lit from under my feet. The shopping cart wheeled over each blip of tile—so smooth. Glossy loops of blond samples down aisles of hair dye—delightful! I grabbed shampoo, a pack of Slims (oh, sweet aroma through the plastic), and a can of white paint.

I thought about a card. I went to Thank You and Thank You For Her. Fanned through the options of embossed sayings. "Life is measured not by the number of breaths we take, but by the moments that take our breath away." Um. Can you say no way? I stuffed them back and went to Accessories. She said she liked jewelry, so.

I loaded up. Like I was tearing stuff off the spinning Y-shaped displays. Clinking necklaces and heavy bangles and crystal rings and something called a toe clutch. A dozen watches—who wore watches? I had a field day. I filled my cart like they do in the movies when a shooter's on the loose or the neighborhood's on fire, grabbing for my Angel like I'd never do for myself.

At Checkout the glittering pile moved down the conveyor belt. The girl beeped her gun around the stash and said that'll be $193.80. Whoa now. Hold up.

She looked through my face. She wanted to know did I want to put something back. Um, yeah, you think? So I came home with a pendant, the toe clutch, and two bracelets on clearance. $34.17 total. But nobody would know.

"What in God's name?" said Bao. He found me kneeling on newspaper in the foyer, holding a paintbrush wet with harsh chemicals.

"Our trims," I said. "They're a wreck."

Bao breathed through his nostrils. "Baby," he said. "This isn't taking it easy."

"I know, I know." I tried getting to my feet, but pain like a snapped trap unfolded with my body. Bao grabbed my arm. I was dizzy and restless. I didn't know what to do. I didn't want her here.

⋮

"Can you move your stuff?" said Bao. I wiped down the coffee table. I gathered the crap on the staircase.

I ripped the tags off the jewelry and rummaged for a box. No box. Fetched a Gladware and buried them in there with Kleenex, pretty-like. Found an old gift certificate to Olive Garden and put that in too. Wrapped it up—technically Christmas paper, red with snowflakes, but pretty ambiguous, and anyway it was November. No card. What was I supposed to say?

Bao painted some crackers with cream cheese. I warmed potato skins. "We cooked!" he said, marching the plate to the living room. I watched his excitement. I wanted a drink. Instead I went to the fridge and checked on my apple juice. Slipped into my pocket two harmless Slims.

At 10:56 the doorbell went off. Bao almost dropped the plate in his rush to the door. I stayed behind, neatening things, my fingers shaking rudely like they belonged to someone else.

I heard her voice before I saw her. So much exclaiming, hugging, everything loud. They came gliding toward me, Bao grinning anxiously and searching my face. She was even more radiant than the photo. Slightly older-looking—crinkly eyes, thin hair—but emanating a glow that no camera could capture without filters. Out came her arm and her long, elegant hand, the delicate fingernails, tips creamy white.

"Baby?" said Bao. His eyebrows urged me on.

"Hi!" I said. "Hi hi hi. Come in, come in." I guess I was staring. We shook. Her hands were cold from outside. Mine were sweaty and I wiped them on my pants, though I worried maybe that would look rude, like I didn't want her germs. I watched her shoes, two sculptures of soft green suede. She was too shiny to look at. It was like squinting at the sun.

"This," she said, eyes probing my socks, my sweatshirt, the whole of me, "is incredible."

"Right on," I said. "Sorry. I feel super weird right now."

The lips of Rose Rothario spread in a generous smile. "I can't believe it either, Chuntao. Am I saying it correctly?" I nodded that she was. She placed her hand on her chest. She gazed around our house, at our weird stuff and the carpet slashed with lines from the vacuum cleaner.

Bao chatted with Rose Rothario, both nodding vigorously. The crescendo of a siren, of trucks guzzling by: the voice of Rose Rothario rose above them all. It was like a singing melody, exuberant and controlled. She stepped around our living room. Bao followed, explaining photos and stuff on the mantle, a breeze of high-pitched peaches trailing in her wake. I felt like a zoo animal watching human onlookers make their way toward more interesting exhibits. Suddenly my arms were too long, hair was sticking to my face. At least they were moving, killing time.

"Is this a family heirloom?" Rose Rothario lifted her glasses from her nose. She bent to examine the carvings on the zitan chair.

"I guess so," said Bao, hands folded like a docent. "It's Chuntao's."

"It's mine," I said.

"It's a stunning relic," said Rose Rothario, roving her head along the back, the armrests, the deflated cushion. A stunning relic? It was a chair. I imagined Grand-mah hunched in the seat, raising her furry eyebrows, wondering *Who the hell?*

Bao suggested that we sit around the coffee table. "We got some snacks," he said. "Nothing special."

"Oh my goodness," said Rose Rothario, admiring the Ritz crackers fanned around the plate. I hated the sight of them: everything the same pale color. But Rose didn't seem to care. She sat, folding her skirt and holding her abdomen on the way down. I wondered if it hurt: the hole inside of her. I wondered if she missed it. But I sort of didn't want to know.

Rose pulled her phone from her purse.

"Pardon," she said. "I just love this so much." She aimed the phone at the crackers, concentrating. Then—satisfied—she put it away.

We faced each other, the triangle of us. Nobody ate. Finally I lifted a cracker and put it in my mouth. It tasted like nothing, like water, just cold and crumbs and creamy stuff, mashing around.

"You sure don't look like you just had surgery," Bao said to Rose Rothario.

"Thank you," she grinned. "Everyone's been so supportive. So many cards and flowers. And from people you'd never expect." I went in for my apple juice. The eyes of Rose Rothario snagged on my glass, following my hand as it floated from the table to my lips. "Is that wine?" she said.

I stopped mid-sip. "No. It's a Welch's."

"Oh!" she said, bursting into a nervous smile. "Ha ha ha." She peered at Bao, then at me, then the hands in her lap.

We were quiet. I drank my drink. And I tried to remember the things I've had to learn: don't react, don't react. I tipped back into the cushions, the air fuzzy with shapes and colors. Bao and Rose Rothario discussed the neighborhoods of Charlestown—which restaurants were nice and which ones you should skip. They were talking holidays, or somebody's pet, or the best commute from this place to that. "But this neighborhood is also beautiful," she said, ridiculously. "Do you like to go for walks?"

"We're definitely going to," said Bao. "We're going to get into that."

"Not me," I said, swirling my glass. "I'm still healing. So, yeah."

Bao cleared his throat. Rose Rothario studied me tenderly. "Of course," she said. "I found that yoga and gentle stretching was all I could do at first."

"I've been thinking about the yoga," I said. "But I bet I'd be bad."

"Maybe Rose could teach you," said Bao.

The woman's eyes perked up. "Truly?"

He nodded and tipped his drink in her direction. "You could go together. You could show her the ropes."

"I could show you the ropes," said Rose, turning my way. My face must have been doing something, because then she said, "Or. We could not. Whatever you prefer."

"What? What?" Bao gaped at me, hands up in surrender. "I thought you wanted someone to go with!"

Rose waved everyone off the subject. "It's really not important." She smoothed her skirt. "It's okay, Bao." And I didn't like her saying my husband's name.

"Excuse me," said Bao, and stood up to make for the bathroom.

I followed him. Inched open the door and slipped myself inside. Bao was peeing into the toilet, and when he saw me he had to hold himself in place. "Are you out of your mind?" he hissed in a soft-loud voice.

I hissed back. "Yoga with her? Are you crazy? I would rather die."

"That's great," said Bao, shaking and zipping his pants. "That's just what I want to hear." He scrambled with his buckle and pushed passed me to the sink.

"And that photo?" I said. "She'll like, show it to everyone . . ."

He twisted the faucets and splashed all over. "I happen to be thankful," he said. "The woman saved my wife. You—you scared the shit out of me. But then she comes along and helps a person in need."

"So I guess she's a saint?" I said. "She's the kindest bitch on the planet?"

"Can you just go be with her?" he said, hurrying a towel up his arms. "Can you just go be a good person?"

"You go," I said.

"No, you," he said. And we stood there in the bathroom, panting and scared of the woman in our house.

We exited. In the living room Rose was sitting pin-straight on the couch, waiting just like we'd left her, like somebody's dog.

Bao squared his eyes on her. "Before we let another moment pass, Rose, we just want to say . . . we just want to express to you . . ." He glared at me, but I couldn't say it. That angry puppy face made me want to say nothing at all.

"Well!" said Bao, rocking on his heels. "I think I'll leave you two alone now."

Air leapt down my throat. "What? Where are you going?"

"You must have a lot to say to each other." He jerked on his jacket.

Don't, I pleaded silently. *Don't you dare.* But he snapped up his helmet, rushing his feet into shoes with the ankles smashed flat. Rose Rothario sat still, eyes roving between us. And I felt through my heart the spear that would orphan me.

The click of the door left a loud and bristling silence. Like the world tipping over. I was in my living room, I was standing on the carpet, a bus rumbling by like it was any old day.

⋮

I hurried up and gave Rose her present. She practically squealed in delight, there were little tears in her eyes. Okay. That was done. I sunk into the cushions. She lifted the pendant—long chain with a copper sunburst—and eased it over her head. Wrapping paper remains were cracked open on the coffee table. She hid the Gladware in her purse, saying she'd fully relish the rest later.

"It was fun to buy," I said. "I had to figure out the bus, but that was actually totally fine."

Rose Rothario frowned, leaning forward. "Forgive me, but I was told there was an accident."

"Yup," I said.

She bit her worried lip. "That must have been terrifying."

"You bet," I said, but the truth was that I couldn't remember. I just remembered going for my stash in the basement, the icy vodka in the Sullivan Square mug. Washing machine and stray coins vibrating across. When had I decided to go downtown? How had I even gotten in the car? It was the logic of a dream. "Trees!" I said, saluting with my glass. "They come out of nowhere."

"There was a storm?" She followed along with goony eyes.

"Big time," I lied. I described fierce winds, driving hail, windshield wipers that flapped like my hands. I marveled at my voice, making this stuff up. It sounded correct. "The dash slammed me all over. They even took out a rib—it was total smithereens." I pointed at the torso of Rose Rothario. "Hey, you got any extras in there?"

I chuckled. Rose Rothario let out a strained little laugh. Immediately I felt terrible and wished that she would go. I thought about the cigarettes—I'd told Bao I wouldn't smoke in the house. But he had left, so.

Rose Rothario squeezed the hem of her skirt. "Has your recovery been very difficult?"

I sipped my juice. "I'm not *in* recovery, if that's what you're asking."

"What?" she blinked. "Oh. That's not what I mean. I hope you know that's not what I mean."

I could see that she was uncomfortable. So what? I leaned in for a cracker and put the whole thing in my mouth. "I'm great," I said. "I can walk up stairs, catch the bus."

"I'm glad to hear it." I chowed down and she watched. "I do find that yoga helps," she said. "But I still can't quite sleep through the night."

"Neither can I," I said. "I keep getting up to pee."

"Are you finding it hard to tie your shoes? And just to bend over, generally?"

"Yeah," I said.

"Me too."

"What a bitch," I said.

Rose Rothario took a cracker and bit off an edge. She chewed in silence. More and more it seemed hard for her to look at me. Her eyes drifted to the window, to the ceiling, to her free hand in her lap. Finally she turned my way, her jaw working the cracker, but she looked right through me, as if to some far-off mountain. Then I realized. She was watching my torso. She was thinking about her kidney, buried inside of me. "Do take care of it," she said quietly.

"You think that I wouldn't?" I said.

"No, that's not what I mean." She turned away, waving off the thought. "It's yours, of course. Never mind. It's yours now."

"Well, sort of," I said, feeling bad. "You gave it to me. It's still sort of yours." She squirmed and knocked her knees together. "Hey," I said. "Don't you worry." Her head lowered, hair shielding her face. "So much is different now. I'm going to treat it so good. I'm going to take good care."

"I'm sure," she said. "Of course."

"Look," I said, "I have to be honest with you." I concentrated on the limp hand in her lap. "I'm not really looking for connections right now. Like I'm not really looking to hang out. Don't get me wrong: I am totally grateful. Like one hundred percent. But I've got too many friends already. I can barely keep up."

"Oh, no no no no," she said. "I'm not interested in friendship."

"Like I don't want to offend you, but."

"I just wanted to meet you," she said. "I just thought it would be a meaningful experience."

"It is," I said. "No doubt."

I looked up. She was chewing and cupping her palm to catch the crumbs. My heart pooled with relief. I'd said what I needed to. Now she could leave.

But she didn't. She kept on munching her cracker like that. What was she waiting for? What did she want? "Is there something that you want?" I said.

And that's when the face of Rose Rothario blotched and crumpled. Her eyes squeezed up, her hair fell forward. She was crying into her hand. The other hand pinched her bitten cracker, keeping it aloft. "I'm sorry," she said. "It's all just so much."

I didn't know what was happening. What I thought was: What is this, this white woman, crying on my couch? Crying to *me*. I felt bad for her, but I also wanted to slap her. Instead I leaned forward and put my hand on Rose Rothario's knee. It was warm, shivering, faceted with bone.

Her mouth contorted with sobs, articulating nothing. But I knew what she was thinking. She was thinking it was supposed to be different. "I hear you," I said quietly. "When I was dying, people were nicer."

Rose Rothario swallowed. "What—what are you saying?" She was whimpering now, fingers pressed into her eyes like she didn't want to look.

I saw my hand and I saw her knee. But they weren't as sharp as the thought in my head. That when I was dying none of it mattered: what I'd done or what I was. People bared their love and I thought I had my hands on it.

"I can't explain," I said. "Things were different. But now . . ."

Rose Rothario uncovered her shiny, bloated face. Then her fingers fluttered down and with no warning at all they rested themselves on my hand. I flinched. Her skin was cold, hovering and weightless, but I still could feel the warmth of her, pinning me.

"Have you told people about me?" she said.

I was tense, dutiful, careful not to move. "Of course," I said.

"And what do they say?" Her eyes were strained and glistening, as if from hunger.

What do they say? Just: eager things, stunned things. Like people who'd glimpsed promised lands, or had been spared by magnificent storms. "All the things you'd expect," I said.

Rose Rothario let out a strange, sloppy laugh.

"Come on," I said. "People worship you. That's pretty clear."

She pinched the bridge of her nose, squinting as if from pain. Then the water-works started up again. "Never mind," I said, sliding out my hand and rubbing my muscles. My wrist bones sank and shifted, accompanying her sad song. I covered them. Didn't look at her. Maybe I'd just wait this one out.

But after a while Rose Rothario quieted. She reached around for the Gladware and fetched some Kleenex, dabbed her eyes. "I'll tell you what I would like. I would love to have a photo with you." She smiled weakly through her wet face. "That would mean a lot to me. To the people in my life."

I imagined my face immortalized next to Rose Rothario's. I didn't like this move. But if that's what it took to get her out, to get on. "If that floats your boat," I said.

She rose. Balled the Kleenex in her fist and looked for the spot that she wanted. I watched her circle the living room, thinking It's okay. It'll only take a second. She traced her steps around the foyer, the mantel, the photos on the wall. But I knew what she was after. She curled her hands on it. My chair.

I hesitated. "You're not going to post this somewhere, are you?"

"Do you want me to?"

"Never."

"Then no," she said. I stood, shuffled over. The black wood gleamed with white lines of lighted grooves. "Do you want to sit in it?" she offered.

"Doesn't matter," I said. But then I changed my mind. "Actually, yes. I want to sit in it." I lowered myself onto the knotty cushion. I rested my elbows. Beside me Rose Rothario crouched down, touching the armrest for balance.

"Careful," I said.

"Wow—how old is this?"

"Old," I said. Rose Rothario knelt on the carpet. She smelled like peach sham-poo. There were squiggly grays in her hair and a bumpy mole behind her ear.

She fussed with her phone, stuck out her arm. I didn't know where to look until she angled it toward me and I saw our faces looking back. The photo would be fuzzy, rough with sediments of darkness, but I knew that she would treasure it always. Because the thing about the dying is they command the deepest respect, respect like an underground river resonant with primordial sounds, the kind of respect that people steal from one another.

"Ready?" she said. And we peered into her outstretched hand. I saw my grandmah's chair. I saw the face of Rose Rothario. I saw that I was smiling, my eyes cast slightly sideways, looking at something off the screen but I didn't know what it was.

My City in Two Dog Parks (excerpt)

*With respect to every urban space we should ask ourselves how
it functions: for whom, by whom and for what purpose. Are we
merely impressed by its sound proportions or does it perhaps also
serve to stimulate improved relations between people.*

—Herman Hertzberger, "The Public Realm"

I live in a neighborhood called Over-the-Rhine, in Cincinnati, Ohio. When I walk my dog, Betts, she mashes her nose into the ground, excavating smells—communicating with the space in a way I cannot. I don't know what information she receives, how far back she can read. Can she smell the dog that walked by an hour ago? The gnawed-on chicken wings dropped the night before? The box of moldy clothes that sat there last week? Or can she go back further? Whatever she smells, it must be interesting, because she often tries to rip my arm off for one more whiff.

However, she is a dog, and her knowledge is limited. She certainly can't smell that this used to be a German neighborhood, supported 45,000 people, almost seven times its current population. She is likely unaware of the 300-plus empty buildings, but she's certainly fascinated by the trash strewn across 700 vacant lots. She doesn't know that the buildings she trots under are ancient, the largest collection of nineteenth-century Italianate architecture in the US, or that they are endangered. She can't smell the ash and blood from the 2001 race riots, which have washed away long ago. Does the odd juxtaposition of businesses mean anything to her? Does she pause to see the strange mix of check cashing centers and yoga studios, corner stores and organic groceries, fried fish establishments and overpriced urban eateries, art galleries and homeless shelters, all in the same few blocks? Unfortunately, she mostly pays attention to food and pee.

For all she doesn't know, she is the medium through which I know my neighborhood. Although I take her for walks, she also walks me, through neighborhood streets, spaces, and people. As much as she's my beloved pet, my dog is also a furry and badly behaved ontological instrument. As I walk my dog through my neighborhood, I see the battle being fought for its future. Will it be a gentrified enclave, a dark ghetto, or a diverse urban village? I don't know, but my dog really has to take a piss.

Northern Row Park

Northern Row Park is not an official dog park, but that's mostly what it's used for. When we approach its cast-iron gate, Betts wheezes against her choker collar to see if another dog is inside. When there is, every muscle in her forty-pound stocky build strains to get closer. She yaps like a psychotic squeeze toy, and on her back forms a stripe of raised, brown fur. She forces her head under the gate, snarling and flashing fangs, and the other owner, someone I haven't met before, looks nervous. He asks, "Is he friendly?" which really means: "Don't let *that* in here" and "Your dog looks like a boy." He winces as I open the gate, and just as my monster is about to rip into the soft of his dog's throat, she stops, sniffs its privates, and wags her tail—a white flag. The owner squints: "What kind of dog is that?"

That is how I meet most of my neighbors. My dog is a slobbering conversation piece. She looks hilarious, a breeding experiment gone wrong. She has the head of a pit bull and the legs of a wiener dog, with a muscled jaw and body atop four stubby legs. I adopted her from the SPCA last year, and to date, she's dug five holes in the carpet, eaten three remote controls, chewed five pairs of shoes, and munched half a string of Christmas lights. The dog she most closely resembles is whatever kind you find in junkyards. "I don't know," I say. "Maybe basset hound and pit bull? Something that shouldn't have mated."

We watch our dogs wrestle around the park's cobbled court and run through the grass and dirt perimeter. I turn to the owner and ask: "You live around here?" It's a dumb question. They always do. They live on Main and Sycamore, Orchard and Fourteenth Street, in the old tenements that are now rehabbed apartments and condos. They are lawyers and actors, janitors and store owners, PR men and bartenders, students and salespeople. They have lived here fifteen years, five years, six months, a week. They work downtown or in the adjacent neighborhoods, and they mostly have mutts, though there is the occasional purebred. When their dogs have to take a shit, they come here, one of the only greenspaces in the area, if you discount vacant lots.

This is not a public park, not anymore, but they have a right to be here. The park was made not by city planners but by the residents, reclaimed for the community from asphalt-cracked urban decay. Northern Row Park has existed for as long as anyone can remember. It's named for the northern row of houses on the edge of the city, which used to be at the end of the block on Liberty Street. With the Miami and Erie Canals (now Central Avenue) delineating the neighborhood's southern and western boundaries, and with its substantial German population, the neighborhood was nicknamed: "Over-the-Rhine."

Most of its buildings were constructed between 1865 and the end of World War I, when German Americans dominated the area. OTR was one of the most densely populated neighborhoods in the country, second only to Manhattan, and in 1900 was home to more than forty-five thousand people. The neighborhood was bustling and vibrant, but certainly not idyllic, reeking with thick smog from the various industries and stench from the packed-in humanity. With the advent of the automobile, much of the middle class migrated out to the expanding suburbs, leaving OTR's tenements to the working class and poor. In the 1960s, African Americans migrated from the south and from surrounding neighborhoods razed for a new highway. The latter half of the twentieth century follows the tragic plot of every rust belt city: investment in the surrounding suburbs and disinvestment in the urban core, leaving the buildings to decay and blight, and the people to fight for city services and quality education from a dwindling tax base. Most of the white residents left, and OTR became predominantly black and poor, with high crime. The population has shrunk to seven thousand in 2010 (36 percent white, 62 percent black, mostly low income).

When John Spencer discovered Northern Row Park in 1990, it mirrored the state of the neighborhood. It had an island of greenspace in the middle, sur-rounded by a sea of cracked blacktop, and a rusting swing set from the 1950s that no sane kid would sit on, a teetering death trap. A pair of shoes hung from the telephone wires above, marking the territory for drug dealers. Homeless people used the park as a bathroom. Spencer, a local architect and developer, had just moved into an adjacent building, and with his business and life partner, Ken Cun-ningham, he aimed to rehabilitate OTR's architecture. He reported the dangerous equipment to the city, but they merely took the swing set away, leaving the space empty. "We decided it could be something," he said. "We could take it over and make it into a park worthy of a new neighborhood."

But nothing gets done quickly in Cincinnati. After seven years in negotia-tion with the park board, in 2004 they were allowed a ninety-nine-year lease for a pittance. They had just converted their building into condos and the new residents were excited about rehabbing the park as a neighborhood project. Over the course of a year, about forty neighbors worked to transform the park. They wrote grants and raised $100,000, convinced the city to donate old granite pavers from the downtown bus terminal, and did the grunt work. They freed the existing haw-thorn and elm trees from asphalt encasements. They dug up drug paraphernalia and railroad irons, and in their place left a natural dirt area on one side and grass and a rose bed on the other. They installed street lamps and floodlights hanging down from the trees, and wrapped the space with a cast-iron fence, punctuated on a diagonal by two gates.

Spencer said he wanted the space to be a "passive area of recreation," as a "nice green space that people could enjoy." People have used the park for neighborhood parties, concerts, movie nights, weddings, chiminea campfires, picnics, and lunches. But to Spencer's mild regret, the space has mostly gone to the dogs: "There is such a need for dog space, it's overrun." The dogs have dug up flowers and trampled the grass into sad clumps. When they're in the park, they dissuade most people from passing through or loitering, and they've left land mines of crap all over the green.

However, as Spencer noted, the dogs signify a strong pulse for the neighborhood, a sign of health. "As you get more people with dogs, it indicates two things: more people with disposable income, and more people meeting each other," he said. "It's a great mixer. That's what is important about living in an urban area: the opportunity to meet and find out about other people."

A dog park is a space to fight against the anonymity of the city, where neighbors are forced to interact in a common space. We have no other tasks to complete. We have nowhere else to go. We must loiter long enough for our dogs to do their business, and even if you're socially awkward like me, you'll eventually interact with the other human being across from you. We get to know each other.

But this knowledge is often limited by and filtered through the dogs. For instance, I know my neighbors value fairness. My dog often plays with a beagle terrier mix named Spence (no relation to John Spencer). His owner, a professional woman of about forty-five, cheers for him as if he's a child playing soccer: "Get her, Spence, get her!" She spends her time clapping. It's hard to have a conversation. But when my dog bites Spence's collar and throws him around, she objects: "Hey, Betsy. Play fair." She separates them like a referee.

"Fair?" I say. "Look where we live. These are street rules." She disagrees.

They also seem to think their dogs' private space should be respected. Several people have bitchy ankle-biters that are not at all friendly. The pugs in particular strike me as hissing, furry lizards, as Betts' attempts at play are met with hard nips from their little fist mouths. One small and black French thing with an actual French name, Miniot, also snaps at my dog. His owner excuses its aggression: "Say, 'I'm too delicate to play.'" There are dogs too delicate to play.

In addition, I know most of my neighbors don't have kids, because they treat their pets like children. Besides the cheering, they confess to buying soy products at gourmet pet food stores. They have taken their dogs to expensive obedience classes. They often greet the dogs first and the people second. One yuppie couple even named their dogs Sophie and Addison, which are not at all dog names, as if they wanted to practice the names on other living things before they moved to the suburbs and bequeathed them to their children. They cheer, correct, and scold.

As our dogs tear up the park and slam into one another, they look at me with ex-asperation, as if to say, "These kids . . ." I too am guilty of this anthropomorphic infantilization. I live alone, and in my weaker moments of existential loneliness, I might vocalize what my dog would be thinking if she had the intelligence of a spunky, eight-year-old child. But let me be clear: Betts eats regular dog food, is hopelessly misbehaved, and though her name is not Fido or Ace, it's still one sylla-ble and not as yuppie-child as Sophie or Addison.

Lastly, I know that we don't necessarily trust one another. People hang plastic grocery bags on the iron fence. This is understandable, as the park can only function if everyone does their part, and if the system of personal respon-sibility breaks down, things could get pretty crappy. If others aren't playing fair, why should you, and then everyone has poop on their shoes. So the bags are tied around the fence in case you need them, but are also devices of shame, as if your neighbors expected you to not plan ahead, to forget your bag, and are such good people that they make sure you're good too. *Bastards.* You remember your bag next time.

But as much as dog park culture sometimes annoys me, it has also opened my neighborhood. Sometimes, while we watch our dogs fight over sticks, we have genuine conversations. We learn where people used to live and what brought them to the neighborhood. We share intel on favorite restaurants and bars. We learn that the owner of the German shepherd also bikes to work every day, and share stories of car aggression. We learn that the wine salesman is taking a business trip to Argentina, and when he comes back, we ask him how it went. The actors tell us about upcoming productions. We learn that someone's sister is having brain surgery. And, if there's a horrific act of violence in the neighborhood, we have a place to worry and vent. Some of us are even close friends. Some of us kiss when we see each other.

Even if most of these interactions are trivial, they draw us out of private life and make us feel included in the fabric of the neighborhood. It's akin to how urban critic Jane Jacobs characterizes interactions on city sidewalks in *The Death and Life of Great American Cities*: "Most of [the contact] is ostensibly trivial but the sum is not trivial at all. The sum of such casual, public contact at the local level . . . is a feeling for the public identity of people, a web of public respect and trust, and a resource in time of personal or neighborhood need."

While not a city street, the dog park is similarly vital to my public identity. While exercising my dog, I form lasting, if mostly superficial, relationships with the people around me. But those interactions add up into a public identity. I am Betsy's owner. I live on Main Street and ride my bike to work. I am an English teacher and writer. My politics are fairly liberal. I patronize local bars and like good beer. I am thankful that John Spencer and other residents have given me a place to be this public self, have built a space for me and my dog.

But this dog park is also a limited space. As Spencer said, having a dog in the city allows you to "find out about other people," but what kind of other people? Almost all of the dog park attendees are middle-class or upper-middle-class, have no children, and are white, like me. Where is everyone else? If this is Spencer's "new neighborhood," where is the old one?

Data Pit/Pit Data

If you aint from here, don't come round here.

> —*Spray-painted on an OTR building,*
> *Thirteenth and Main, September 2010*

When I first moved to the neighborhood, I discovered one of the great OTR dog-walking benefits: you don't need to bring a bag. When your dog pops a squat, the streets are so filthy that, almost without fail, you will have a variety of trash to choose from. Do you luck into a shriveled plastic bag under the curb, or is there a spare White Castle bag overflowing from a trash can? Like the local organic grocery store suggests, I like to reuse and recycle.

But once, when Betts squatted on Fourteenth Street, I couldn't find a piece of trash right away. I panicked. How far could I walk before people think I'm just leaving? Apparently, I passed the boundary. An old lady called down from a third-story window: "Hey! Don't be leaving that shit right on the street! We gotta live here! We *gotta . . . live . . . here!"* How could I explain the great dog-walking benefit?

So I shouted back: "I gotta live here too!" I eventually found an appropriate piece of trash and made a great show of cleaning up. But this incident underscores the hostility toward middle-class white people coming into OTR. For a long time, as Spencer notes, Main Street was primarily an entertainment district for people like me. Young suburbanites and university students would drive in for night life, and the young white people who did rent had more interest in partying than investing in the neighborhood. When this lady saw me and my shitty little dog, she probably assumed that we were invaders who didn't care about the community, about the people who actually "gotta live here." But this is not the typical reaction I get when I'm walking Betts on the street. At least once on any given walk, I am asked a version of the same question: "What kind of dog is that?" And if they're local black or white working-class residents, they usually have a hunch. Sometimes they just say it: "Dat'a pit." They see the pit bull in the ball of muscle on each side of her head, in her large mouth and Egyptian eyes, in her chest thrown forward and stocky build. But what is up with those legs? "It looks crossed with a wiener dog," they often say, and might be right. The conversations don't go much farther than that, but sometimes they do. Mostly, they make comments about her physique and praise her leash-pulling power: "She's built. Look at that, long and strong." They might offer advice: "You should mate her with a tiger pit." When she sees another dog walking across the street, lunges against her leash, and squeak-barks, I hear: "Get 'em, killer."

Consequently, sometimes they get the wrong idea about why I have her. Once, when Betts jumped up on a homeless guy and I apologized for her bad behavior, he offered me training advice: "Don't let anyone pet her. You want a guard dog, right?"

"No," I said. "I want a companion dog."

"Okay. Let them pet her, but never as much as you."

In a 1990 study of an unidentified gentrifying urban neighborhood, sociologist Elijah Anderson points out that "within the black community, dogs are used mainly as a means of protection, whereas the middle-class whites and blacks in the Village generally see them as pets as well." In other words, if lower-class black and white people have dogs, they often don't see them as fur children. In a poor area with high crime, you need a dog that is aggressive and intimidating, that will convince criminals to move on to the next guy. This is not the kind of dog you want fighting over a stick with a labradoodle.

I'm not saying all lower-class people view their dogs this way. And I'm not saying all of my conversations on the street take on this tenor. Sometimes the conversation will start with my dog's pit-bull strength, but then move on to other topics. One black man I see regularly praised Betts's muscle, but has since taken a liking to her as a pet. He hangs out on a stoop near my building and insists that Betts calls him "Uncle James" while he calls her "princess" and "queen of the block." Sometimes after initial exchanges about my dog, one of us will ask: How you doing? His mother is visiting or his grandkids stopped by. He's been sick all week or he's feeling young and how about this weather? Sometimes we talk about women. Sometimes we talk about changes in the neighborhood. "It's changing much too fast," he said. "I don't like it. A lot of people have moved away." He recently told me that he used to work in demolition and I told him I was a teacher. But what we did for a living didn't seem to matter much. He's the guy who sits on the stoop and I'm the guy who walks his dog. We don't talk about much beyond my dog, but we often say "hi."

Still others on the street act like my dog is public property. I've had all races and classes kneel to my dog without asking and whisper sweet nothings in her ear: "Hi. You're pretty and sweet." Recently, a Hispanic man asked if my dog spoke Spanish, and then proceeded to whisper Latinate as he scratched her ear. I've had a wealthy-looking white man at the farmer's market publicly humiliate himself as he knelt and made out with my dog's head. My canine has a democratizing effect. She is a public object of affection for all.

These interactions on the street are perhaps even more trivial than in Northern Row Park. We are on the move with less time to loiter for sustained conversation. But for feeling part of the neighborhood, the old one not cut off by a cast-iron fence, this contact is much more important. Over-the-Rhine has a terrible reputation. Mention you live here to some Cincinnati suburbanites, and it's as if you've confessed an elaborate plan for suicide. I would be lying if I said OTR's bad reputation doesn't sometimes loom in my mind, especially when it seems confirmed by crime reports and pops of gunfire. I spent my teenage years in a homogenized, upper-middle-class suburb outside Cleveland, with five black people in a high school of 520. With my upbringing, it would be easy to feel threatened.

But Betts provides a reason to interact with anyone on the street. When I'm with her, she forms my public identity. I am not some dorky white guy invading the neighborhood. Foremost, I am the owner of a funny-looking dog. I cannot control whom she sniffs or jumps up on, and I cannot control who talks to her. For all her ferociousness with other dogs, she loves people, and is as amiable with the black homeless man who compliments her strength as she is with the white soccer mom who babbles baby talk in her ear (though I hope she likes the homeless man better). A dog can break down the defenses we build to protect us from each other.

But I know she can provide a false sense of security. If threatened, she could take a good chunk out of a perp's leg. She might persuade a criminal hunting for a victim to keep looking. But you're still playing with probability. You think: *If I bring my dog, I will be safe. If I don't sell or buy drugs, I won't get shot. If I don't go on Race Street at night, I won't get robbed.* But the terrifying thing about violence, especially in a poor, urban neighborhood, is its randomness. On my street a few months ago, a pregnant woman was shot during a robbery by a fourteen-year-old kid. Months before that, two innocent women were shot with stray bullets in a failed drug hit inside Tuckers, a diner known for its vegan burgers. My dog, long and strong, will not protect me from desperate kids or stray bullets. But she will have to pee. She will get me into the street and talking pit bulls with people I might otherwise fear. She facilitates the trivial interactions that build trust, that make you less afraid, that give you a place to start a conversation: "What kind of dog is that?"

When my dog pulls me down the street, people often ask: "Who's walking who?" It's a better question than they know.

Camp and Locust

House on the corner where I grew up,
second-floor flat I still find in dreams,

window from which I see Candy
squirm out of his collar again.

It is always a lurid, purple night,
the middle of summer. He is taking off,

having figured it out, and is headed toward
all that existence promises, even to dogs.

Bête Noire Ranch

"You've got a tick in your eye." My cousin, five years older than me, infinitely cooler than me, in cut-off jean shorts and vinegary Sun-in blond hair, says this with only slight alarm as she leans down to peer at me, under a rusty swing set, somewhere at the end of an Oklahoma dirt road that no longer exists. "See?" she says to her sister, just as wonderful, leggy and ethereal in her blue eyeliner and shiny toenails, a red plastic cup of sweet tea in her hand, held as languidly as that cousin does everything.

I have never been languid a day in my sweaty eight-year-old life. Languid is not a word that has been used to describe me.

I am marched down the dirt lane to sit next to the midcentury pool at my aunt's low-slung ranch house, the only smudge of glamour in a neighborhood of open fields, unruly honeysuckle, and fighting-rooster coops. My aunt went to art school in Kansas. She is always going to be different in just the right way. My back is close enough to her Lincoln Continental to feel the heat off the metal as I face the pool and everybody stares at the tick in my eye.

It is a glorious, humid, dusty, hay-scented, exotic Oklahoma summer day.

NOTHING MY parents ever offered, once they'd moved north to a wealthy suburban Wisconsin town, held anything like the heady intimacy of being part of the community of that county in Oklahoma. Slow waves on back roads, neighbors lining the driveway to put in your cattle guard, trucks pulling over to chew the gossip till it's used up next to intersections, were way better to my mind than the sailboats and tall fences we moved to, everything in the new place about otherness and getting away from and having or not having. There's a difference between everybody knowing your business and accountability for your public actions. Accountability gets you a serious conversation in a kitchen somewhere, but the other only gets you a side-eye and a snicker at the arcade. I found out both the long way.

I've been searching to find that net again, that invasive and advice-doling citizen body, my whole life.

I've tried a lot of neighborhoods.

MY DAD was the local Episcopalian priest in that wealthy Wisconsin town, and our family occupied a genteel poor church mouse status as the succor to the elite rich white folks who populated the parish. Episcopalians, if I allow myself a broad generalization, seem to come in two stripes: hippy community organizers who make unleavened wheat bread for communion, and rich white people who seriously like ceremony, tradition, and wine. We would have tended to be in the first crowd, but this town had the rich white version. We were not rich, and in retrospect, not terribly white: our minimal but mixed Native American ("Oklahoma: The Native State" say the license plates) blood made us a little muddy, just the tiniest bit olive, with cheekbones that didn't make any sense in a sea of Germanic ruddiness.

We had a kidney-bean-shaped pool on the church's dime at the clergy house, and our backyard's chain-link fence divided us from the local high school principal's house, so I managed a convenient crush on the principal's son for a bit, but couldn't maintain it in the face of his absolutely regular boringness. Across the small street next to us was a sprawling and deep cemetery full of hills and mausoleums, and it is a mark of the town that that place was about the best thing going on at the time park-wise. I found a deer leg bone there once and was able to convince myself it was probably a human leg bone, by proximate causes, until at least college when I faced the fact that this had been wishful thinking.

I remember nothing else about the people in the neighborhood. Nothing. We lived there ten years, and the whole time felt transient.

Even so, that was some solid middle-class life.

My parents' relationship to their neighborhoods is still a mystery to me. I think when I ask them, it's going to tell me a lot about them, and perhaps that's why I haven't asked, afraid of that Rorschach-like accuracy about their lives in the decades when each liked or hated a job, their relationship to and expectations of each other, their relationship to and expectations of the world at large. The answer will be the larger circle of the Venn diagram of what I knew of them at home, navigating us. Long before Wisconsin, in a small Pennsylvania army town, my mother remembers my oldest brother choking as an infant and her running flat out the front door of the house straight down the middle of the street toward the army base hospital, her neighbors peeling out in cars to try to catch her and put her in the car and drive there faster.

MOSTLY MY own adult neighborhoods feel like they are chasing me. Old identities I can't squelch, more unburnable than journals, each holds proof of how well or badly I have behaved. Neighborhoods hold such promise and in my experience at least, later such crushing weight. The weight of the memories: hopes played out, time squandered, inadequacies revealed, ignored or faced; any crucible that held all these is doomed to provoke such intensity in me I might mistake it for hate. But that would be a mistake.

Welcome to the Neighborhood

Shocked by the gaps I have in my childhood, the sheer absence of credit for time spent, I have tried as an adult to be committed to deeply knowing the places I live, and while I would like to imagine that knowing a place means learning the wildlife and the plants in the area, I know now that knowing involves the humans. What a surprise. I lived for a long time everywhere at a remove: as the young girl, the white girl, the grad student, the liberal, me using any identifier that would get me a pass out of becoming engaged with whatever the dominant feel at work on the block was. It got in my way and it won me absolutely nothing. It stunted my growth, and I spent my thirties catching up to all of the emotional lessons and showing up I had dodged before.

So my neighborhoods have become my parish, of sorts, the people I'm handed without choice, to navigate a relationship with. Notice that neighborhoods is plural, though, even now—the mark of a grown-up who has never quite found a particular job or way of life that has stuck.

Presently I have one and half neighborhoods. Neither is very nice. I do not have the big square midwestern ivy and clapboard home I imagined I would by now, and I'd guess I never will. I still feel a punch of yearning, some moonlit nights and some hazy mornings, walking by houses with deep side yards and swing sets, porch chairs and front halls. But I am always surprised that I haven't squelched that longing yet when it rears its atavistic head, because it's evident even to me that I have not pursued the life that would have led to that end.

My Los Angeles neighborhood is in accurate ways the culmination of my adult life. All the major races are represented. All ages. And in fact, all economic statuses, because at the end of our tidy cul-de-sac are the five houses that climb the mountain foothill to look down at those of us on the flats. We all know every car, and every car has its regular de facto parking spot, and if a guest should throw that off for more than a few hours, heaven forbid. A new car in a new spot is an actual conversation here.

In the regular passing of a day, I walk the Vietnam vet's chihuahua with my own dog. Mike the vet of the Iraqi war knocks and gives me fish he caught in Mexico and asks for the avocados off my tree and I say take them all, and also take the Meyer lemons, because I will never do this fish justice. The mother and son next door stop me to tell me how good I look after my new workout plan and haircut, and I say the same to them because one of them just took up boxing and the other got a haircut and I'm too shy by a mile to just say thank you. Also, the mother's mother hands me grapes off their vines while the mother's father zealously guards the yard cat that will only come to him anyway. Mary down the way washes her car religiously—perhaps for church? The only place she ever seems to go—and covers it, again, with the tarp. She will give us a note at Christmas

that will be addressed, in elemental and evocative English, to "The Good Family."
The husband of the woman who is as mean as a snake to everyone dies at their
home across the street and two mornings later, the keening of the daughter hits
the dawn sky. The baby of the psychologist and her professor husband grows
seemingly on every walk until I wait for it to spring from the bassinet of its own
volition, an Alice in Wonderland nightmare. The unsmiling man who lives kitty-
corner to us leaps to help my husband work on a truck, stomping the gas pedal,
unsmilingly, as my husband turns things in the engine. "It's like with my father,"
he says, and I am never quite sure if he means the process or perhaps the truck
itself, full of grit, truculence, and mysterious quirks.

A half a neighborhood can only happen because you are there part-time, not
because you only get half of it. Neighborhoods only come in whole portions.
My other neighborhood is in undeniable and inconvenient ways my heart, my
bête noir, the thing I wish I didn't love. To describe it is to see my id. It's new to
me and as in all new love affairs I give it whatever it wants. In that neighborhood,
I have a too-small cabin in the desert, on land no one wants and thus was very
cheap. In fact, no one had wanted that land before 1954, and then no one wanted it
since 1954, when the government tried to give the land away, and one new Italian
immigrant thought it was worth at least the price of the cinder block cabin he put
there, but nobody thought so since.

When I drove up to the cabin, it was with something I would call un-surprise
that I realized I couldn't even get off the dirt road to park. The house had been
plowed in, years of grading the dirt road throwing a berm of red sandy desert into
a trench in front of the ignored place. No matter. I knew how to play hard to get.
The low gray cinder-block cabin crouched there in the blazing sun. It looked like
if you touched it the walls would be cool, as if in rebellion to the elements. Even
made of brick, the house had a kind of transparency, turned in on itself but with
windows lined up front and back, the desert the view from front to back. I stood
there till dark and listened to the dogs and coyotes howl at the twilight wind as the
heat bowed out and the uninhabitable desert reasserted itself.

The next day I drove back. At the newest house in the area, twenty acres from
the cabin, a thirtysomething man brings water to his goats in a pen. Nearby, the
oldest man I've ever seen picks something nearly imaginary it is so small off of the
dirt of his yard next to the dirt that is the road. An alarmingly fit seventy-year-old
woman hoofs it down the road with a Walkman on. A heavyset girl about twenty
wrings out a towel heavy with water into a bucket in her driveway, fifteen acres
from the cabin in the other direction. Have I mentioned none of these cabins have
water or power? How inconvenient they are? How like me, in spatial space and
utility and charm?

Every one of the people waves except the girl. And she's my closest neighbor. But I figure I'll be back for her later, I'll get her. Every one of the people I saw is a perfect specimen of desert types, including me, city-transient overeducated wound-up-on-desert-dream, and so the fabric of the neighborhood feels complete. I wonder what I'll learn about them one driveway snippet at a time over years. I wonder what they'll learn about me, by knocking on my door when I don't want them or catching me on a low-resistance day. I wonder what I'll learn about myself, listening to that wind so meaningless it's existential, staring at the long view, interrupted only and pointedly by the houses of other people who also came here to be alone, when none of us are, and in fact what we are honing is really only the power to pretend that we could ever be, and then we go and we tell each other about it.

The Real West

" . . . the frontier is productive of individualism. The tendency is anti-social. It produces antipathy to control, and particularly to any direct control."

> *—Frederick Jackson Turner*

The guy who sells smoked trout at the farmer's market—he's got a Ph.D. in Classics, but he left his professorship for fish farming. *I was always interested in history,* he smiles, and his white beard bristles. *But never politics. This is more my speed.*

Cowboys and oil rigs. Knowing how to dig a firebreak. Or mill your flour. Or prep seed potatoes for planting. Or pickle beans. Knowing where to take the antelope you shot for butchering.

Rows of flat-slatted snow fence all along the I-80 corridor. Still, a blown-out bigrig tipped into the ditch.

Yucca. Aloe. Ladies' night at the shooting range. Sage.

Sitting in steam rising off the hot springs, snow mounded all around, sipping wine while an eagle hovers above the river watching for a glint of fish.

I walk out of the university auditorium in Billings after the reading and drum circle, head back to the hotel with its bucking-bronco carpet. The air is acridly sweet. *What is that?* I ask. *O,* says my host. *It's the sugarbeet factory.*

Mutton-buster kids at the rodeo, their little aluminum spurs.

Mobile-home meth labs.

Rows and rows of Big Jim chiles transubstantiating sun into heat. Buy them at a roadside stand, roast them over an open flame. They'll go into chile verde, tortilla soup, pizza, quiche, bagels, apple pie. And it'll all have that tangy savor, a little sting in the cheek, the sun inside warming your throat.

A church without a cross on it. A church with a cross and a statue of Our Lady. Our Lady of the Desert Passage. Our Lady of the Wildfire. Our Lady of the Snakeoil Salesman. Our Lady, Pride of the Penitent. Our Lady of the Snows. Our Lady of the Unknown Variable. Our Lady of the Birdsong. Our Lady of the Beggar's Ball. Our Lady of the Green Glass Sea. A church with a basketball court. A church in a warehouse, sign written in Korean. A church in a shopfront. La Iglesia Evangelica. La Iglesia Pentecostal. A double-wide church on a compound comprising bomb shelters and gunracks and bathtubs planted with tomatoes and mint.

A church whose plastic movie-times marquee reads: Get Right or Get Left.

A McDonald's with a smoking section. A church-run charity shop stocked with musty sofas, an armchair with some hard substance caked onto its wing, remoteless TVs, bins of bent shoes, bins of tinny kitchen equipment, beveled yellow water glasses, twee teacups.

A sign on the road that says: Bureau of Land Management. That says: Trespassers Will Be Shot. That says: Next Services 78 Miles.

At the coffee shop, a little clutch of hipsters wear their colored tattoos and ear gauges and expensive denim like they'd thought them up. A work-booted dude in a flannel shirt with his sleeves rolled up orders a chai soy latte. I notice his raw knuckles.

A taco cart in a Sear's parking lot. A dim sum cart by the bus station.

In a dry arroyo miles from anything but lizards and scrub, a pair of beatup Adidas. No laces.

A redrock spire. A redrock cliff, windowed with an arch. A butte like a stone ship run aground. Goblin Valley. Virgin River Gorge. Dead Horse Point. Moki Dugway. A canyon pass, at whose entrance a brass memorial plaque says: This Is The Place.

The Summer of Whooping Cough

Up and down our street, coughs pepper the night, soft gunfire from scattered positions. Our efforts to fall into a deep sleep are futile, as our windows are wide open to catch any bit of tepid air flow over our sweating bodies. No air-conditioning in these small ranches.

When the cough entered the five children across the street, nights became even more desperate struggles for rest and peace.

On those hotter nights, when I feel something burning me up from inside, and I hear a front door creak open and a screen door pushed aside, I rise. And watch. The neighbor's Ford truck, patched with spackle, has been gone for days now. He's out on the ocean somewhere, dragging in lobster. When he is home, you can smell the sea from the truck bed. So Catherine, his wife, is alone with the kids, trying to keep them breathing till morning.

Light behind her from their hallway silhouettes curves, a dark shape that holds up her translucent, damp gown. When the steam from the shower doesn't work, she brings them outside to clear their lungs. Under the red maple in the corner of the lawn, in full leaf now, they are little wilting forms, barely visible away from the window light. Just rumbling sounds and exhausted wails.

When things are really critical, she is just in bra and panties. Too overburdened to care who sees, kids on bent hips. Night seems heavier with small cries to get air.

Heavy, but beautiful on those black nights. Sometimes strobing lights from an ambulance flicker across the white clapboards. And I am coming home from the sea, the truck bed smelling of ocean catch. A well-lit house full of fever-flushed. Comforting one, smoothing another's brow, holding my wife close, feeling some of the night's coolness still on her freckled skin. The roughness of her lace-edged bra.

Stop looking, my wife says from behind me. Chastened, I follow her back to the bedroom. The wall clock in the kitchen ticks loudly and firmly. The refrigerator vibrates. Floorboards groan under our sullen weight.

The comforter on the floor. On our backs, arms and legs spread out, only our hands between us touch. I stroke her hand, her concave stomach that hollows out between her sharp hip bones. When I pull my hand back to my side, she grabs it and won't let go.

The coughs continue to ricochet against our mildewed shingles. They rattle and shake and call us out of a place we can no longer sink into.

the war of all against all

welcome to the bellicose beauty of true tooth and nail, a warcry that isn't all bye-bye-biplanes, espionage and cryptography. or, for you new world orphans, that isn't all hacktivist drones, wikileaks and cyborg oil barons. after two thousand years cryogenically frozen in clone plasma, we'll likely wake up to a dystopian cityscape repeat of the same old pre-national battle: *bella omnia contra omnes,* the all-encompassing something that sifts the fittest four-legged fish from the inbred and the invalid, the vindictive sickle-bearing bitch who brings the fits and starts of existence to fisticuffs dripping guts and vestigial gills. beyond my childhood windowsill, the goldfinch never stood a chance against the tabby, but its absentminded capture still felt like telltale tabloid tragedy, the whole neighborhood standing around enraptured by the outlying fraction of grass that still smelled feral. and all the way back to their houses—single-file through the turnstiles—they kept their noses held aloft like they were searching.

Into the Limen: Where an Old Squirrel Goes to Die

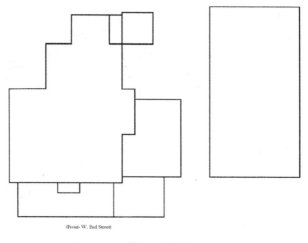

(Plan of Site)

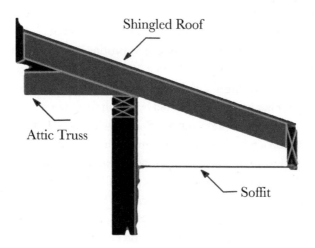

I.

A **Soffit** is an architectural element resulting from the combination of two dissimilar spaces. It is the underside or inside of a construction component such as an arch, a flight of stairs, a ceiling space, or the exposed surface beneath a section of roof that bridges the gap between a house's siding and roofline, otherwise known as its eaves.

A.

1.

The man calls himself
The Critter Gitter. He has seven
fingers and "not many teeth," says my
grandmother offhand, worrying the high collar
of her fleece. When I meet Jim on the back steps he
greets me without a handshake, keeping two right knuckles
at rest along the hip of his jeans. He has the kind of dry tan that
doesn't fade. The hollows of his cheeks are suede-like and wrinkled as palms.
He's rope-thin and wears the tattoo of a black pheasant in flight along his fore-
arm, a Bass belt buckle, a soft lisp.

In my first few minutes with Jim I resume the bad habit I've had all my life.
The one of asking hasty, precise questions about a stranger's profession, which
reads as if I'm starved for work and on the immediate market for anything,
though this has only now and then been the case. I ask Jim what it looks like up
inside ceilings, how he gets in there, what a squirrel's tail feels like, if I can possi-
bly take some notes. My grandmother addresses me with an insistent, knowing
look but Jim begins to talk more quickly and seems to treat me as a kind of
job-shadower, and maybe I sort of am one, so I don't elaborate.

The snappy old-timers that I favor call Muscatine, Iowa, "both the west
coast and the east bank"—of the Mississippi. I'm visiting my grandparents there
under the premise of writing about the town's pearl button industry. When I
wake the first morning in my mother's old bedroom there is a whiteness to the
paneled sunlight that tells of a sky outside flocked with snow. But it's June, I
remember, and soon a scuttling picks up in the ceiling, and then the event that
woke me—black dust spurting from the air vent, clouding the foot of my quilt.
"Attic squirrels," says my grandmother from the hall. They cut a tree down last
month, but still, she's calling someone. So I carry a ladder from the carriage
house and up the soggy, carpeted steps as my lithe granny jogs up behind. I pluck
my fingers from the slats that tick and pinch and crank the vent tight as we wait
for Jim to arrive.

246   Welcome to the Neighborhood

2. For the past fifty years, my family has lived in what's known as the Lambert-Musser house on West Second Street in Muscatine. It's a three-story, late Victorian that sits among others on a bluff above the Mississippi, just across from Illinois. The walls are gray frame weatherboard and the roof is shingled asphalt. It has a skinny side yard and a red brick chimney and a second-story glass porch where my grandparents sleep facing the river in all seasons. Daniel Lambert, attorney, built the trunk of the house in 1866, three decades before the button boom came to give the Pearl City its nickname. When the Lamberts fell on hard times they sold the place at a sherriff's auction, and the house lay vacant, furnished but uninhabited, for almost a decade. Then the lumber baron, Clifton R. Musser, bought the place in 1904, the year the caterpillar tread was invented to allow the tank and the verdant steel thresher to roll continuously. Musser was head of the Weyerhaeuser Timber Company and president of the Muscatine Bank. He built the brick stable and the auto house at the back of the property. He added a solarium, a small elevator, and an attic to what Lambert had made. He planted five pines in the backyard, of the same species his company stripped from the banks not a mile away.

3. For ten years an area of six square feet slept at the crown of my head and I never knew its color. Then, on a morning in September, my father quit our house and his life there, and that spring the rest of us followed suit, with the dog, in a truck. We left our nicks on the corners, a box on the high shelf, our layer of paint like a recent tree ring. But there are bits of my skin that stayed there. Long hairs still wound into carpet, our echoes caught up in the walls.

When a house is measured in square feet, there are places unaccounted for. Cabinets and bathtubs open into recesses where no wall leans its back against another. Some areas get sealed just after being built and not aired again until disaster or demolition arrives. I have this idea about a house like a coat with holes in its pockets. An idea about intangible additions. I like the wild and functional places behind walls that listen to and collect us. These margins that belong to less human things.

4.

Jim carries a
flashlight, a catch pole,
and a pair of gauntlet gloves.
When we step onto the porch he
leans elbows to knees. He's a talker and a
smoker and the conversation between us is oddly
familiar because of his steady ease, but I lurch around what
I want to ask him. This house is where we were sent when we
needed to momentarily disappear during the divorce. Like when our mom
was hospitalized for dehydration or when our parents left the country separately.
But I get the feeling that Jim knows the place much better than we do. I want to ask
him about the short doors at the backs of closets, those manholes to the house. I
want him to hand over maps of its inner territories. But my questions feel crazed and
private when I realize that it could matter to me if those depths were finite or barren.
So instead I ask Jim about pests as he takes a short drag.

J: Well, they get into crawlspaces, vents in the attic. Raccoons look for dark spots
along a roof and climb up. A coon'll hunch herself up under a soffit and stand up on
her hind legs to push the metal away. Then she'll rip out the wires and insulation.

S: Soffit? Is that a kind of room?

J: (Pointing) See? Where the roof attaches to the house, that triangular space. That's
not part of any room. It's a very intimidating place for a person. Dead airspace with a
pitch to the roof.

S: In our old house there was this tiny door in the attic leading to this hallway lined
with sheet metal. There was a turn at the end but I never went far enough to see past.

J: Oh well that's where you'll find the 'coon. It's mostly like that. Metal and wires. Some-
times it gets hard to breathe. This real fine, heavy dust, almost silver. You can see tracks
real clear. There's lotsa cobwebs, mice. We're so big compared to a critter ya know? But
it's the perfect place for them, safe and warm. It gets about 120 degrees, so you don't
wanna pass out, and the only way out is the way you come in, so you don't wanna get
turned around neither. Wasps too, they'd kill you right there in the attic if you got stuck.

S: Do you ever feel scared?

J: 'Course, sometimes. Sometimes there's just short planks that lay across ceiling
joints to walk on. When a raccoon comes charging out of the dark you have two
choices, to fight or flee. Once I fell clean through the ceiling. The critter run me
outta there! That's why I got insurance. I laugh and ask about other run-ins and
about scratches and bites. I stare hard at anything but Jim's right hand.

J: I never been bitten, and I've got a couple thousand of 'em . . . No, that's not true! I
got bit by a dang ground squirrel once, blood and everything.

I grimace and try to hide it but Jim snickers.

Welcome to the Neighborhood

5. In 1959 when Musser's widow, Margaret, was moved to a retirement facility, the windows on Second Street darkened for another decade. In those years my grandmother Sarah had two babies that she bathed a double-bowl sink on 8th Street. The first one, my mother Margaret, was named after her grandmother like I am. To specify, my grandfather calls her "The Peach," his wife "Cherry," and me "#2." He and my grandmother weren't looking to move, but something about the old house made them pick up and invest. They bought it for $35K using a loan from my great-grandfather. But when they arrived they found the house in a state of partial decay. The place had been unkempt for perhaps many years before it was abandoned, and the Mussers had taken nothing but personal effects. Moth-eaten drop cloths described heavy sofas and cabinets. The closets were stacked with linens yellowing along the fold. My grandparents didn't have much, and they kept most of what could be salvaged. So growing up, I sat in Musser dining chairs, read by their lamplight, sounded the creaks they wore into floors. Today their traces still linger in shelves of books that disintegrate when opened, lacquered toys left in the basement, chairs with hand-carved feet. Sometimes my grandmother brings out pieces of Musser crystal at holidays and the family may as well be upright again and around the table with us.

6. If a lineage is marked by both chance and inevitable likeness, a kind of lingering aesthetic in china settings and sets of eyes that reflect a river, then the Mussers are some version of our ancestors. Their possessions are hallowed, their stories significant to ours. We speak about them abruptly, but keep their trunks of photographs in the attic in case someone comes back after all this time. As a kid I knew that reverence, as if parts of the house were never ours, as if somewhere there were rooms kept back. My family appeared to be contracting and I had a lot of time. So I felt for buried hallways where the doorframes didn't match. I pressed my eye to cracks that might filter light into rooms where our voices had blended with pocket change and socks, floss and silver. Today when I look into a split wall I still think of that state of affairs as a kind of wreckage, as if all deep interiors should really be furnished for the purpose of collecting.

7. Jim is
trying hard not
to curse around me,
but he's also trying to get me
to laugh. I gather that he could talk
for hours, and that among his talents Jim
is a seasoned salesman and a storyteller, roles
that may prove interdependent in a town where every
conversation has a cellar.

S: Do you ever find anything in those extra places? Like furniture or belongings?

J: Never furniture. Those aren't really spots where people went to, you know, social-
ize. Once I crawled way back in an attic and found a big trunk. I asked the guy if he
wanted me to bring it down. He had to be about 75. It was a box of his grandfather's
pictures from college in the 1920s that he'd never seen before. All yellow. He was sur-
prised. Folks don't even know what's inside their own habitat. I find tools a lot too. A
chisel or a file, jack planes and hammers, things that workers left behind.

S: Do you carry those out too?

J: No. I always put the tools back, I tell 'em right where it is, but I leave it just there.
Sometimes dead animals too. I found a perfect squirrel skeleton in your Grandma's
attic once. Completely intact.

S: Really? Here? Was it rotting?

J: No just like that. Bare bones, nothing left. You can't tell at the time, all that smell
gets vented out the roof.

S: Do you think something ate it?

J: No, no, multiple generations living in there. That's why I keep comin' back here
every time. They think this is their home now. Where does an old squirrel go to die?
He goes where he lives.

S: I guess so.

3. The house that my parents left separately stood on a hill in Illinois. It was another first investment. Double-porched and river-facing and in rough shape. On three sides were graveyards and on the other, an interstate. Our attic had a fireplace that rung as if recently vacated and low, wide sills that smelled of glue and sunbaked dust. The stairs creaked when they wanted to and the heating popped and sung. As soon as the wind was kept out it found a new way in. Our father worked late and left early, and my mother and I kept our eyes ahead as we locked up the big doors at night. We didn't talk God, or death, or the reasons for a haunt. We were Iowans and we didn't have to look directly at anything to know it was there. This was the year Mom picked up our hands and walked out of church during a sermon about her and my father. She dropped fifty pounds and bought a leopard print dress. It was the year I told her that one day I would buy our house from whomever was living there and put everything back the way it was and she told me that I might need to speak with a psychiatrist about that someday. We moved forty minutes from Muscatine. When my grandparents held Christmas parties they invited the whole town and my friends and I worked coat check in party dresses and snuck tumblers of champagne into the elevator shaft. We pulled the rusty door shut, jammed the emergency stop, and got first-drunk in the space between floors. Within a year my sister and I had a new father, two new brothers, and a new-new house stale with plaster.

9.

Bachelard writes:
"Thus we cover the universe with drawings we have lived. These drawings need not be exact. They need only to be tonalized in the mode of our inner space."
So always, I dream inside houses where I have lived or loved someone and never find myself beneath open sky. Most often, the interiors splice my grandparents' and parents' first homes haphazardly. The floors of the two houses alternate, their first story, our second. For a year, bits of my boyfriend's family home attached itself to my old one. Staircases and their landings extend into others, triple-jointed. Additions of other houses bloom from hallways like extra limbs. To my sleeping brain all seems navigable, familiar. My mother and sister don't dream this way, though they both admit that they never want to live again in the first iteration of a home.

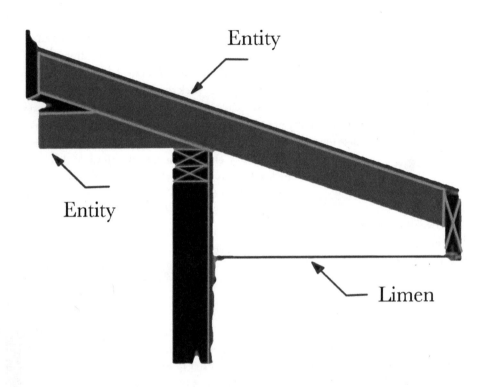

Entity

Entity

Limen

II.

A **Liminal Space** is an ambiguous zone between two definitive entities as applied to both spatial and temporal dimensions. It is a space or state that simultaneously divides and unites and exists only in the presence of an outer and inner, a perceived set of doubles. When two planes meet, it's the limen that remains between. Or, when a cabinet door fits loose in its socket, the liminal space is the ever-present gap, however miniscule, that persists. To name a few examples, airports are liminal spaces, as are shorelines, porches, puberties, graveyards, drag shows, skins, comas, and step-siblings.

D.

10.

S: How you
catch them—what do you
do with the animals afterwards?

J: You know, you have to think like a coon
sometimes. I have to be patient. Some folks think I
can just blow a flute and the critter will come running to
the cage. You know, I have to go in with what I call "extreme
prejudice," because sometimes the folks just want the critter eliminated.

Jim looks at me without blinking, couching his answer in a way I will come to
think of as his mode of gauging a listener's politics.

S: So . . . sometimes you kill them.

J: Yes, he says, looking gravely at me, and then at his hands. I don't have malice,
I love animals. Sometimes I get real emotional.

S: Yeah, I'm into animals too.

J: You gotta have emotions. It's a real necessary thing! The job's not for everyone.
You've gotta have some mustard. You have to be outgoing. It's a kinda entre-
preneurial thing.

S: Brave?

J: Yes, brave. My grandpa used to say "grow a hair!" that meant buck up and get
in there, get that thing! You have to look at your fears. Get the critter where it
waits.

S: Well, it sounds like you've had time to practice.

J: I mean, I have a lot of experience. But I still have to, you know, mentally
prepare, come in with my extreme prejudice, as I say. I pray that it's not a dam-
nable practice. Once I had to take out 11 adult coons. That was a terrible thing.
I've cried when I had to eliminate a family with baby foxes, too. There's a fox
downtown that I know, I know right where his hole is in the middle of town,
but no one else knows and I'm not gonna say nothing.

11. Sometimes, the hunting dogs are smiling and cataracted and graying at their tips and sometimes they are massive, sloppy pups thatshake the door hinges as I approach the old house. There are always exactly two of them, and my grandmother always needs to walk them to the park. Then we cook or pick out frames together or trouble-shoot at the desktop. She always has an afternoon meeting before we dress for dinner and go get stewed at some empty restaurant and have a loud conversation that I always try to hush. So it's no surprise when we end up alone in the Thai place that night, at the hour my family calls "wine o'clock." They kick us out long after close and back at the top of the hill we are breathless and tipsy and she wants to walk out to the cliff and look over the river. This part is new. A long barge chases its spotlight against the current, pushing hard at five compartments and one long horn. In the months between the duplex and Second Street, my mother's family lived in an old clammer house on stilts that the Mussers rented out as they got their affairs in order. The Peach says the sound of this barge horn is the first thing she remembers.

12.

A place that can't
be measured gets erased
by its descriptions. Which is why
I can't separate the idea of ghosts from
these spaces. These spots nested just beyond
the path of the inhabitant. I know that houses keep
our bits, but they also get stuck with our decisions. Some
do regret. This is what makes a ghost—the remnants of several
lives and a place for them to gather quietly. This is the way a house *knows*.
Why it aches at the stairwell. This is what's meant by something lingering at the
threshold like a soul.

E.

13.

S: Do you
ever think you'll
see a ghost?

This is the first time Jim doesn't
answer me straight away. Instead he
sits back in his chair, folds his cigarette cross
his buckle and holds my gaze.

J: I look for them. It's strange, my brain knows I'm back in a place
where no one has been maybe in a century. I wonder who was here, and
ya know they're gone now, but they were the last ones before you.

S: Right.

J: Some of these old mansions (motioning to the neighborhood), you just
don't know. I've been startled a few times. I hear a sound real close and turn
around, and nothing's there! But a ghost won't make a noise, that's what I tells
myself.

S: Is that why you don't take the tools?

J: Yep. These planks have gone to shit, but those are somebody's!

He takes a sip of water from the bottle at his hip as I write quickly. I begin a
question and my grandma steps through the glass door to tell me we better
get going. We're late for our dinner down the hill. I stand up and Jim smiles
and there's a pause and a lurch. A near-hug that we turn from, sheepish.

J: You know, you could come up there with me, if grandma was okay with it.

The static between my shoulders takes me by surprise—I'm scared. Bits of the
house are staring. They search the small of my neck.

My grandma raises her eyebrows very slowly as I falter. "Another time?" she
says, thinking I need an out. "Another time?" I say to Jim, and he nods. We
clasp left hands instead of right and hold for a second. "Nice to talk with you."
"You too."

Jim hands me a card. He lifts his tools toward the craggy back staircase and
looks over his shoulder. "You give me a ring!" he says, winking.

14. The next morning I go for a tired run along the Muscatine Riverwalk lit by cloudy vintage bulbs. The wind from the river brings the reek of moldering fish and the briny, electric scent of an incoming storm. I take a hot shower and search my mother's drawers for lip balm. The white built-ins have rows of keyholes that stretch to the ceiling. I climb on the sink to reach the highest, snooping, and find small wicker baskets of brittle hairpins, pill boxes, silk jewelry bags, perfume that could be from '56 though the smudged 5 is maybe a 7. It's been thirty years since my mom and her brother moved out and left my grandparents to themselves. Thirty years with just the two of them and three floors of centenarian house. Lately, my grandparents drive the forty minutes to us for holidays. They garden and sit by the fire, they get another puppy they can't train. They've been losing control of the place for some time and none of us knows what's packed into the varied storage. We're wondering quietly how long it will be until we need to open all the hatches. It seems like my grandma might go the way Margaret did, watching each room slip beneath dust until she is the last thing to go. People like us no longer die in their houses. When this one goes, our name will not be added to the Lambert-Musser chain. We built no tangible additions. We shored things up. We leaked into what came before.

15.

In many old houses a slit was once made in the back of medicine cabinets for disposing used razors into the wall space behind. This is why remodelers sometimes encounter a cascade of antique blades. More than sharp edges, stingers and teeth, close darkness, what I'm afraid of about these crawlspaces are the things they might know abstractly. I worry that something lies forgotten there that doesn't want to be left alone. This feels something like the guilt I have knowing that I won't be the one to take up the house for the very reasons that houses like this go to ruin. For their size and their dying towns and their upkeep. I worry about that time when the old place is divided, when it gets cut down or memorialized, when our remnants have nowhere to go.

16.

When I finally do
call, Jim is a bit reluctant
to make plans. The only weekend
I'm available is the first weekend of deer
season, so he tells me I should go up in there on
my own.

J: It ain't that scary. Some people asked me once if I was afraid
of ghosts goin' into old houses. They musta been watching those
paranormal shows or something.

S: Jim, that was me who asked you. When we first met!

J: Oh ho! Well sometimes I think about it now. You know when I go into a place, now
I talk to the house sometimes.

S: Yeah?

J: I says, I'm here to help. Those critters are gonna chew you to hell inside. I'm like a
doctor coming in to stop the bad stuff.

Two weeks later, Jim meets me on the porch with a pointed skull in hand. My
grandma is at her meeting, and the house is ours to crawl through unsupervised.

J: Look what I brought ya, I thought you might like it

S: What is it?

J: It's a badger, them's about the meanest animals we got in this state. See these canines?

S: Yeah. Did you find it somewhere?

J: No, I caught this one by the golf course bothering some people.

S: On a golf course? So you skinned it?

J: No, I just boiled it clean to get the skull, like a cat. You know the best way to catch
a coyote is to get a cat. They can't resist a cat.

S: Do you let the cats . . . go? After they serve as bait?

J: Well. You know . . . You don't use a live cat for trapping. Easier to get one dead.

Jim tells me about things he traps accidentally. About how, at the humane society in
town, he is known as "the bounty hunter." The gentle Critter Gitter is letting me see
a different side. This time, I've brought a digital recorder, and a bit more gumption.
Jim is curious too, but he's performing more this time around. He has good lines
and he knows it. Git is a part of the language that leaks out of him, and one that he
inserts for effect. He peddles the Critter Gitter like a ware to the fine people of Mus-
catine who want someone to crawl behind their walls.

17. After my mother's family settled in at Second Street, the Mussers' daughter, Margaret II, asked to come back and visit three times. My mother's room had been hers, and though she hadn't lived there for years, my grandma said she had loved the house so much she needed to see it every so often. She felt the way we do, I think, about houses like containers of people, even once gone. The Mussers' daughter died in a car accident and only afterward did they find a stack of her letters in the back of one of the cabinets.

18.
Margaret names my
mother, her grandmother,
and me by middle name. Three
more have come and gone among the
Mussers. Most of us have lived in the white
bedroom on the second floor where I finger these
dusty, comingled things. I look into the dimpled mirror, the
one as old as the house, and imagine all our faces in there, as if it could
know the difference.

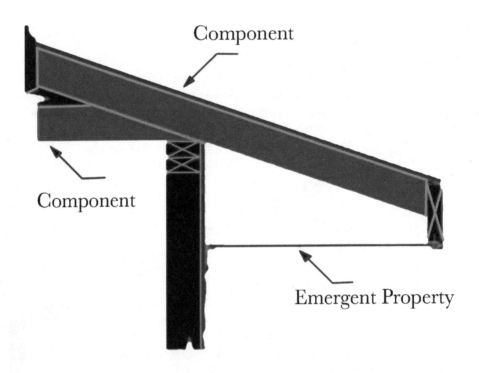

Component

Component

Emergent Property

III.

An **Emergent Property** is one that results when simple components are joined
in constraining relations to produce a unique element that is present in neither
of the individual elements. This concept is captured by the phrase, "the whole is
greater than the sum of its parts." Consciousness is an emergent property result-
ing from the combined parts of the human brain; we do not know where or how
it resides, only that it does when these parts combine. An example from nature
is hive mentality, or the pulsing of hundreds of fireflies in tandem. To highlight
emergence at work, we might look to a soffit, to the internet, to collaborations, to
a nest built between eaves.

19. We start
in the basement.
The recorder in my front
pocket digs into a hip crease
while the industrial beam swings from
Jim's hand, showing me exactly what he's
looking at. We crawl upwards through the house.
I choose the route and Jim narrates, his rough voice
itinerant through the recording. We find pipes cushioned in
asbestos, a silver shaving mirror receding into black, a hand drill for
punching buttons from clams, a toilet unhitched from its plumbing. I lift a
hatch while Jim sticks his head down the laundry chute and yells his report,
"Hoses, powerlines, debris, don't guillotine me please!" Then Jim shows me where
he caught the first squirrels in the attic.

J: I trapped 'em here with the wedding dresses. They ate a hole through the ceiling
up there, and they were climbin' all over the clothes and makin' a mess. I set some
cages and it took a while, but I did get 'em and your grandma was real happy.

We crawl inside our first soffit on the third floor, through a door about a third of
Jim's height.

J: This is one of those, what did you say, indigenous spaces?

S: Yeah. Liminal, actually.

J: Well, the critter, he'd be right around that corner, maybe you're gonna find
something there.

S: Back there?

J: Yep. You gotta watch and not step in a hole, if you step through that one there
you'll go right through the ceiling.

I inch down the triangular, exposed hall, empty but for scattered acorns and what
looks very much like a fleshy down comforter stuffed between the beams.

J: This pink stuff, you know, this is fiberglass. It itches, and you don't necessarily
really want to stir it up too bad . . .

S: Fiberglass, got it. Is that a kind of insulation?

J: Well lookit, they really chewed the hell out of . . . No, fiberglass is really a new
stuff. This gray matter insulation you see here, that's shredded up newspaper,
cellulose fiber stuffed in a lining. Old stuff, extras.

S: Gray matter, hm.

20. Certain traits skip generations, bloodlines, helix railings. My mother swears emphatically that she has never seen a ghost. "Yuck," she says, when I ask. "Let's not talk about creepy things." On the way back to the house, my grandmother wants to be straight, "You know, I can't really say. A ghost doesn't sound like a very nice thing. Isn't that about revenge? I'm not sure about seeing anything but I hear sounds over the years. It's just me here a lot. Makes you wonder what's been going on. They're not bad things. Mostly I say it's just the dogs." Maybe it's the spirits, the conversation, the cold night, but when we sway back up the hill and into our beds I'm not wary of sleeping in my mother's room, of my inherited spaces and what they contain.

21.

"The state of
your house is the state of
your mind," my mother would nag
when I insisted that my room was cozier
beneath a layer of paper leaves and clothing.
Her aphorism seemed intended to induce the
organization of both spaces, but mostly it just
made me feel shameful about revealing my most
inner struggles so obviously in the arrangement of
my things.

22.

Up in the attic we
peel apart cartoon-sized
cobwebs, our voices on the
recording edging into focus as the
house begins to taper and constrain.

J: Yeah, the squirrels were drivin' her nuts here and
she thought, well this guy's an interesting character.

S: Well . . . you do have an interesting job.

J: Yes I'm sure that's exactly what she thought. Yeah that! (pointing at a
ladder leading into a door in the ceiling) The skeleton is up there.

S: It is? Now?

J: Well, no . . . I took it a course. Watch your eyes, cause there's dirt. (scuffling) So let's see.
Well, that hinges back real easy, and it's not gonna hurt you, so you can just push it open with
your head. And just go easy and then you can shine the light in there. And you can see why . . .
why I didn't wanna crawl in.

S: (climbing) Okay . . .

J: (snickers) When they call you and say ooh yeah Jim I want you to catch that squirrel for me,
and you have to go into a space like that . . .

S: Um, can I have the light? I'm not tall enough to . . .

J: Just take another step and put your back against that door. The skeleton was in that hole there.

S: (scuffling) Ugh. And what's all the stuff hanging down?

J: Well, let me see, can I sneak up on the ladder?

Jim and I perch together on a single rung with our heads between the ceiling and the roof. It
smells of rot and the heat is oppressive even in October. I direct my beam onto the materials
that hang about our ears. Tar paper. A patch of dead moss. Electrical wires threaded through
glass insulators and abandoned. A lead water tank riveted to the rafters.

J: The thing is when they redone the heating and stuff, the couldn't get this sun of a gun out.

S: And what's this? (pointing up) Is it like a handle? For holding on?

J: Yep, I guess so . . . No : . . That looks like a hatch.

S: What?

J: It's a hatch! To the roof!

S: Okay . . . wait? Can we . . . ?

J: You can get that out of . . .

S: Can we just push it . . . ?

J: Grandma ain't gonna get mad . . . ?

S: No no no, she said we can go . . .

J: Careful, cuz you don't wanna . . .

(wind) (light)

23. The storm ends and clouds disperse like rubble in the sky. It's time to leave the gray house again. Time to drive the forty minutes back to my city and the life advancing there. Before I leave, my grandma wrenches an orange binding from deep in bookshelves. It's a book by Margaret's daughter, Marion Musser. A handwritten note inside the cover reads: "Dear Rodger and Sarah, Since this tale starts in your house, I thought you might be interested. It comes with all good wishes for you and yours for the new millennium. Cordially, Marion. Jan. 2000."
"I was born in our house at West Second Street," she writes, "in Muscatine, Iowa on September 11, 1910—at least my Uncle George testified to that when I applied for my first passport, as there were no birth certificates then." Marion describes her father, who called her "peaches," and tells the story of a Muscatine boy who once told her that he'd overheard men plotting to kidnap her and hide her on a boat going down the Mississippi for ransom. About her travels to more than twenty countries as a woman in the early '40s.

24.

Soffits, it turns out,
are pretty treacherous.
They feel like somewhere
between an animal den and a back
alley. They guard nests and original poisons,
refuse, and jagged metal scraps. A soffit measures
time inside the way a landfill can outdoors. It chronicles
eras of retired technology like flood lines that that rise up a bank.
Even the air decays. Inside it is plain that before they described a house,
the walls were once soil and are on their way back to it.

Lately, in describing third-spaces, I've been thinking in colors. Black seemed easy, the color of being lost, sealed, in the absence of light, but I've decided on its opposite. White contains the entire spectrum, but still reads as empty. It houses all the hues we can and will never perceive.

25.

S: Okay, comin' up.

J: There.

(train horns)

S: You can see the river bend from here.

J: Grandma prolly never done that!

S: No, I don't know if anyone's done this in a while.

(wind)

S: Is it okay to walk on this roof?

J: Just don't get near the edge. Cause you can, what can happen is, is a . . . there's a funny phenomena, you just go to the edge you'll automatically want to go over it. It's really weird, I can't explain it.

S: Yeah I . . . I've actually been writing about that feeling lately.

J: Ah there's a chimney cap up here, or the raccoons would be right in there!

S: Ah, yeah.

J: And turds.

S: Really.

J: Yeah, he'd be like, hey this is my new territory, and then he'd crap all over.

Jim sits and lights a cigarette. I ask him if I can have one.

J: Well, are you gonna get in trouble?

S: No.

J: How old are you?

S: Twenty-five.

J: Yeah, you most certainly can have one. (holding up lighter) You just put that on there . . . watch it.

Jim tells me about thinking like an animal; always having an escape route. About dogs he's seen jump straight off a cliff. He talks about finding his grandfather's newspapers boxed up in a family barn. About his life in Iowa and his soft spot for forgotten things. On the roof, with smoke between us, I remember that I'm following a man who traps animals for a living through my family's historic home. Officially, Jim is an exterminator for whom the animal is alternately a pest, a product and a body deserving his respect. He knows how to separate a carcass and boil the bones, and he'd probably rather be doing that right now. Jim owns black dogs, roots for my teams, and traces his roots to this same river city. But I'm a middle-class white girl doing research for an arts program, and he's a man seasoned by backwoods and the wild indoors. Jim grew up trapping his food three decades before I was raised in my suburban neighborhood. And now he's here, just doing his job, sitting beside me on a house built by lumber barons, telling me about friends of his that live under the bridges downtown. Friends, he says, who'd be happy to move into the carriage house, as we dangle our legs over the gutters and watch the big dogs wear holes in the yard. We look back down into the house and close the hatch up behind us. When he leaves, Jim doesn't wink. We shake right hands for the first time, my fingers gripping haphazardly around his and into empty space.

26. This time is wine o'clock and I'm home at the bar with my mother, describing the innards of her childhood house. She seems lacking interest, or perhaps disappointed, as I admit that I am too. It's not that the crawlspaces of my mind and those we clambered into are mutually exclusive, exactly. I came out carrying old medicine bottles without threads, stacks of photos from both my family and the Mussers', a silk glove, three shotgun shells, bites on my ankles and wrists from some infesting insect, coatings of dust that alternated by century, and some sounds—a human-like hum on the recording that we didn't hear while shuffling around. But I didn't see squirrels, and no ghosts followed me home. In stepping beyond hatches meant to be sealed forever, what we found, mostly, were a lot of unsightly things.

27.

A soffit
is home undomesticated.
A place for estranged things to
mend. A place for unlikely encounters,
where boundaries get thin. Comfortable at
the animal level, collecting at the human. And maybe
what we heard there were squirrels in the walls—the dust
was from their bones, after all, and never ours. But a house
collects more than tangible artifacts and grows with its inhabitants—a
process somewhere between the way a snail shell adds spiraling rims
as an inner mollusk expands, and the way shells of various crabs are
discarded, and gather new tenants. Of this I am assured. I was a small
thing myself, once added into these rooms.

Neighbor

The knock—shave
and a haircut—led her
to open the door,
the front door that was
made of wood,
no window, thinking it
was the neighbor,
a jokester, an intimate.
It happened
months ago
and maybe the man before
her meant no harm,
maybe his freckled,
young face and lanky
form was sincere
—she'd had people
from Gospel Rescue
Mission knock, wanting
work, or food, a blanket
once, these ghosts
of need that floated
through her daily life, ones
that made of air, until
the hand shook, or stink
of his jeans wafted,
or the story
emerged about a bus ticket
to Amarillo, the baby
and its fucking mother,
and maybe he will go
to Amarillo,
and maybe not.
Terrible the moments of

belief, trust, when you open
your face
to a stranger. Because
you are tired
of your mean self. Because
you remember your own
poverty. Because you
thought it was
someone else. She was settling
her child down
with food, a winter
afternoon in the desert, precise
sun, a leaf blower
somewhere moaning.
The child was eating
slowly, her eyes
in a book about fairies choosing
a mortal life for
reasons of love and loyalty.
Other kids
from the Boys and Girls Club
chattering down the sidewalk
toward the park
disappeared in the
blower's drone
which sounded
like a man's grief,
an unmitigated sadness
from his gut to his throat
and over the public
spaces of the run-down
neighborhood where dogs
chewed at chain link
and once her husband, at
dawn, walking the girl
in his arms when she
was a baby with
colic, found a man
in the gazebo

with a shotgun. She had been
standing on the porch,
watching them, drying
her own tears in a milk-stained
nightgown, who would
see her? and did she care?
The man had said I am
in a bad bad way.
She saw them talking,
the baby had stopped crying
as if she felt the
moment. The man had said
I am going to do something
I will be sorry for
and my license and papers
are in that car. I've got
my baby here,
said her husband and as
he backed away,
he said, I know
there are reasons
for not doing this.
In the house,
the small family
lay on the floor
as the man shot himself and
the sirens found
the bright red stain, the body
fallen on the path.
The wedding booked for
that afternoon
went on as planned, the woman
in white, the retinue
of girls in blossom shades
scattering petals
ahead of her. I realized,
a friend of hers once told her,
that I was
planning how to cut

my own hand off—the when,
the how, and how not to
die from it, but just to do it
and get it over with. That's when
I called my neighbor.
That was 20 years ago,
and she wishes
she could say that he's not still
suffering or that this man
at the door was in pain
for this reason or that—one he could
retch, spit out. The thing
about the man
at the door was he
was in shock, his voice strangely
loud when he spoke and
he wanted to know if Sergio
was home. As if Sergio
could contain his body
which was young
and thin and sewed with ink, shapes
askew up his neck.
Or to put it another way,
the death in a person
was drawn
on his skin, for another's
eyes, the hope being
the death inside might be
assuaged by a face that looks
clearly and directly,
that says what?
how? may I? She looked
at him and thought
of her beautiful
boy in high school who loved
to get high, how he's
been dead now a year,
found in his bed
in Aspen where he

made snow for a living.
How still was the snow day
a week ago—
the cacti covered
in it, the day and night
of waiting
for the melt since there were
no plows, the
dirty, stunted snowmen
that populated the park,
were pocked with sticks
and debris, awkward
expressions of joy, opportunity, delirium.
Not very sturdy,
nor long-lived. No one drove,
no one wandered
the streets looking for
what they needed that day,
no one risked crashing,
confrontation or shame.
The street was white
and still. And early
it was very clean, that sacred
blankness associated
with nothingness or the sublime.
It was like the state
her friend's daughter desired for herself
as she ate only blueberries
and peas, as she carved
from her body a self
that was not body, not family,
not food or defecation.
No one saw her
orchestrating her patient
pilgrimage toward
oblivion. The horizon of that
is the question—
at fourteen, she wanted a world
that is utterly pure,

a grassy field the right
green, a lushness
made impossible by anything
living or moving,
by weather and drought,
by trees that shed their
dead leaves and branches,
and animals who must
do their business of shitting
and digging and burning
sometimes.

Cottage Industry

Fat bumblebees have commandeered the lavender
Two or three to a slender stem, dulled by competition
They've occupied the green and purple hedge
outside the kitchen door.
Leaning down, I hear a low rumble.
Mindlessly they hang on the purple nodes.
They're stuck between harmony and desire,
their motors so loud they're
unaware of the earth mover's sounds
the house being built, the road being paved,
the grinding punctuated by beeps
in the middle distance.

The bees will stay at their work till sundown
Drunk with lavender juice
I'm stuck between harmony and desire myself
Our old apple trees have dropped their fruit too soon.
Tomorrow there'll be rain.
Few bees will report for duty.
The lavender will stand tall, unweighted by these busybodies.
I'll be on the road back to the city,
Radio says
All news all the time.
The bees will take no notice.

Valediction

The backyard lives of cat and bird
and the way leaves give themselves
away this instant to the all-but-no breeze
creeping across the silver-painted roof where clouds,

reflected, pass dark, then bright
above a book left out by the vacant deck chair
fluttering its pages, signalling to the reader somewhere out of sight
to come back, come back and start the book over,

this all arrives without a valediction forbidding anything,
just the sense of seeing something
or someone for the last time: the poet's faded fedora

in a tea store window haunting this October's primary
blues bringing back mid-May and the missing mate
of the nightingale singing "day-long and night late."

i.m. Seamus Heaney

What the Living Do

Johnny, the kitchen sink has been clogged for days, some utensil probably fell down there.
And the Drano won't work but smells dangerous, and the crusty dishes have piled up

waiting for the plumber I still haven't called. This is the everyday we spoke of.
It's winter again: the sky's a deep, headstrong blue, and the sunlight pours through

the open living-room windows because the heat's on too high in here and I can't turn it off.
For weeks now, driving, or dropping a bag of groceries in the street, the bag breaking,

I've been thinking: This is what the living do. And yesterday, hurrying along those
wobbly bricks in the Cambridge sidewalk, spilling my coffee down my wrist and sleeve,

I thought it again, and again later, when buying a hairbrush: This is it.
Parking. Slamming the car door shut in the cold. What you called that yearning.

What you finally gave up. We want the spring to come and the winter to pass. We want
whoever to call or not call, a letter, a kiss—we want more and more and then more of it.

But there are moments, walking, when I catch a glimpse of myself in the window glass,
say, the window of the corner video store, and I'm gripped by a cherishing so deep

for my own blowing hair, chapped face, and unbuttoned coat that I'm speechless:
I am living. I remember you.

Perhaps the World Ends Here

The world begins at a kitchen table. No matter what, we must eat to live.

The gifts of earth are brought and prepared, set on the table. So it has been since creation, and it will go on.

We chase chickens or dogs away from it. Babies teethe at the corners. They scrape their knees under it.

It is here that children are given instructions on what it means to be human. We make men at it, we make women.

At this table we gossip, recall enemies and the ghosts of lovers.

Our dreams drink coffee with us as they put their arms around our children. They laugh with us at our poor falling-down selves and as we put ourselves back together once again at the table.

This table has been a house in the rain, an umbrella in the sun.

Wars have begun and ended at this table. It is a place to hide in the shadow of terror. A place to celebrate the terrible victory.

We have given birth on this table, and have prepared our parents for burial here.

At this table we sing with joy, with sorrow. We pray of suffering and remorse. We give thanks.

Perhaps the world will end at the kitchen table, while we are laughing and crying, eating of the last sweet bite.

Neighborhood Talks

Opening the Discussion

Close Reading:

1. Compare and contrast the following two poems: "Watch" by Gary Jackson and "To the Fig Tree on 9th and Christian" by Ross Gay. How would you describe the mood of the speaker in each poem? Why does each speaker feel this way? In what ways do these mostly dissimilar poems overlap or allude to a shared reality? Be sure to evidence your ideas with specific lines from each poem.

2. Reread the following short stories: "The Kindest" by Sonya Larson and "Religion" by Christine Schutt. Although neither of these stories centers around neighbors or neighborhoods in a conventional sense, what forms of neighboring do you see taking place in each story? How do the themes of Larson's and Schutt's stories fit in with the other works in this anthology?

3. In the essays "Shelter" by Sarah Einstein and "Occupants" by James Miranda, each writer develops a profile of a nonfictional character (or group of characters). What aspects of these characters' descriptions do you find most memorable and/or compelling? What compelled Einstein and Miranda to write about them? What ethical principles, if any, do you think essayists should follow when writing in a documentary style about the people they meet and befriend in their neighborhood?

4. U.S. Poet Laureate Joy Harjo's poem "Perhaps the World Ends Here" closes the book. What do you think the kitchen table symbolizes in this poem? What do you notice about Harjo's patterning of various uses of the kitchen table? Is this a celebratory poem?

5. What do you think is the "moral" of Jarod Roselló's comic "The Neighbor"? How does it resonate with contemporary social issues?

Writing:

1. Picture your childhood street. Which sensory details stand out the most to you? What childhood memories do they evoke? Are these memories solitary or shared with others? Why do you think these particular moments stood out to you? Note: If it is challenging for you to choose a particular childhood location, pick the one that you have the strongest sensory memories of; alternately, write about what makes this exercise challenging for you.

2. Describe your relationship with your current neighborhood. How long have you lived there? What do you know about its history? How has it changed over the years? What landmarks and people have you come to know well? What parts of it (if any) are mysterious and/or alienating to you? Do you think everyone who lives there feels welcome? Why or why not?

3. Think of a moment when your assumption about a neighbor was disproven—perhaps during your childhood, because of your limited perspective as a child. Write both the backstory and a scene describing how the shift in your perception happened.

4. Draw a map of your current neighborhood. Provide as much detail as possible, including streets, houses, trees, alleys, and any other little details you can remember. What parts are the most vivid for you? Mark locations where memorable events occurred. What were they and why have they stayed with you? What parts of the map are less detailed or even blank? Write about the process of drawing this map and what it reveals about your relationship to your neighborhood. How might you get to know your neighborhood better?

5. Invent a neighborhood. Make your narrator omniscient, and write a scene in which you describe what several characters are doing (and thinking) at the same moment –say, 3 p.m. on a Tuesday—in different homes/yards. No one character needs to stand out. Let the shared neighborhood setting be another character with which they all interact. Find ways for the neighbors to connect without necessarily interacting directly (for example, a bee shooed away by one neighbor drifts into another neighbor's yard; one neighbor tapes a flyer to another's door; a sudden burst of rain affects everyone).

Group Discussion:

1. In a small group, introduce yourselves in turn with your name and the neighborhood you call home. Tell the group about your neighborhood. What are your favorite places in your neighborhood? Who are some of your neighbors? What

makes your neighborhood feel like home? Does anything about your neighborhood make you uncomfortable?

2. In your neighborhood, what does "neighborliness" look like? What are some ways people in your neighborhood help each other? How does your community welcome new members to the neighborhood? What can sometimes make it challenging to build community where you are? What community-building ideas can you think of that have not yet been tried, or that existed in the past in your area but could be profitably rekindled?

3. What contribution stood out as your favorite (or most memorable) piece in the anthology? Does this piece remind you of your own neighborhood and experiences? Why or why not?

4. What are some of the primary themes you notice among pieces included in *Welcome to the Neighborhood*? Which pieces do you think best exemplify concepts like neighborliness, community, and altruism?

5. What do you remember about the ways your family gave and received neighborly aid when you were a child? Does a particular person stand out in your memory as the embodiment of a welcoming neighbor?

Share!

Welcome to the Neighborhood can be a great tool for getting to know your neighbors and your community. Organize a potluck and invite people who might be interested in forming a book discussion group. Plan some meetings and use these prompts to spur conversation. Let people create their own connections and observations. Your local library and bookstore are also good places to check for book club information if you're not yet ready to organize your own gathering.

Feel free to contribute to the *Welcome to the Neighborhood* Facebook page here: https://www.facebook.com/welcome2theneighborhood/

Acknowledgments

A special thanks to Gillian Berchowitz, Dinty W. Moore, Eve Bridburg, and Wayne Miller for their advice and encouragement throughout the book's progress, to Robert Pinsky and Edward Hirsch for their early support of this project, to Bruce Simon for additional feedback, and to all of the contributors who made it possible for me to include their stories, essays, and poetry. This neighborhood exists because you wrote it.

Credits

"Hungry" from *Never-Ending Birds* by David Baker. Copyright © 2009 by David Baker. Used by permission of W. W. Norton & Company, Inc.

"Upon Hearing about the Student Arrested at the Gun Shop" by Katie Berta previously published in *Salt Hill*.

"Pornograph, with Americana" from *The 44th of July* by Jaswinder Bolina. Copyright © 2019. Used by permission of Omnidawn Publishing. All rights reserved.

"Neighborhood" by Betsy Brown previously published in *B. O. D. Y.*

"Aubade in the Old Apartment" by Leila Chatti previously published in *Southern Indiana Review.*

"Forest Ridge Farms Nocturne" by Sean M. Conrey reprinted with the permission of Brick Road Poetry Press.

"A Map of the World" by Jennifer De Leon previously published in *Brevity* (Fall 2012).

"A Small Guest" by Jennifer Kwon Dobbs appears in *Interrogation Room*, published in 2018 by White Pine Press.

"Daystar" from *Thomas and Beulah,* Carnegie-Mellon University Press, Pittsburgh, PA ©1986 by Rita Dove. Reprinted by permission of the author.

"Reading Celan in a Subway Station" by Carolina Ebeid reprinted by permission of Noemi Press in Blacksburg, VA.

"Not Trash Day" by Claire Eder previously published in the *Colorado Review.*

"Shellar" by Sarah Einstein previously published in *The Sun.*

"The Invincible" by Jonathan Escoffery previously published in *Salt Hill Journal.*

"City Morning" by Rebecca Morgan Frank from *Little Murders Everywhere* (Salmon Poetry, 2012).

"As I Wander" from *The Loss of All Lost Things* by Amina Gautier reprinted by permission of Elixir Press.

Contributors

DAVID BAKER is a poet, editor, and educator who lives in the village of Granville, Ohio, where he teaches at Denison University and serves as poetry editor of *The Kenyon Review*. His most recent book is *Swift: New and Selected Poems* (W. W. Norton, 2019).

LINDA BAMBER is a writer and professor of English at Tufts University. Her poetry collection, *Metropolitan Tang,* was published by David R. Godine. Bamber has published widely in periodicals such as *The Harvard Review, The Nation, Ploughshares, The New York Times, The Kenyon Review, Raritan,* and *Tikkun.*

KATIE BERTA lives in Phoenix, Arizona, where she works as the supervising editor of *Hayden's Ferry Review.* Her poems have appeared in *Prairie Schooner, The Kenyon Review Online, Blackbird, Sixth Finch, Indiana Review, Salt Hill,* and *Washington Square Review,* among other journals. You can find her book reviews on the *Ploughshares* blog. Her poetry has received support from the Vermont Studio Center and the Virginia G. Piper Center for Creative Writing. She has her PhD in poetry from Ohio University and her MFA from Arizona State.

DAVID BLAIR lives in Somerville, Massachusetts. He is the author of three books of poetry, *Ascension Days,* which was chosen by Thomas Lux for the Del Sol Poetry Prize; *Friends with Dogs;* and *Arsonville;* and a collection of essays, *Walk Around: Essays on Poetry and Place* (www.davidblairpoetry.com).

JASWINDER BOLINA is author of *The 44th of July* (2019), *Phantom Camera* (2012), *Carrier Wave* (2006), and the digital chapbook *The Tallest Building in America* (2014). His poems and essays have been included in anthologies including *The Best American Poetry* and *The Norton Reader.*

BETSY BROWN is author of *Year of Morphines,* a National Poetry Series winner. She is a poet and writer based in Minneapolis.

STEVE BRYKMAN left med school to become managing editor of *National Lampoon.* He's written for *A Prairie Home Companion,* Comedy Central, NPR, and the Food Network, and was featured in *Ars Technica, Tablet, Cognoscenti, Playboy, Nerve,* and *The New Yorker.* As a UMass writing fellow he was awarded the Harvey Swados prize.

NICOLE CALLIHAN's poetry books include *SuperLoop* (2014) and *Translucence* (with Samar Abdel Jaber, 2018), and the chapbooks *A Study in Spring* (with Zoe Ryder White, 2015), *The Deeply Flawed Human* (2016), *Downtown* (2017), and *Aging* (2018). Her novella, *The Couples,* was published by Mason Jar Press in summer 2019.

LAUREN CAMP is the author of four books of poems, including *One Hundred Hungers* (Tupelo Press, 2016), winner of the Dorset Prize and finalist for the Arab American Book Award, and *Turquoise Door* (3: A Taos Press, 2018). She lives and teaches in New Mexico.

PETER CAMPION is the author of three books of poems and a literary critical collection, *Radical as Reality: Form and Freedom in American Poetry,* all from the University of Chicago Press. He lives in Minneapolis.

LEILA CHATTI is a Tunisian American poet and author of *Deluge,* forthcoming from Copper Canyon Press in 2020, and the chapbooks *Ebb* and *Tunsiya/Amrikiya.* The inaugural Anisfield-Wolf Fellow in Publishing and Writing at Cleveland State University, her work appears in *Ploughshares, Tin House, The American Poetry Review,* and elsewhere.

SEAN M. CONREY's most recent collections are *The Book of Trees* (2017) and *The Word in Edgewise* (2014). Recordings of his experimental music project, *Mercury City Suburbs,* are available online. He lives in Syracuse, New York, with his wife, Carol Fadda, and their two daughters.

DOUGLAS K CURRIER has published work in many magazines both in the United States and in South America. He lives with his wife in Winooski, Vermont.

JENNIFER DE LEON is the author of *Don't Ask Me Where I'm From* (forthcoming from Atheneum/Simon and Schuster in 2020) and the editor of *Wise Latinas* (University of Nebraska Press). An assistant professor of creative writing at Framingham State University and a GrubStreet instructor and board member, she lives in the Boston area.

AARON DEVINE is a lecturer in the Honors College and ESL instructor at the University of Massachusetts Boston. He cofounded Write on the DOT, a reading series and literary platform that supports and promotes local writing in Boston's Dorchester neighborhood.

JENNIFER KWON DOBBS is the author of *Paper Pavilion* (White Pine Press Poetry Prize, 2007), *Interrogation Room* (White Pine Press, 2018), and the chapbooks *Notes from a Missing Person* (Essay Press, 2015) and *Necro Citizens* (Hochroth Verlag, 2019, German/English edition). She is associate professor of creative writing and directs race and ethnic studies at St. Olaf College.

RITA DOVE, Commonwealth Professor at the University of Virginia, is a former U.S. Poet Laureate, the 1987 Pulitzer Prize winner in poetry, and the only poet who has received both the National Humanities Medal and the National Medal of Arts. Her latest poetry collections are *Sonata Mulattica* and *Collected Poems: 1974–2004*.

CAROLINA EBEID was born in West New York, New Jersey, and is the author of *You Ask Me to Talk about the Interior* (Noemi Press). She holds an MFA from the Michener Center for Writers and a PhD from the University of Denver. She teaches at the Lighthouse Writers Workshop and has won fellowships from CantoMundo, the Stadler Center for Poetry, and the National Endowment for the Arts, and a Lannan Foundation Residency. Recent work appears in *Poetry, PEN America, jubilat,* and *The American Poetry Review.* She helps edit poetry at *The Rumpus.*

CLAIRE EDER's poems and translations have appeared in *Gulf Coast, The Cincinnati Review, PANK, Midwestern Gothic,* and *Guernica,* among other publications. She holds an MFA from the University of Florida and a PhD from Ohio University. She lives in Madison, Wisconsin, where she works for the University of Wisconsin Press. Find her online at claireeder.com.

SARAH EINSTEIN is the author of *Mot: A Memoir* (University of Georgia Press, 2015), *Remnants of Passion* (Shebooks, 2014), and *The Tripart Heart* (Sundress, 2019). Her work has been awarded a Pushcart Prize, a Best of the Net, and the AWP Prize in Creative Nonfiction.

JONATHAN ESCOFFERY's recent honors include a Distinguished Story in *The Best American Short Stories 2018,* a Glenna Luschei *Prairie Schooner* Award, and the Waasnode Fiction Prize. His writing has appeared in *AGNI, Prairie Schooner, Pleiades, Passages North, Creative Nonfiction,* and elsewhere. He holds an MFA from the University of Minnesota.

C. E. FORT hails from Northern California and currently resides in Massachusetts. Her poems have appeared in *St. Mary's Magazine* and *Loop.*

REBECCA MORGAN FRANK is the author of *Sometimes We're All Living in a Foreign Country* and *The Spokes of Venus,* both from Carnegie Mellon University Press, and *Little Murders Everywhere* (Salmon Poetry), a finalist for the Kate Tufts Discovery Award.

LEORA FRIDMAN is author of *My Fault,* selected by Eileen Myles for the Cleveland State University Press First Book Prize, in addition to other books of poetry, prose, and translation. More at leorafridman.com.

AMINA GAUTIER is the author of three short story collections: *At-Risk, Now We Will Be Happy,* and *The Loss of All Lost Things.* Her stories appear in *AGNI, Glimmer Train, Oxford American,* and *The Southern Review,* among other places. For her body of work she has received the PEN/Malamud award.

ROSS GAY is the author, most recently, of the poetry collection *Catalog of Unabashed Gratitude,* and the collection of essays *The Book of Delights.* He teaches at Indiana University.

SARAH GREEN is the author of *Earth Science* (421 Atlanta, 2016). A Pushcart Prize winner, New Women's Voices Series Prize winner, and one of the Best New Poets 2012, she is currently at work on her second collection of poetry. She teaches at St. Cloud State University.

MARK HALLIDAY teaches at Ohio University. His seventh book of poems, *Losers Dream On,* appeared in 2018 from the University of Chicago Press.

JOY HARJO, current United States Poet Laureate, is the author of nine books of poetry, including her forthcoming, *An American Sunrise.* She has been honored with the Ruth Lilly Poetry Prize from the Poetry Foundation, the Wallace Stevens Award from the Academy of American Poets, and a Guggenheim Fellowship. Her memoir *Crazy Brave* won the PEN USA Literary Award.

SARAH C. HARWELL is the author of the poetry collection *Sit Down Traveler.* Her poems have appeared in *Three New Poets* as well as various journals. She is associate director of Syracuse University's MFA program in creative writing where, out of necessity, she has developed a deep fondness for snow.

EDWARD HIRSCH's most recent books of poems are *Gabriel: A Poem* (2014) and *Stranger by Night* (2020).

RICHARD HOFFMAN is author of seven books: the poetry collections *Without Paradise, Gold Star Road, Emblem,* and *Noon until Night;* the memoirs *Love & Fury* and *Half the House;* and the short story collection *Interference and Other Stories.* He is senior writer in residence at Emerson College.

KATHERINE HOLLANDER is a poet and historian. She is the author of *My German Dictionary,* a collection of poetry, from Waywiser Press. She has taught most recently at the University of Hartford and Colby College.

MARIE HOWE is the author of four books of poetry, the latest *Magdalene* (W. W. Norton).

Born and raised in Topeka, Kansas, GARY JACKSON is the author of the poetry collection *Missing You, Metropolis,* which received the 2009 Cave Canem Poetry Prize. His poems have appeared in *Callaloo, Tin House, Tuesday,* and elsewhere. He is an associate professor at the College of Charleston in Charleston, South Carolina.

DANIEL B. JOHNSON is the author of *How to Catch a Falling Knife,* published by Alice James Books. Johnson's poetry has been featured on National Public Radio and *PBS NewsHour,* in *The Washington Post,* and elsewhere. He currently serves as the executive director of Mass Poetry.

JENNY JOHNSON is the author of *In Full Velvet* (Sarabande Books, 2017). Her poems have appeared in *Harvard Review, The New York Times, Waxwing,* and elsewhere. Her honors include a Whiting Award, a Hodder Fellowship, and an NEA Fellowship. She currently lives in Pittsburgh, Pennsylvania.

DANIELLE JONES holds an MFA from the University of Massachusetts Boston, and is associate director of The Writers House at Merrimack College. Her work has appeared in *Beloit Poetry Journal, Memorious, Southern Poetry Review, Zone 3,* and elsewhere. She is a recipient of a 2014 Rona Jaffe Foundation Writer's Award.

ESON KIM's stories appear in *Sycamore Review, Stories from the Stage,* and more. She was a New Jersey Council on the Arts Fellow and earned the David B. Saunders Award. She holds an MFA from Emerson College and directs Community & Youth Programs at GrubStreet. She is currently writing a novel.

DYLAN KRIEGER is a repository of high hopes from hell in south Louisiana. She is the author of *Giving Godhead* (Delete, 2017), *dreamland trash* (Saint Julian, 2018), *no ledge left to love* (Ping Pong, 2018), and *The Mother Wart* (Vegetarian Alcoholic, forthcoming). Find her at dylankrieger.com.

BECCA J. R. LACHMAN works in the magical world of public libraries and is a writer/educator/singer-songwriter living in Appalachian Ohio. She is editor of *A Ritual to Read Together: Poems in Conversation with William Stafford* (Woodley Press). Her poetry collections are *Other Acreage* (Gold Wake Press) and *The Apple Speaks* (Cascadia).

SONYA LARSON's work has appeared in *The Best American Short Stories, American Short Fiction, The American Literary Review, Poets & Writers, Writer's Chronicle, West Branch, Salamander, Memorious, The Harvard Advocate,* and more. She directs GrubStreet's "Muse and the Marketplace" conference, received her MFA from Warren Wilson College, and is writing a novel.

SARAH LAYDEN is the author of *The Story I Tell Myself about Myself,* winner of the 2017 Sonder Press Chapbook Competition, and *Trip through Your Wires* (Engine Books, 2015), a novel. She is an assistant professor of English at Indiana University–Purdue University Indianapolis.

REBECCA LINDENBERG is the author of *Love, an Index* (McSweeney's) and *The Logan Notebooks* (Mountain West Poetry Series).

GERI LIPSCHULTZ is grateful to be here. Some of her work has seen daylight in *Ms, BLARB, The New York Times, Black Warrior Review, College English,* and Pearson's college literature anthology. Once upon a time, she was awarded a CAPS grant, which led the way to a one-woman show.

DORA MALECH is the author of four books of poetry, including *Flourish* (Carnegie Mellon University Press, 2020) and *Stet* (Princeton University Press, 2018). She lives in Baltimore, where she is an assistant professor in The Writing Seminars at Johns Hopkins University.

FRED MARCHANT is the author of five books of poetry, the most recent being *Said Not Said* (Graywolf Press, 2017). Founding director of the Suffolk University Poetry Center, he is also the editor of a collection of the early poetry of William Stafford, and a cotranslator of several Vietnamese poets.

GRETCHEN MARQUETTE is the author of *May Day* (Graywolf Press, 2016.) Her poetry has appeared in *Poetry, Harper's, The Paris Review, Tin House, PBS NewsHour,* and elsewhere. She lives in Minneapolis.

TARA LYNN MASIH is editor of *The Rose Metal Press Field Guide to Writing Flash Fiction* and *The Chalk Circle: Intercultural Prizewinning Essays.* She founded *The Best Small Fictions* series. Her recent novel, *My Real Name Is Hanna,* won four book awards, including the Julia Ward Howe Award for Young Readers, and was translated into Slovak.

JAMAAL MAY's books are *Hum* and *The Big Book of Exit Strategies* (Alice James Books). He teaches in Detroit at Wayne State University, where he guides the [re]launch of Organic Machine Books as well as the sonic co-op Jamtramck Beat Systems, fostering personal, social, and financial empowerment through sound technology education.

GAIL MAZUR is author of seven collections of poetry, including *Zeppo's First Wife, Figures in a Landscape,* and *Forbidden City.* Her eighth collection, *Land's End,* is forthcoming 2020 from University of Chicago Press. She lives in Provincetown and Cambridge, Massachusetts, where she is founding director of the Blacksmith House Poetry Series.

D. R. MCCLURE lives and works in Iowa.

Three-time Pushcart prize winner JILL MCDONOUGH teaches in UMass-Boston's MFA program and in a Boston jail. Her books include *Habeas Corpus, Where You Live, Reaper,* and *Here All Night.*

WAYNE MILLER is the author of five collections, including *We the Jury* and *Post-,* which won the Rilke Prize and the Colorado Book Award. His cotranslation of *Zodiac* by Moikom Zeqo was shortlisted for the PEN Center USA Award in Translation. He teaches at the University of Colorado Denver and edits *Copper Nickel.*

SARAH MINOR is the author of a collection of visual essays forthcoming from *Rescue Press* (2020), *Slim Confessions* (Noemi Press 2021), and *The Persistence of the Bonyleg: Annotated,* a digital chapbook from Essay Press (2016). She is the video editor at *TriQuarterly Review* and assistant professor of creative writing at the Cleveland Institute of Art.

JAMES MIRANDA's writing has appeared in *Gulf Coast, Mississippi Review, Cimarron Review, Indiana Review, Alaska Quarterly Review,* and elsewhere. He is a lecturer in the Writing and English Departments at Ithaca College and SUNY Cortland.

BRAD AARON MODLIN is the Reynolds Endowed Chair of Creative Writing at the University of Nebraska, Kearney. *Everyone at This Party Has Two Names* (The Cowles Prize) contains the poem "What You Missed That Day You Were Absent from Fourth Grade." *Surviving in Drought* (fiction) won The Cupboard contest.

DINTY W. MOORE is author of the memoir *Between Panic & Desire,* the writing guide *Crafting the Personal Essay,* and other books. He has published in *The Georgia Review, Harper's,* and *The New York Times Sunday Magazine,* among others. He lives in Athens, Ohio, where he grows tomatoes and edible dandelions.

TOMÁS Q. MORÍN is the author of *Patient Zero* and *A Larger Country,* winner of the APR/Honickman First Book Prize. He is coeditor with Mari L'Esperance of the anthology *Coming Close: 40 Essays on Philip Levine,* and translator of *The Heights of Macchu Picchu* by Pablo Neruda.

LADAN OSMAN is the author of *Exiles of Eden* (2019) and *The Kitchen-Dweller's Testimony* (2015). She lives in Brooklyn.

KATIE PETERSON is the author of four collections of poetry, including *A Piece of Good News.* She is the director of the Creative Writing Program at the University of California at Davis. She lives in Berkeley, California, with her husband and daughter, but she used to live in Massachusetts.

ROBERT PINSKY was born in Long Branch, New Jersey. Like his parents, siblings, aunts, uncles, and cousins he graduated Long Branch High School, where his class poll named him Most Musical Boy. His honors include the Italian Premio Capri and the Korean Manhae Award.

DONALD PLATT has published six books of poetry, most recently *Man Praying* (2017) and *Tornadoesque* (2016). He has been awarded two individual artist's fellowships from the NEA and three Pushcart Prizes, and his poems have been included three times in *The Best American Poetry*. He teaches in the MFA program at Purdue University.

DAVID RIVARD's most recent book, *Standoff*, received the 2017 PEN New England Award in Poetry. His five other books include *Otherwise Elsewhere, Sugartown,* and *Wise Poison*. The recipient of awards from the Guggenheim Foundation, Civitella Ranieri, and the NEA, he teaches at the University of New Hampshire.

KIP ROBISCH's stories and essays have appeared in *Puerto del Sol, Necessary Fiction, Juked,* and other journals and magazines. His book, *Wolves and the Wolf Myth in American Literature,* was published by University of Nevada Press. He is a freelance writer and editor and lives in Indiana with Elizabeth Hensley and their cat, Roxie, who they are certain will like a dog.

DANA ROESER's fourth book, *All Transparent Things Need Thundershirts,* won the Wilder Prize at Two Sylvias Press and was published in Spring 2019. Her earlier books won the Juniper Prize and Morse Prize (twice). Other honors include an NEA fellowship and Pushcart Prize.

JAROD ROSELLÓ is a Cuban American cartoonist and writer. He is the author of *The Well-Dressed Bear Will (Never) Be Found* and the middle-grade graphic novel *Red Panda & Moon Bear*. He teaches in the creative writing program at University of South Florida.

CHRISTINE SCHUTT is the author of three novels and three collections of stories. Finalist for both a National Book Award (*Florida*) and Pulitzer Prize (*All Souls*), she is also a multiple O. Henry Award winner and recipient of Guggenheim and NYFA fellowships. Her most recent book, *Pure Hollywood,* was a *New York Times* Notable Book for 2018.

LLOYD SCHWARTZ teaches in the MFA program at UMass Boston, reviews classical music for NPR's *Fresh Air,* and is coeditor of the Library of America's *Elizabeth Bishop: Poems, Prose & Letters*. His latest poetry collection is *Little Kisses*. He is the Poet Laureate of Somerville, Massachusetts.

MATTHEW SIEGEL is the author of *Blood Work,* winner of The Felix Pollak Prize in Poetry. His poems have appeared in the Academy of American Poets Poem-A-Day, *The Guardian, PBS NewsHour, San Francisco Chronicle, Tin House,* and elsewhere. A former Wallace Stegner fellow at Stanford, he is a professor of humanities and sciences at San Francisco Conservatory of Music.

TOM SLEIGH's many books include *The Land between Two Rivers: Writing in an Age of Refugees* (essays) and *House of Fact, House of Ruin* (published simultaneously), *Station Zed, Army Cats* (John Updike Award from the American Academy of Arts and Letters), and *Space Walk* (Kingsley Tufts Award), all published by Graywolf. He has received a Guggenheim Fellowship, an American Academy in Berlin Fellowship, and two National Endowment for the Arts grants, among many other awards. He is a distinguished professor at Hunter College and works as a journalist in the Middle East and Africa.

LIZ STEPHENS runs Mojave Desert Arts, an off-grid residency cabin and land. She is a memoirist and essayist and is working on a screenplay about desert kids. Her works include her memoir, *The Days Are Gods; Brief Encounters: An Anthology of Contemporary Nonfiction;* and the interdisciplinary anthology *Dirt: A Love Story.*

SETH STEWART is the author of two poetry collections: *The Ending I Imagined* (2016) and *In the Future Room* (2019). He received his MFA and MA degrees from CalArts, and is currently pursuing his master's degree in counseling to enhance his work with survivors of sexual abuse and assault.

NOMI STONE is a poet and an anthropologist, and the author of two poetry collections, *Stranger's Notebook* (TriQuarterly, 2008) and *Kill Class* (Tupelo, 2019). Winner of a Pushcart Prize, Stone's poems appear recently in *POETRY, The American Poetry Review, The New Republic, The Best American Poetry, Tin House, New England Review,* and elsewhere.

BRIAN TRAPP has published stories and essays in *The Kenyon Review, The Gettysburg Review, Ninth Letter, Narrative, New Ohio Review, Brevity,* and elsewhere. He directs the Kidd Creative Writing Workshops at the University of Oregon. His dog misses the city but enjoys the large yard and the many possums.

KATRINA VANDENBERG is the author of two books of poetry, *The Alphabet Not Unlike the World* and *Atlas,* both published by Milkweed Editions. She teaches at Hamline University, where she also serves as poetry editor for *Water~Stone Review.*

LYNNE VITI is the author of *Baltimore Girls* (2017), *Punting* (2017), *The Glamorganshire Bible* (2018), and *Hollyhocks* (2019). She received Honorable Mentions in the WOMR/Joe Gouveia Outermost Poetry Contest (2018, 2019), Concrete Wolf Chapbook competition (2017), Grey Borders Wanted Works Contest (2016), and the Allen Ginsberg Poetry Award (2015). She blogs at stillinschool.wordpress.com.

CONNIE VOISINE is the author, most recently, of *And God Created Women* (2018) and *The Bower* (2019). She lives in the Alameda Depot neighborhood in Las Cruces, New Mexico.

PHOEBE WAYNE is the author of the chapbooks *Transit* (Magnificent Field, 2019), *The Sleep Volumes* (dancing girl press, 2017) and *Lovejoy* (c_L press, 2010). She lives in Portland, Oregon, with her family.

MARCO WILKINSON's work has appeared in *The Kenyon Review, Seneca Review, Bennington Review, DIAGRAM,* and elsewhere. His memoir, *Madder,* is forthcoming from Coffee House Press. His neighbors include a gray manx cat whose name is Little but who he calls Space Ghost, black raspberries whose canes are ghostly white in the winter and whose berries are luminously black in the summer, and a dogwood tree planted in memory of Dr. Martin Luther King Jr. in 1968.

AMY YELIN considers herself a good neighbor. Her work appears in *The Gettysburg Review, The Missouri Review, Salon,* and more. She's received two Pushcart nominations, a notable *Best American Essays* mention, and fellowships to VSC and The Writer's Room of Boston. Amy is also assistant nonfiction editor for *Solstice.* Yelinwords.com.

DAVID YOUNG likes his neighborhood because it is full of poets he knows—Stafford, Levertov, Charles Wright, Franz Wright, Charles Simic—but also poets he has visited as a translator—Rilke, Petrarch, Neruda, Montale, Celan, Holub, and a number of classical Chinese poets. His Selected and New Poems is *Field of Light and Shadow.*

JOSEPHINE YU is the author of *Prayer Book of the Anxious* (Elixir Press, 2016). Her poems have appeared in *Ploughshares, The Southern Review, Crab Orchard Review, TriQuarterly, 32 Poems, Nimrod International Journal, Best New Poets 2008,* and other journals and anthologies.

ANDRENA ZAWINSKI's poetry has received accolades for lyricism, form, spirituality, and social concern. Her newest collection is *Born Under the Influence,* forthcoming from Main Street Rag. Others are *Landings, Something About* (PEN Oakland Award), and *Traveling in Reflected Light* (Kenneth Patchen Prize). Born and raised in Pittsburgh, PA, she lives in the San Francisco Bay Area, where she runs the Women's Poetry Salon.

Author Index

Title Index